ENGLISH - THAI

AND

THAI - ENGLISH

DICTIONARY

Mini : English-Thai
and Thai-English Dictionary

A total English-Thai and Thai-English
vocabulary of more than 7,000 selected
useful words and terms. With Thai
words shown in easy English phonetics
and also in real Thai writing. Designed
especially for those who cannot yet read
the Thai language but want to speak and
understand Thai.

by

Gordon H. Allison, B.A.

published by

CHALERMNIT

108 Sukhumvit 53 Bangkok 10110 Thailand
Tel (66-2) 662-6264 Fax (66-2) 662-6265
E-mail : chalermnit@hotmail.com
Website : www.chalermnit.com

RTAF (Royal Thai Air Force)
RTN (Royal Thai Navy)
SEAP (Southeast Asia Peninsula)
sgt. (sergeant)
sl. (slang)
Th. (Thailand)
univ. (university)
v. (verb)
veg. (vegetable)
v. i. (verb, intransitive)
v. t. (verb, transitive)

Numbers in Thai

Note. The main numbers are also listed in the
body of the dictionary. Both Thai and
Arabic styles of numbers are used in
Thailand, as shown in the following
summary. (The Thai-style number is
shown last.)

0 (zero) r)soon! ศูนย์ ๐
1 l)neung! หนึ่ง ๑
2 r)sawng ("tho" in some cases) สอง ๒ (ไท)
3 r)sam สาม ๓
4 l)see สี่ ๔

```
 5 f)ha    ห้า ๕
 6 l)hok!  หก ๖
 7 l)jet!  เจ็ด ๗
 8 l)paet  แปด ๘
 9 f)kao!  เก้า ๙
10 l)sip!  สิบ ๑๐
11 l)sip!-l)et!  สิบเอ็ด ๑๑
12 l)sip!-r)sawng  สิบสอง ๑๒
13-19 ["l)sip!" + 3-9]
20 f)yee-l)sip!  ยี่สิบ ๒๐
21 f)yee-l)sip!-l)et!  ยี่สิบเอ็ด ๒๑
22 f)yee-l)sip!-r)sawng  ยี่สิบสอง ๒๒
23-29 ("20" + 3-9)
30-99 (same system as for 20-29)
100 l)neung! h)rawy  หนึ่งร้อย ๑๐๐
101 l)neung! h)rawy l)et!  หนึ่งร้อยเอ็ด ๑๐๑
102-199 ["l)neung! h)rawy" + 2-99]
200 r)sawng h)rawy  สองร้อย ๒๐๐
201 r)sawng h)rawy l)et!  สองร้อยเอ็ด ๒๐๑
202-999 (same system as for 102-199)
1,000 l)neung! phan!  หนึ่งพัน ๑,๐๐๐
1,001 l)neung! phan! l)et!  หนึ่งพันเอ็ด ๑,๐๐๑
1,002 l)neung! phan! r)sawng  หนึ่งพันสอง ๑,๐๐๒
1,003-1,999 ["l)neung! phan!" + 3-999]
```

2,000 r)sawng phan! สองพัน ๒,๐๐๐

2,001 r)sawng phan! l)et! สองพันเอ็ด ๒,๐๐๑

2,002 r)sawng phan! r)sawng สองพันสอง ๒,๐๐๒

2,003—9,999 (same system as for 1,003—1,999)

10,000 l)neung! l)meun หนึ่งหมื่น ๑๐,๐๐๐

20,000 r)sawng l)meun สองหมื่น ๒๐,๐๐๐

100,000 l)neung! r)saen หนึ่งแสน ๑๐๐,๐๐๐

1,000,000 l)neung! h)lan หนึ่งล้าน ๑,๐๐๐,๐๐๐

1,000,000,000 l)neung! phan! h)lan หนึ่งพันล้าน

๑,๐๐๐,๐๐๐,๐๐๐

Note. "1" at the end of numbers, beginning
with "11", is usually expressed as "l)et!"
instead of "l)neung!"

Time and Telling Time in Thai

There are two ways to tell time in Thailand: the official system (24-hour system) and
the colloquial system (which breaks up the
24-hour day into various parts).

It is very easy to express the time in Thai
by simply saying the hour plus the number of
minutes past the hour. There are other ways
of course, but this is the simplest way.

Here are the hours from 1.00 a.m. to 12.00 midnight, with the official way shown first and the colloquial way shown last. ("na-li!-ka" = "o'clock".)

1.00 a.m. 1)neung! na-li!-ka, tee 1)neung! หนึ่ง นาฬิกา, ตีหนึ่ง

2.00 a.m. r)sawng na-li!-ka, tee r)sawng สอง นาฬิกา, ตีสอง

3.00 a.m. r)sam na-li!-ka, tee r)sam สามนาฬิกา, ตีสาม

4.00 a.m. 1)see na-li!-ka, tee 1)see สี่นาฬิกา, ตีสี่

5.00 a.m. f)ha na-li!-ka, tee f)ha ห้านาฬิกา, ตีห้า

6.00 a.m. 1)hok! na-li!-ka, 1)hok! mong h)chao! หกนาฬิกา, หกโมงเช้า

7.00 a.m. 1)jet! na-li!-ka, 1)jet! mong h)chao! เจ็ดนาฬิกา, เจ็ดโมงเช้า

8.00 a.m. 1)paet na-li!-ka, 1)paet mong h)chao! แปดนาฬิกา, แปดโมงเช้า

9.00 a.m. f)kao! na-li!-ka, f)kao! mong h)chao! เก้านาฬิกา, เก้าโมงเช้า

10.00 a.m. 1)sip! na-li!-ka, 1)sip! mong h)chao! สิบนาฬิกา, สิบโมงเช้า

11.00 a.m. 1)sip!-1)et! na-li!-ka, 1)sip!-1)et! mong h)chao! สิบเอ็ดนาฬิกา, สิบเอ็ดโมงเช้า

12.00 noon l)sip!-r)sawng na-li!-ka, f)thiang
สิบสองนาฬิกา, เที่ยง

1.00 p.m. l)sip!-r)sam na-li!-ka, l)bai mong
สิบสามนาฬิกา, บ่ายโมง

2.00 p.m. l)sip!-l)see na-li!-ka, l)bai r)sawng
mong สิบสี่นาฬิกา, บ่ายสองโมง

3.00 p.m. l)sip!-f)ha na-li!-ka, l)bai r)sam
mong สิบห้านาฬิกา, บ่ายสามโมง

4.00 p.m. l)sip!-l)hok! na-li!-ka, l)see mong
yen สิบหกนาฬิกา, สี่โมงเย็น

5.00 p.m. l)sip!-l)jet! na-li!-ka, f)ha mong yen
สิบเจ็ดนาฬิกา, ห้าโมงเย็น

6.00 p.m l)sip!-l)paet na-li!-ka, l)hok! mong
yen สิบแปดนาฬิกา, หกโมงเย็น

7.00 p.m l)sip!-f)kao na-li!-ka, f)thoom!
l)neung! สิบเก้านาฬิกา, ทุ่มหนึ่ง

8 00 p.m. f)yee-l)sip! na-li!-ka, r)sawng
f)thoom! ยี่สิบนาฬิกา, สองทุ่ม

9.00 p.m. f)yee-l)sip!-l)et! na-li!-ka, r)sam
f)thoom! ยี่สิบเอ็ดนาฬิกา, สามทุ่ม

10.00 p.m. f)yee-l)sip!-r)sawng na-li!-k.., l)see
f)thoom! ยี่สิบสองนาฬิกา, สี่ทุ่ม

11.00 p.m. f)yee-l)sip!-r)sam na-li!-ka, f)ha
f)thoom! ยี่สิบสามนาฬิกา, ห้าทุ่ม

12.00 p.m. f)yee-l)sip!-l)see na-li!-ka, f)thiang kheun สิบสองนาฬิกา, เที่ยงคืน

Notes. The word for minute is "na-thee". Thus, any time can be expressed, either in the official or the colloquial way, by simply adding the number of "na-thee" after the hour. For example, suppose it is 7,15 p.m. One could say "l)sip!-f)kao! na-li!-ka l)sip!-f)ha na-thee" or "l)neung! f)thoom! l)sip!-f)ha na-thee". The colloquial words "h)chao" (of the morning) and "yen!" (of the late afternoon) need not be expressed when it is obvious what part of the day it is, but "l)bai" and f)thoom!" are usually expressed.

Useful Tips on Thai Grammar and Usage

1) If you are a male, it is recommended to use "r)phom!" for "I" or "me". If you are female, it is recommended to use "r)chan!" for "I" or "me". If you want to show respect to elders, important people, or Buddhist priests, then males can change "r)phom!" to "l)kra!-r)phom!" and females can change "r)chan!" to "dih!-r)chan!".

2) If you are a male, always say "h)khrap!" to mean "sir, yes sir, ma'am, or yes ma'am." If you are female, always say "h)kha!" to mean "sir, yes sir, ma'am, or yes ma'am".

3) Adjectives come after the noun in Thai, except for numerical adjectives (1, 2, etc.), which come before. Example: khon! dee = good person ("khon!" = person; "dee" = good); r)sawng khon! = two persons ["r)sawng" = two].

4) Adjectives can be used after a noun or pronoun to make a complete sentence in Thai, without it being necessary to have a "be" verb. Example: r)khao! r)suay = She is beautiful. ["r)khao!" = he or she; "r)suay" = pretty or beautiful.]

5) Adverbs qualifying adjectives generally come after the adjective. Example: r)suay f)mak = very pretty ["r)suay" = pretty; "f)mak" = very].

6) The Thai verb "mee" has many meanings: have, has, had, there is, there are, there was, there were. Examples: r)chan! mee nguhn = I have money; f)mai! mee nguhn f)thee-f)nee = There is no money here.

7) The most-used negative word is "f)mai!", in front of a verb. Example: r)chan! f)mai! f)sap = I do not know.

8) Many words necessary in English may be omitted in Thai, as everyday Thai is very flexible about grammar. If the listener understands, then it is not necessary to express every word. For example, such English words as "a", "an", "the", "some", "any" can be expressed in Thai (with more or less the same meaning as in English) but are often omitted when the meaning is clear without them. Other words may also be omitted when the meaning is clear without them, especially nouns and pronouns used as the subject of verbs. Example: f)mai! pai! can mean "I'm not going." or "I don't want to go.", although the literal meaning of the two words is only "not go".

9) Thai verbs are always in the same form. Tenses and different persons are shown through other words. Following are some of the most useful helping words to know in Thai.

   a) l)yak = would like to, as in "l)yak pai!" = would like to go.

b) l)ja! = shall or will, as in "l)ja! pai!" = will go.

c) f)dai! used in front of another verb usually shows the past tense, as in "f)mai! f)dai! pai." = did not go. However, the same word "f)dai!" when used after another verb usually means "can", as in "pai! f)mai! f)dai!" = can not go.

d) khuan = should or ought to, as in "khuan pai!" = should go.

e) l)thook! used in front of a verb shows a passive construction, as in "r)khao! l)thook! tee" = He was beaten.

f) f)tawng = must, as in "f)tawng pai!" = must go.

g) f)hai! = let, as in "f)hai! r)chan! doo" = let me see. When used after other verbs or at the end of phrases or sentences, "f)hai!" shows an idea of doing something for someone else, as in "r)chan! l)ja! tham! f)hai!" = I will do it (for you).

h) f)hai! f)dai! used at the end of requests or orders shows that something must be done without fail, as in "khoon! f)tawng ma f,hai f)dai!" = You must come, without fail.

    i) l)yang in front of adjectives or adverbs = "in a certain way" or "to a certain extent", as in l)yang f)mai! f)na f)cheua" = in an unbelievable manner.

    j) kan used in front of a verb gives a gerund: kan kin = eating.

    k) khwam used in front of other words gives an abstract-idea word: khwam dee = goodness.

    10) The verb "tham" can mean either "make" or "do". Example: tham! l)kha!-r)nom! = make candy or sweets; tham! ngan = do work.

    11) Possession in Thai can be shown by putting the possessed thing before the possessor or by using the word "r)khawng" between the possessed thing and the possessor, as in "my friend" = "1)pheuan r)chan!' or "f)pheuan r)khawng r)chan!".

    12) There are many ways to say the same pronoun in Thai, depending on sex, age, and importance of the person concerned, but the

most-used forms in everyday life are: I (male) r)phom!, (female) r)chan!; you, khoon!, (respectful) f)than; he, she, or they, r)khao!, (respectful) f)than; it, man!; we, rao! or f)phuak rao! The same pronoun can be used as either a subject or an object, and there is only one form for each pronoun.

13) There are many ways to say "please" in Thai. Examples: ka-roo-na ma f)duay = please or kindly come too; l)prot ma f)duay = please come too; f)chuay l)bawk r)khao! = Please tell him. (Help me by telling him.); h)na! (at the end of requests), as in "pai! h)na!" = Please go. (Oh come on, please go!).

14) Classifier nouns. In theory at least, all Thai nouns are classified under "classifier nouns", giving us expressions that sometimes sound redundant in English. However, you have to get used to this language phenomenon gradually, and please don't fight the language! For example, some of the most-used classifier nouns are "khon!" (for persons), "tua" (for animals and certain objects), "khan!" (for

vehicles and certain objects), and "f)look" (for
fruit, balls, round objects in general). Examples: f)phoo-r)ying! r)sam khon! = (literally)
women, three persons, or (simply) three women.

Note. The best things to do when trying to
learn to speak or understand Thai are to
control one's temper, be patient, and be
generous with the word "h)khrap" (for
males) or "h)kha!" (for females). If you
follow this simple advice, you will probably be well-liked by Thai people. The
simple truth is that most Thai people
do not like people who are loud, abrupt,
overly blunt, temperamental, impatient
or impolite.

PART ONE
ENGLISH TO THAI

a, an l)neung! หนึ่ง

abbreviate f)yaw ย่อ

abdomen h)thawng h)nawy ท้องน้อย

ability khwam r)sa-f)mat ความสามารถ

able r)sa-f)mat สามารถ

abnormal (not sane) f)ba บ้า; (deformed) h)phi!-
kan พิการ; (unusual) l)phit! l)pok!-l)ka!-l)ti!
ผิดปกติ

aboard ship bon! reua บนเรือ

abolish h)yok! f)luhk ยกเลิก

abortion h)thaeng f)look แท้งลูก

about (to) (almost) l)keuap เกือบ; (approximately) pra!-man ประมาณ; (concerning) l)keeo
l)kap! เกี่ยวกับ

above (higher than) r)soong l)kwa สูงกว่า; (over,
in price) kuhn เกิน; (over, in space) r)neua
เหนือ; (upper side) f)khang bon! ข้างบน

abroad l)tang l)pra!-f)thet ต่างประเทศ

abscess pen! r)fee เป็นฝี

absent f)mai! l)yoo ไม่อยู่

absent-minded jai! lawy ใจลอย; (forgetful f)khee leum ขี้ลืม

absolutely l)det!-l)khat เด็ดขาด

absorb l)doot, kleun ดูด, กลืน

accelerate f)reng เร่ง

accelerator (of vehicle) f)thee f)reng h)nam man! ที่เร่งน้ำมัน

accent (in speaking) r)sam!-niang สำเนียง

accept yawm h)rap! ยอมรับ

accept an invitation h)rap! chuhn รับเชิญ

accident oo-bat-ti-het อุบัติเหตุ

accidentally doy bang-uhn โดยบังเอิญ

accident insurance pra!-kan! oo-bat-ti-het ประกัน อุบัติเหตุ

accompany (go with) pai! f)duay ไปด้วย

accomplish tham! jon! r)sam!-l)ret! ทำจนสำเร็จ

according to tam ตาม

account (n., fin.) ban!-chee บัญชี

accountant (n., fin.) sa!-moo!-ban!-chee สมุห์บัญชี

accurate l)thook-f)tawng ถูกต้อง

accuse (of) 1)klao r)ha กล่าวหา

accustomed to khuhy chin! เคยชิน

ache 1)puat ปวด

across (from) trong! f)kham ตรงข้าม

actor, actress da-ra ดารา

add (numbers) 1)buak, ruam บวก, รวม; (add to) 1)taw tuhm ต่อเติม

addict n. f)phoo 1)sep-1)tit! ผู้เสพติด

addicted (to) 1)sep-1)tit! เสพติด

additional f)phuhm tuhm เพิ่มเติม

address n. 1)thee 1)yoo ที่อยู่

adhesive tape plas-tuh ปลาสเตอร์

adjust 1)prap!-proong! ปรับปรุง

administer v. baw-ri-r)han บริหาร

admirable f)na chom!-chuhy น่าชมเชย

admiral (5-s.ar) jawm-phon! reua จอมพลเรือ; (4-star) phon! reua 1)ek พลเรือเอก; (3-star) phon! reua tho พลเรือโท; (2-star) phon! reua tree พลเรือตรี

admire chom! (chuhy) ชม (เชย)

admission (fee) f)kha 1)phan pra!-too ค่าผ่านประตู

admit yawm h)rap! ยอมรับ

adopt a child ao! 1)dek! ma h)liang เอาเด็กมาเลี้ยง

adult n. f)poo l)yai! ผู้ใหญ่

advanced (modern, prosperous) l)ja!-ruhn h)laeo เจริญแล้ว

advantage(s) l)pra!-l)yot! ประโยชน์; (have advan. over someone) f)dai! l)priap ได้เปรียบ; (take advan. of opportunity) r)theu oh-l)kat ฉวยโอกาส; (take advan. of someone) ao! l)priap เอาเปรียบ

adventurous l)pha!-jon! phai!, f)lot r)phon ผจญภัย, โลดโผน

advertise kho-sa!-na, f)jaeng khwam โฆษณา, แจ้งความ

advice n. kham' h)nae!-nam! คำแนะนำ

advise h)nae!-nam! แนะนำ

advisor f)thee l)preuk-r)sa ที่ปรึกษา

aerial (antenna) r)sao! ah-l)kat เสาอากาศ

a few r)sawng r)sam สองสาม

afraid (of) klua กลัว

after(wards) thee r)lang! ทีหลัง

afternoon tawn l)bai ตอนบ่าย; (late afternoon) tawn yen! ตอนเย็น

again l)eek (thee) อีก (ที)

again and again h)sam! h)sam! ซ้ำๆ

against (next to) l)tit! l)kap! ติดกับ; (not in favor of) f)mai! r)hen! f)duay ไม่เห็นด้วย

against the law 1)phit! 1)kot!-r)mai ผิดกฎหมาย

age ah-h)yoo! อายุ

agent f)poo thaen ตัวแทน

ago f)meua.... เมื่อ....

agree 1)tok! long! ตกลง; (in favor of) r)hen! f)duay เห็นด้วย

agriculture n. kan 1)ka!-1)set การเกษตร

ahead (in front) f)khang f)na ข้างหน้า

ahead of time (in advance) f)luang f)na ล่วงหน้า

aid v. f)chuay [r)leua] ช่วย (เหลือ)

aim (a weapon) leng! (peun) เล็ง (ปืน)

air n. lom!, ah-1)kat ลม, อากาศ

air base r)than h)thap! ah-1)kat ฐานทัพอากาศ

air-conditioned 1)prap! ah-1)kat ปรับอากาศ

air-conditioner f)khreuang 1)prap! ah-1)kat เครื่องปรับอากาศ

aircraft-carrier reua ban!-h)thook! f)khreuang-bin! เรือบรรทุกเครื่องบิน

airfield 1)sa!-r)nam bin! สนามบิน

air force kawng h)thap! ah-1)kat กองทัพอากาศ

airline r)sai kan bin! สายการบิน

airmail prai!-1)sa!-nee ah-1)kat ไปรษณีย์อากาศ

airman h)tha!-r)han ah-1)kat ทหารอากาศ

airplane f)khreuang-bin! เครื่องบิน

airplane crash f)khreuang-bin! l)tok! เครื่องบินตก

airplane ticket r)tua kan bin! ตั๋วการบิน

airport f)tha ah-l)kat-sa-yan ท่าอากาศยาน

air raid kan jom-tee thang ah-l)kat การโจมตีทาง
อากาศ

airsick mao! f)khreuang-bin! เมาเครื่องบิน

alarm clock na-li!-ka l)plook! นาฬิกาปลุก

alcohol n. aen-kaw-haw แอลกอฮอล์

alcoholic (person) f)phoo pen! f)rok h)phit!
l)soo!-ra ผู้เป็นโรคพิษสุรา

alcoholic beverages l)soo!-ra, f)lao! สุรา, เหล้า

alert (wide awake) l)jaem-r)sai แจ่มใส

alert n. (mil. or police) triam h)phrawm เตรียม
พร้อม

algebra n. phee-h)cha!-h)kha!-h)nit! พีชคณิต

alias (false name) f)cheu plawm ชื่อปลอม

alien (person) khon! l)tang-f)dao คนต่างด้าว

alien papers (alien ID card) bai! l)tang-f)dao
ใบต่างด้าว

alike r)meuan kan! เหมือนกัน

a little bit h)nit! l)nawy นิดหน่อย

alive mee chee-h)wit! มีชีวิต

all h)thang! l)mot! ทั้งหมด

all day h)thang! wan! ทั้งวัน

all gone (all used up) l)mot! h)laeo หมดแล้ว

alligator jaw-h)ra!-f)kheh จระเข้

all night h)thang! kheun ทั้งคืน

allow ah-noo-yat อนุญาต

all right f)dai!, O.K. ได้, โอ. เค.

All right? (Okay?) f)dai! r)mai!? ได้ไหม ?

all set (ready) l)set! h)laeo เสร็จแล้ว

all the time l)ta!-l)lawt weh-la ตลอดเวลา

almost l)keuap เกือบ

alone khon! deeo คนเดียว

alongside f)khang f)khang ข้าง ๆ

a long time weh-la nan เวลานาน

a long time from now l)eek nan อีกนาน

a lot (very much) f)mak f)mak มาก ๆ

already h)laeo แล้ว

also (too) f)duay ด้วย

altogether (total) ruam h)thang! l)mot! รวม
ทั้งหมด

always l)sa!-r)muh เสมอ

am v. (See BE.)

amateur (person) f)phoo l)sa!-l)mak! f)le:
ผู้สมัครเล่น

amazed l)plaek jai! แปลกใจ

ambassador f)thoot ทูต

ambulance h)rot! h)pha!-ya-ban รถพยาบาล

ambush f)lawp jom-tee ลอบโจมตี

America(n) (a-meh-ri-ka(n) อเมริกา (กัน); (person) chao a-meh-ri-kan ชาวอเมริกัน

ammunition l)kra!-r)soon! peun กระสุนปืน

among nai! h)ra-l)wang ในระหว่าง

amount n. jam!-nuan จำนวน

amphoe (Thai district) am!-phuh อำเภอ

amplifier f)khreuang l)kha!-r)yai r)siang เครื่อง ขยายเสียง

amusing l)khop!-r)khan! ขบขัน

an (same as a)

anchor n. l)sa!-r)maw สมอ; v. f)thawt l)sa!-r)maw ทอดสมอ

ancient bo-ran โบราณ

and h)lae! และ; (meaning "with") l)kap! กับ

and so on (etc) h)la! ฯลฯ

angle n. mom! มุม

angry l)krot โกรธ; (suddenly) mo-r)ho โมโห

animal l)sat!, tua สัตว์, ตัว

ankle n. f)khaw-h)thao! ข้อเท้า

announce l)pra!-l)kat ประกาศ

annoy h)rop!-kuhn รบกวน

annually l)pra!-jam' pee ประจำปี

another (thing) l)eek an! l)neung! อีกอันหนึ่ง;
  (person) l)eek khon! l)neung! อีกคนหนึ่ง;
  (animal) l)eek tua l)neung! อีกตัวหนึ่ง

answer v. l)tawp ตอบ; (the telephone) h)rap!
  tho-h)ra!-l)sap! รับโทรศัพท์

ant n. h)mot! มด

antenna (T.V., radio) r)sao! ah-l)kat เสาอากาศ

anti-aircraft artillery (AAA) peun l)yai! l)taw-
  f)soo ah-l)kat-l)sa!-yan ปืนใหญ่ต่อสู้อากาศยาน

antidote ya f)kae h)phit! ยาแก้พิษ

antiseptic n. ya f)kha h)cheua-f)rok ยาฆ่าเชื้อโรค

anxious kang-won! กังวล

any (some) bang, f)bang บาง, บ้าง

anybody, anyone khrai! f)kaw f)dai! ใครก็ได้

anyhow l)yang-rai! f)kaw! tam อย่างไรก็ตาม

anything l)ah!-rai! f)kaw! f)dai! อะไรก็ได้

any time f)meua-rai! f)kaw! f)dai! เมื่อไรก็ได้

anywhere f)thee-r)nai! f)kaw! f)dai! ที่ไหนก็ได้

apartment n. f)hawng f)chao!, "flat" ห้องเช่า,
  แฟล็ต

apologize r)khaw f)thot ขอโทษ

appear (seem) doo r)meuan ดูเหมือน

appearance (shape) f)roop-r)rang รูปร่าง; (way one looks) f)tha thang ท่าทาง

appendicitis f)rok f)sai! l)ting! โรคไส้ติ่ง

appetite n. khwam r)hew ความหิว

apple n. aep-pun แอปเปิ้ล

applicant (person) f)phoo l)sa!-l)mak! ผู้สมัคร

apply (put on) tha, l)sai! ทา, ใส่; (make written application) l)sa!-l)mak! สมัคร

appoint v. l)taeng f)tang! แต่งตั้ง

approach (come near) f)khao! ma f)klai! เข้ามาใกล้; (go near) f)khao! pai! f)klai! เข้าไปใกล้

approve (of) r)hen! [f)chawp] f)duay เห็น (ชอบ) ด้วย

approximately l)pra!-man ประมาณ

April meh-r)sa-yon! เมษายน

apron n. f)pha kan! f)peuan ผ้ากันเปื้อน

architect l)sa!-r)tha-l)pa!-h)nik! สถาปนิก

are v. (See BE.)

area (amount of land) h)neua f)thee, h)pheun f)thee เนื้อที่, พื้นที่; (vicinity) baw-h)ri!-wen บริเวณ

argue v. (quarrel) h)tha!-h)law! kan! ทะเลาะกัน

arise (get up) h)look! f)kheun! ลุกขึ้น

arithmetic n. f)lek h)kha!-h)nit! เลขคณิต

arm (of body) r)khaen แขน

armed forces kawng h)thap! กองทัพ

armored (cavalry) yan l)kraw! ยานเกราะ

army kawng h)thap! l)bok! กองทัพบก

around (all around) f)rawp f)rawp รอบๆ

arrange v. l)jat! (kan) จัด (การ)

arrest v. l)jap! koom! จับกุม

arrive (reach) r)theung! ถึง

art, arts r)sin-l)la-l)pa! ศิลป

artery (blood vesssel) f)sen lo-l)hit' daeng เส้น โลหิตแดง

artillery (mil.) peun l)yai! ปืนใหญ่

artist (painter) f)chang r)khian f)roop ช่าง เขียนรูป

ashamed h)la!-ai ละอาย

ashes f)khee f)thao! ขี้เถ้า

ashtray f)thee l)khia l)boo!-l)ree ที่เขี่ยบุหรี่

Asia(n) eh-sia(n) เอเชีย(น)

ask (a question) r)tham ถาม; (ask for something) r)khaw ขอ

asleep nawn l)lap! นอนหลับ

aspirin aes-phai-rin แอสไพริน

assist (aid) f)chuay-r)leua ช่วยเหลือ

assistance n. khwam f)chuay-r)leua ความช่วยเหลือ

assistant (person) f)phoo-f)chuay ผู้ช่วย

association n. sa-ma-khom สมาคม

as soon as possible reh-o f)thee l)soot! เร็วที่สุด

astrology n. r)ho-rah l)sat โหราศาสตร์

astronomy n. da-ra-l)sat ดาราศาสตร์

as usual tam khuhy ตามเคย

as you like (wish) tam jai! ตามใจ

at (a place) f)thee ที่

at ease l)sa!-bai สบาย

at first thee f)raek ที่แรก

athlete h)nak! kee-la นักกีฬา

at last nai! thee l)soot! ในที่สุด

at least l)yang h)nawy อย่างน้อย

at night klang kheun กลางคืน

attach v. l)tit! h)wai! ติดไว้

attaché (dipl.) f)phoo-f)chuay f)thoot ผู้ช่วยทูต

attack v. jom tee โจมตี

attend a meeting f)khao! l)pra'-choom! เข้าประชุม

Attention! trong! ตรง

at that time we-la h)nan! เวลานั้น

at the same time we-la deeo kan! เวลาเดียวกัน

attitude h)that!-l)sa!-h)na! ทัศนะ

attorney-at-law h)tha'-nai khwam หนายความ

at what time? l)kee mong? we-la f)thao!-rai!? กี่โมง? เวลาเท่าไร?

at your convenience h)laeo l)tae l)sa!-l)duak
แล้วแต่สะดวก

auction n. kɔn r)khai leh-r)lang! การขายเลหลัง

audience (listeners) f)phoo fang! ผู้ฟัง

August r)sing!-r)ha-khom! สิงหาคม

aunt (younger sister of father) ah ɑɑ; (younger sister of mother) h)na น้า; (elder sister of father or mother) f)pa ป้า

Australia(n) aws-treh-lia(n) ออสเตรเลีย(น)

author h)nak! l)pra!-phan! นักประพันธ์

authority n. (power) am!-f)nat อำนาจ

automatic doy at-ta-no-mat โดยอัตโนมัติ

automobile h)rot!-yon! รถยนต์

antomobile accident h)rot! chon! รถชน

autumn reu!-doo bai!-h)mai f)ruang ฤดูใบไม้ร่วง

average (math.) doy l)cha!-l)lia โดยเฉลี่ย; (medium) pan klang ปานกลาง

avoid l)leek f)liang หลีกเลี่ยง

awaken l)teun nawn ตื่นนอน; (wake up someone) l)plook! ปลุก

award n. rang-wan! รางวัล

a while f)chua f)khroo ชั่วครู่

awkward f)mai l)tha!-l)nat! ไม่ถนัด

axo n. r)khwan ขวาน

baby n. l)dek! tba-h)rok! เด็กทารก

baby ayah, baby-sitter khon! h)liang l)dek! คนเลี้ยงเด็ก

bachelor (male) chai l)sot ชายโสด; (female) r)ying! l)sot หญิงโสด

back (of body) r)lang! หลัง

backache l)puat r)lang! ปวดหลัง

back of (in back of) f)kbang r)lang! ข้างหลัง

back up (a vehicle) r)thawy h)rot! ถอยรถ

backwards l)klap! kan! กลับกัน

bacon (meat) r)moo khem', r)moo "bacon" หมูเค็ม หมูเบคอน

bacteria (germs) h)cheua f)rok เชื้อโรค

bad (not good) f)mai! dee ไม่ดี

badge f)khreuang-r)mai เครื่องหมาย

bad luck f)chok f)mai! dee โชคไม่ดี

bag n. r)thoong! ถุง

baht (official Thai currency) baht บาท

bake v. l)op อบ

balance (n., acct.) f)yawt ban!-chee ยอดบัญชี

bald (no hair) r)hua l)lan หัวล้าน

ball (for games) f)look bawn ลูกบอลล์

balloon n. f)look l)pong ลูกโป่ง

ballpoint pen l)pak-ka f)look f)leun ปากกาลูกลื่น

bamboo (wood) h)mai! l)phai! ไม้ไผ่

banana f)kluay r)hawm กล้วยหอม

band (musical) wong! don!-tree วงดนตรี

bandage n. f)pha phan! r)phlae ผ้าพันแผล

banded krait snake (deadly poisonous) ngoo r)sam
l)liam งูสามเหลี่ยม

bandit jon โจร

Bangkok (Metropolis) kroong! f)thep [h)ma!-r)ha
h)na!-khawn] กรุงเทพ (มหานคร)

bank (n., fin.) h)tha!-na-khan ธนาคาร; (of a
waterway) l)fang! ฝั่ง

bank account ban!-chee [h)tha!-na-khan] บัญชี
(ธนาคาร)

banknote (currency) h)tha!-na-l)bat, baeng
ธนบัตร, แบงค์

bar (for drinking) bah บาร์

barbecue v. (roast) f)yang ย่าง

barbed-wire f)luat r)nam ลวดหนาม

barber f)chang l)tat! r)phom! ช่างตัดผม

barbershop h)ran l)tat! r)phom! ร้านตัดผม

barefoot h)thao l)plao! เท้าเปล่า

bargain v. (for better price) l)taw ra-kba ต่อราคา

bark (as a dog) l)hao! เห่า

barracks (mil.) rong h)tha!-r)han โรงทหาร

barrel (of a gun) lam! f)klawng peun ลำกล้องปืน

bashful (shy) f)khee ai ขี้อาย

basket n. l)ta!-f)kra ตะกร้า

bat (animal) h)kang-khao ค้างคาว

bath, bathe n.,v. l)ahp h)nam! อาบน้ำ

bathing suit (for swimming) h)choot! l)ahp- h)nam! ชุดอาบน้ำ

bathmat phrom! h)chet! h)thao! พรมเช็ดเท้า

bathroom f)hawng h)nam! ห้องน้ำ

bathtub l)ang l)ap h)nam! อ่างอาบน้ำ

battalion (mil.) kawng phan! กองพัน

battery (mil.) kawng h)rawy h)tha!-r)han peun l)yai! กองร้อยทหารปืนใหญ่; (storage battery, large) f)maw fai!-h)fa, "battery" หม้อไฟฟ้า, แบตเตอรี่; (storage battery, small) l)than ถ่าน

battle v. f)soo h)rop! kan! สู้รบกัน

battlefield l)sa!-r)nam h)rop! สนามรบ

bay (body of water) l)ao อ่าว

bayonet n. l)dap plai peun ดาบปลายปืน

be v. (am, is, are, was, were, been) (be in a place) l)yoo อยู่; (exist) pen! เป็น; (there is, there are) mee มี

beach n. chai l)hat ชายหาด

bean n. l)thua ถั่ว

bear (animal) r)mee หมี

beard n. l)nuat (khrao!) หนวด (เครา)

beat v. tee ตี; (defeat) h)cha!-h)na! ชนะ

beautiful r)suay สวย

beauty shop h)ran r)suhm r)suay ร้านเสริมสวย

Be careful! h)ra!-wang! [l]nawy] ระวัง (หน่อย)

because (of) h)phraw! [f]wa] เพราะ (ว่า)

become v. klai pen! กลายเป็น

bed n. tiang nawn เตียงนอน

bedroom f)hawng nawn ห้องนอน

bedsheets, bedspread f)pha poo f)thee-nawn ผ้าปู
ที่นอน

bee n. f)pheung! ผึ้ง

beef n. h)neua wua เนื้อวัว

been v. (See BE.)

beer n. bia เบียร์

be even (with someone) r)hai kan! หายกัน; (be
smooth) f)riap เรียบ

before l)kawn ก่อน

beg v. r)khaw than ขอทาน; (ask for) r)khaw
ขอ

beggar n. khon! r)khaw than คนขอทาน

begin v. f)ruhm เริ่ม

beginning n. tawn f)ton! ตอนต้น

begrudge v. r)sia dai เสียดาย

Beg your pardon? l)ah!-rai! h)na! อะไรนะ

behind (in back of) f)khang r)lang! ข้างหลัง

belch v. ruh เรอ

believe v. f)cheua เชื่อ

bell n. kra!-ding! กระดิ่ง; (large) h)ra!-khang! ระฆัง

bellboy (hotel) r)bawy f)hawng บ๋อยห้อง

belonging to r)khawng ของ

below f)khang f)lang ข้างล่าง

belt n. r)khem!-l)khat! เข็มขัด; (conveyor) r)sai phan สายพาน

bench n. h)ma f)nang! ม้านั่ง

bend v. tham! f)hai h)khong ทำให้โค้ง

bend over f)kom! (long) ก้ม (ลง)

beneficial mee l)pra!-l)yot มีประโยชน์

bent adj. h)khong โค้ง

beside f)khang f)khang ข้างๆ

besides (in addition to) f)nawk l)jak h)nan! นอกจากนั้น

best dee f)thee l)soot ดีที่สุด

bet v. h)pha!-nan! พนัน

better (than before) dee f)kheun! ดีขึ้น; (than something else) dee l)kwa ดีกว่า

between nai! h)ra!-l)wang ในระหว่าง

beverage n. f)khreuang-l)deum เครื่องดื่ม

bicycle l)jak!-ra!-yan จักรยาน

big l)yai! ใหญ่

bill n. (banknote) h)tha!-na-l)bat! ธนบัตร; (for collection) bin! r)khaw l)kep! ngun บิลเก็บเงิน

binoculars n. f)klawng l)sawng thang klai

bird h)nok! นก

birth certificate bai! l)kuht ใบเกิด

birth control kan khoom! kam!-l)nuht การคุมกำเนิด

birthday wan! l)kuht วันเกิด

bite v. l)kat! กัด

bitter (taste) r)khom! ขม

black (color) r)see dam! สีดำ

blackboard n. l)kra!-dan dam! กระดานดำ

blame v. f)thot โทษ

blanket n. f)pha l)hom! ผ้าห่ม

bleach v. tham! f)hai r)khao ทำให้ขาว

bleed v. f)leuat l)awk เลือดออก

blind adj. ta l)bawt ตาบอด

block the way f)kan! thang กั้นทาง

blood f)leuat เลือด

blood pressure khwam dan! lo-l)hit! ความดันโลหิต

blotter n. 1)kra!-l)dat h)sap! กระดาษซับ

blouse (lady's) f)seua l)sa!-tree เสื้อสตรี

blow v. 1)pao! เป่า; (as the wind) h)phat! พัด

blowout (tire) yang h)ra!-l)buht ยางระเบิด

blue (color) r)see h)nam'-nguhn สีน้ำเงิน; (light blue) r)see h)fa สีฟ้า

blunt (not sharp) f)theu ทื่อ

blush v. f)na daeng หน้าแดง

boa constrictor (snake) ngoo r)leuam งูเหลือม

board n. (wood) h)mai! l)kra!-dan ไม้กระดาน

board v. (get aboard) f)kheun pai!

boast v. 1)uat อวด

boat n. reua เรือ

body n. (of a person) f)rang-kai ร่างกาย

boil n. r)fee ฝี

boil v. (be boiling) 1)deuat เดือด; (boil something) f)tom! ต้ม

boiled water h)nam' f)tom! h)laeo น้ำต้มแล้ว

bold jai! f)kla ใจกล้า

bolt n. klawn กลอน

bomb n. f)look h)ra!-l)buht ลูกระเบิด; v. h)thing! h)ra!-l)buht ทิ้งระเบิด

bomber (airplane) f)khreuang-bin! h)thing! h)ra!-l)buht เครื่องบินทิ้งระเบิด

bone n. 1)kra!-1)dook กระดูก

book n. r)nang!-r)seu หนังสือ

bookcase f)too r)nang!-r)seu ตู้หนังสือ

border (of a country) chai daen ชายแดน

bored l)beua เบื่อ

boring f)na l)beua น่าเบื่อ

born, be born 1)kuht เกิด

borrow v. r)khaw yeum ขอยืม

boss (employer) nai, nai f)jang นาย, นายจ้าง

both h)thang! r)sawng ทั้งสอง

bother v. h)rop!-kuan รบกวน

bottle n. l)khuat ขวด

bottle-opener f)thee l)puht l)khuat ที่เปิดขวด

bottom (of something) f)kon! ก้น

bounce v. 1)kra!-dehn! กระเด็น

bounced check h)chek! t)dehng เช็คเด้ง

boundary n. 1)khet, 1)khawp l)khet เขต, ขอบเขต

bow (of ribbon etc.) bo โบว์

bowels (of body) lam!-f)sai ลำไส้

bowl (dish) cham ชาม

bowl v. f)len bo-f)ling เล่นโบว์ลิ่ง

bowling alley l)sa!-r)than bo-f)ling สถานโบว์ลิ่ง

bow tie h)nek!-thai! l)phook! bo เน็คไทลูกโบว์

box (small to large) l)klawng, l)heep, lang! กล่อง, หีบ, ถัง

box (v., sport) h)chok! muay ชกมวย

boxer n. h)nak! muay นักมวย

boxing n. kan h)chok! muay การชกมวย

boy n. l)dek!-chai เด็กชาย; (houseboy, waiter etc.) r)bawy บ๋อย

boyfriend faen (from Eng. "fan"), f)pheuan f)phoo-chai แฟน, เพื่อนผู้ชาย

Boy Scout f)look r)seua ลูกเสือ

bracelet kam!-lai! f)khaw-meu กำไลข้อมือ

brag (boast) f)oh l)uat โอ้อวด

brain(s) l)sa!-r)mawng สมอง

brake (n., v.) f)ham h)law, l)brek ห้ามล้อ, เบรค

branch (of company or academic field) r)sar)kha สาขา; (of mil. service) l)lao! เหล่า; (of trees) l)king! h)mai! กิ่งไม้

brand n. (comr.) f)yee-f)haw ยี่ห้อ

brass n. thawng r)leuang ทองเหลือง

brassiere bra-sia, h)yok! song! บราเซียร์, ยกทรง

brave adj. f)kla-r)han กล้าหาญ

bread n. l)kha!-r)nom!-pang! ขนมปัง

break (by itself) l)taek, l)hak! แตก, หัก; (cause
to break) tham! l)taek, tham! l)hak! ทำแตก,
ทำหัก

breakfast ah-r)han h)chao! อาหารเช้า

break out (as disease, war) h)ra!-l)bat ระบาด

breast (female) nom!, f)tao! nom! นม, เต้านม

breath (of body) lom! r)hai-jai! ลมหายใจ

breathe r)hai jai! หายใจ

bribe n. nguhn r)sin!-bon! เงินสินบน; v. l)tit!
r)sin!-bon! ติดสินบน

brick n. f)kawn l)it! ก้อนอิฐ

bridge n. l)sa!-phan สะพาน

brig.-gen. (AF) phon! ah-l)kat l)jat!-l)ta!-wa
พลอากาศตรีว่า; (army) phon! l)jat!-l)ta!-wa
พลตรีว่า; (pol.) phon! tam!-l)ruat l)jat!-ta!-wa
พลตำรวจตรีว่า

bright (of lighting) l)sa!-l)wang สว่าง

bring ao! ma, nam! ma เอามา, นำมา

British ang!-l)krit! อังกฤษ

broadcast v. l)kra!-jai r)siang กระจายเสียง

broil v. (barbecue) f)yang ย่าง

broke (sl., without money) f)mai mee l)sa!-
tang ไม่มีสตางค์

broken (out of order) r)sia, cham!-h)root! เสีย, ชำรุด

broken-hearted l)ok! l)hak! อกหัก

bronze n. thawng brawn ทองบรอนซ์

broom n. h)mai! l)kwat ไม้กวาด

brother (older) f)phee chai, (younger) h)nawng chai พี่ชาย, น้องชาย

brother-in-law (elder) f)phee r)khuhy พี่เขย; (younger) h)nawng r)khuhy น้องเขย

brown (color) r)see h)nam!-tan สีน้ำตาล

brush (n., v.) praeng แปรง

bubbles n. (foam) fawng h)nam! ฟองน้ำ

bucket n. r)thang! ถัง

Buddha h)phra! h)phoot!-h)tha!-f)jao! พระพุทธเจ้า

Buddhism l)sat-l)sa!-r)na h)phoot! ศาสนาพุทธ

Buddhist (person) chao h)phoot! ชาวพุทธ

buffalo n. khwai ควาย

build v. l)kaw f)sawng ก่อสร้าง; (a house) l)plook f)ban ปลูกบ้าน

building n. rong (reuan) โรง (เรือน); (stone) l)teuk!, ah-khan ตึก, อาคาร

bull n. wua tua-f)phoo วัวตัวผู้

bullet n. l)kra!-r)soon! peun กระสุนปืน

bullfight (Southern-Thai style) kan chon! wua การชนวัว

bumper (vehicle) f)thee kan! chon ที่กันชน

bump into chon! kan! ชนกัน

burglar n. l)kha!-moy บโมย

Burma, Burmese h)pha'-f)ma พม่า

burn (by itself) f)mai!, (cause to burn) r)phao! ไหม้, เผา

burst v. h)ra!-l)buht ระเบิด

bury v. r)fang! ฝัง; (bury a body) r)fang! l)sop! ฝังศพ

bus n h)rot! meh, h)rot! l)pra!-jam! thang รถเมล์, รถประจำทาง

bush n. f)phoom! h)mai! พุ่มไม้

business (in general) h)thoo'-h)ra! ธุระ; (trade and commerce) h)tnoo!-h)ra!-l)kit! ธุรกิจ

bus station l)sa!-r)tha-nee h)rot doy-r)san สถานี รถโดยสาร

bus stop f)thee l)jawt h)rot! l)pra!-jam! tbang ที่จอดรถประจำทาง

busy (not free) f)mai! f)wang ไม่ว่าง; (telephone line is busy) r)sai f)mai! f)wang สายไม่ว่าง

but l)tae [f)wa] แต่ (ว่า)

butter nuhy l)awn [r)leh·o] เนยอ่อน (เหลว)

butterfly n. maeng r)phee f)seua แมงผีเสื้อ

button n. l)kra!·doom! กระดุม

buy v. h)seu ซื้อ

buzzer n. (bell) l)kring กริ่ง

by doy โดย; (by air) thang ah·l)kat ทางอากาศ; (by boat) thang reua ทางเรือ; (by land) thang l)bok! ทางบก; (by train) thang h)rot!·fai! ทางรถไฟ

by oneself khon! deeo คนเดียว

cabbage l)kra!·l)lam!·plee กระหล่ำปลี

cabinet (furniture) f)too ตู้; (of govt.) h)kha!·h)na! h)rat!·l)tha!·mon!·tree คณะรัฐมนตรี

cable n. (wire) f)luat l)sa!·ling ลวดสลิง

cable(gram) tho·ra!·f)lek โทรเลข

cage n. krong! กรง

cake n. l)kha!·r)nom! h)khek ขนมเค้ก

calculate v. h)khit kham!·nuan คิดคำนวณ

calendar n. l)pa!·l)ti·thin! ปฏิทิน

calf (animal) f)look wua ลูกวัว

caliber (of weapon) l)suan f)kwang l)pak l)kra!·l)bawk ส่วนกว้างปากกระบอก

call v. f)riak เรียก; (by phone) tho. pai! โทร. ไป

call wrong number (on phone) tho. l)phit! โทร. ผิด

calm adj. l)sa'-ngop! สงบ; (not excitable) jai! yehn! ใจเย็น

Cambodia(n), **Khmer** l)kha!-r)men เขมร

camera n. f)klawg l)thai f)roop กล้องถ่ายรูป

camp (n., mil.) f)khai [h)tha!-r)han] ค่าย (ทหาร)

can v. (able to do) f)dai!, tham! f)dai! ได้, ทำได้; (asking if can) ....f)dai! r)mai! ....ได้ไหม

can n. (small) l)kra!-r)pawng กระป๋อง; (larger) r)thang! ถัง

canal n. khlawng (klong) คลอง

cancel v. h)yok! f)luhk ยกเลิก

cancer n. h)ma!-reng! มะเร็ง

candidate n. f)phoo l)sa!-l)mak! ผู้สมัคร

candle n. thian เทียน

candy (sweets in general) l)kha!-r)nom! ขนม

cannot f)mai! f)dai! ไม่ได้

can-opener f)thee l)puht l)kra!-r)pawng ที่เปิด กระป๋อง

canvas n. f)pha bai! ผ้าใบ

capable r)sa-f)mat สามารถ

capital (money) nguhn thoon เงินทุน

capital city meuang r)luang เมืองหลวง

captain (AF) reua ah-l)kat l)ek เรืออากาศเอก;
(army) h)rawy l)ek ร้อยเอก; (navy) na.wa
l)ek นาวาเอก; (pol.) h)rawy tam!-l)ruat l)ek
ร้อยตำรวจเอก; (sea captain) l)kap!-tan! reua
กัปตันเรือ

capture v. l)jap! f)dai! จับได้

car (auto) h)rot!, h)rot!-yon! รถ, รถยนต์

card (name card) nam l)bat!, (playing cards)
f)phai! นามบัตร, ไพ่

cardboard l)kra!-l)dat r)khaeng กระดาษแข็ง

care (be concerned) pen! l)huang, khae (from
Eng.) เป็นห่วง แคร์

care for (maintain) bam'-roong! h)rak!-r)sa
บำรุงรักษา

careful adj. h)ra'-wang! ระวัง

careless adj. h)mai! h)ra'-wang! ไม่ระวัง

carnival n. (fair, etc.) ngan งาน

carpenter n. f)chang h)mai! ช่างไม้

carry something (light to heavy) r)theu, f)hew!
l)baek, r)khon! ถือ, หิ้ว, แบก, หน

cartridge n. f)look l)kra!-r)soon! ลูกกระสุน

car wreck h)rot! chon! kan! รถชนกัน

cash (money) nguhn l)sot! เงินสด

cash a check (cheque) h)laek h)chek! แลกเช็ค

castle n. wang!, pra-l)sat วัง, ปราสาท

cat n. maeo แมว

catch v. l)jap!, l)jap! h)wai! จับ, จับไว้

catch cold pen! l)wat! เป็นหวัด

Catholic (person) chao kha-thaw-lik, chao khris-tang ชาวคาธอลิค, ชาวคริสตัง

Catholic priest l)bat r)luang บาทหลวง

Catholic sister (nun) f)mae chee, sis-tuh (sister) แม่ชี, ซิสเตอร์

cauliflower l)dawk l)ka-l)lam! ดอกกะหล่ำ

cause n. (reason) f)ton! l)het ต้นเหตุ

cause v. (make to happen) tham! f)hai! ....ทำให้

cavalry (mil.) h)tha!-r)han h)ma ทหารม้า

cave f)tham! ถ้ำ

cavity (as in a tooth) roo phrohng รูโพรง

ceiling (of a room) peh-dan เพดาน

celebrate v. l)cha!-r)lawng ฉลอง

cement n. poon see-mehn ปูนซีเมนต์

cemetery n. l)pa h)cha ป่าช้า

center, centre (in the middle) klang, trong! klang กลาง, ตรงกลาง; (headquarters) r)soon, r)soon klang ศูนย์, ศูนย์กลาง

centimeter, centimetre sen-l)ti'-f)met เซ็นติเมตร

ceremony n. phi-thee, ngan พิธี, งาน

certain, certainly f)nae nawn แน่นอน

certificate bai h)rap!-rawng ใบรับรอง

certify v. h)rap!-rawng รับรอง

chain n. f)so โซ่

chair n. f)kao!-f)ee เก้าอี้

chance (opportunity) oh-l)kat โอกาส

change (small money) nguhn thawn, nguhn f)yawy เงินทอน, เงินย่อย

change v. l)plian, l)plian plaeng เปลี่ยน เปลี่ยน แปลง

change one's mind l)plian jai เปลี่ยนใจ

changwat (province) jang!-l)wat จังหวัด

charcoal n. l)than ถ่าน

charge, charge a price h)khit! ra-kha คิดราคา

chauffeur (driver) khon l)khap! h)rot!, cho-fuh คนขับรถ, โชเฟอร์

cheap (inexpensive) l)thook, f)mai! phaeng ถูก, ไม่แพง

cheat v. kong โกง

check (examine) l)truat doo, chek! doo ตรวจดู, เช็คดู

check (cheque, for payment of money) h)chek!
เช็ค; (bounced check) h)chek! f)deng! เช็คเด้ง

cheek (of the face) f)kaem แก้ม

cheese n. nuhy r)khaeng เนยแข็ง

chest (of the body) f)na-l)ohk! หน้าอก

chew (as food) h)kheeo เคี้ยว

chewing gum l)mak l)fa!-l)rang! หมากฝรั่ง

chicken (animal) l)kai! ไก่

chief (boss) nai, r)hua-f)na นาย, หัวหน้า

chief petty officer (navy) phan!-l)ja-l)ek พันจ่าเอก

child, children l)dek!, l)dek! l)dek! เด็ก, เด็กๆ

chin (of the face) khang คาง

China (the country) l)pra!-f)thet jeen ประเทศจีน

Chinese (person) khon! jeen, chao jeen! (language) pha-r)sa jeen คนจีน, ชาวจีน, ภาษาจีน

choke (suffocate) r)hai jai! f)mai! l)awk หายใจ
ไม่ออก

cholera (the disease) l)ah!-l)hib!-wa อหิวาห์

choose v. f)leuak เลือก

chopsticks (for eating Chinese food) l)ta!-l)kiap
ตะเกียบ

Christ (Jesus Christ) h)phra yeh-soo พระเยซู

Christian 1) (Catholic) khrìs-tang, 2) (Protestant) khris-tian คริสตัง, คริสเตียน

Christianity (the Christian religion) l)sàt-l)sà-r)na h)khrìt! ศาสนาคริสต์

Christmas, Christmas Day wan! khrìs-mas วัน คริสต์มาส

church n. l)bot โบสถ์

cigarette l)boo!-l)ree บุหรี่

cigarette-lighter fai! h)chaek ไฟแช็ค

cinema (film) r)nang!, f)phap-h)pha!-yon! หนัง, ภาพยนตร์, (theatre building) rong r)nang! โรง หนัง

circle n. wong! klom!, (traffic circle) wong! wian วงกลม, วงเวียน

circuit (n., elect.) wong! jawn วงจร

circus h)la!-khawn l)sàt! ละครสัตว์

citizenship (of a certain country) r)san!-f)chat สัญชาติ

city n. kroong!, h)na!-khawn กรุง, นคร

civilian (not military) phon!-h)la!-reuan พลเรือน

claim v. f)ang, f)ang f)wa อ้าง, อ้างว่า

"clap" (the "clap", gonorrhea) f)rok r)nawng-nai! โรคหนองใน

class (1st., 2nd, etc.) h)chan! [as in "1st class" = "(h)chan! f)thee l)neung!"] ชั้น

claw (v., with nails or claws) l)khuan ข่วน

clean adj. l)sa!-l)at สะอาด

clean, clean up v. tham! khwam l)sa!-l)at ทำความ สะอาด

clear (easy to see, hear, understand) h)chat! ชัด

clerk (n., person) l)sa'-r)mian เสมียน

clerk-typist l)sa!-r)mian phim!-l)deet เสมียน พิมพ์ดีด

clever adj. l)cha!-l)lat, l)kehng ฉลาด, เก่ง

climate (weather) n. ah-l)kat อากาศ

climb v. peen ปีน

clock n. na-h)lih'-ka นาฬิกา

close (nearby) f)klai!, f)klai! f)klai! ใกล้, ใกล้ๆ

close (v., shut) l)pit! ปิด

cloth n. f)pha ผ้า

clothes n. f)seua f)pha เสื้อผ้า

cloud n. f)mek เมฆ

coat n. f)seua f)nawk เสื้อนอก

coat-hanger n. h)mai! r)khwaen f)seua ไม้แขวนเสื้อ

cobra n. ngoo l)hao! งูเห่า

cockroach (insect) ma-laeng l)sap แมลงสาบ

coconut n. h)ma!-h)phrao มะพร้าว

coffee ka-fae กาแฟ

coffin n. l)heep l)sop! หีบศพ

coins (money) r)rian, nguhn r)rian เหรียญ, เงิน
เหรียญ

cold adj. r)nao หนาว
(have a cold) pen! l)wat! เป็นหวัด

cold season (cool season, in Thailand) h)reu!-
doo r)nao ฤดูหนาว

collar (of shirt) khaw f)seua คอเสื้อ

collect (as a collection) l)kep!, l)sa -r)som! เก็บ,
สะสม

collect money l)kep! nguhn เก็บเงิน

collector (bill-collector etc.) f)phoo l)kep! nguhn
ผู้เก็บเงิน

colonel 1) (full col., army) phan! l)ek; 2) (full
col, AF) na-wa ah-l)kat l)ek; 3) (lt. col.,
army) phan! tho; 4) (lt , col., AF) na-wa ah-
l)kat tho; 5) (pol. full col.) phan! tam!-l)ruat
l)ek; 6) (pol. lt. col.) phan! tam!-l)ruat tho;
7) (special col., army, equiv. to brig.-gen)
phan! l)ek h)phi!-l)set; 8) (special col., pol ,
equiv. to pol. brig.-gen.) phan! tam!-l)ruat l)ek

h)phi!-l)set ๐) พันเอก; ๒) นาวาอากาศเอก; ๓) พันโท;
๔) นาวาอากาศโท; ๕) พันตำรวจเอก; ๖) พันตำรวจโท;
๗) พันเอกพิเศษ; ๘) พันตำรวจเอกพิเศษ

color, colour r)see สี

:omb n. r)wee หวี

:omb the hair (v.) r)wee r)phom! หวีผม

combine (mix) l)pha!-r)som! ผสม

come v. ma มา

come back l)klap! ma กลับมา

come down long! ma ลงมา
  (decrease) h)lot! long! ลดลง

come in, come inside f)khao! ma, f)khao! ma
  f)khang nai! เข้ามา, เข้ามาข้างใน

come near (approach) f)khao! ma f)klai! เข้ามา
  ใกล้

come off (become detached) l)loot! l)awk หลุด
  ออก

come out l)awk ma ออกมา

come up l)kheun! ma ขึ้นมา

comfortable l)sa!-bai dee สบายดี

command (n., order) kham! l)sang คำสั่ง
  (v., order) l)sang! สั่ง

commander (n., person, mil., govt, & pol.) f)phoo
  ban!-cha kan ผู้บัญชาการ

(naval commander) na-wa tho นาวาโท

(naval lt. cmdr.) na-wa tree นาวาตรี

commodore (navy) phon! reua l)jat'-l)ta!-wa พล เรือตรีวา

communist adj., n. khawm-mew-nit! คอมมิวนิสต์

communist terrorists f)phoo l)kaw kan h)rai khawm-mew-nit! ผู้ก่อการร้ายคอมมิวนิสต์

company (mil.) kawng h)rawy กองร้อย

company (n , comr) baw-h)ri!-l)sat! บริษัท

compare v. l)priap f)thiap เปรียบเทียบ

compass n. r)khem h)thit! เข็มทิศ

compete v. l)khaeng kan! แข่งกัน

competent (able) r)sa-f)mat สามารถ

complain v. l)bon! บ่น

complete adj. baw-h)ri!-boon, h)khrop! บริบูรณ์, ครบ

concerning l)keeo l)kap! เกี่ยวกับ

concrete n. khawn-l)kreet คอนกรีต

condition n. (status) l)sa!-f)phap สภาพ; (require-ment) f)ngeuan-r)khai! เงื่อนไข

conduct (behavior) khwam l)pra!-h)phreut! ความประพฤติ

confess r)sa-h)ra!-f)phap สารภาพ

confidential adj. h)lap! ลับ

confused (in one's mind) ngong! งง
(mixed up) f)yoong, l)sap!-r)son! ยุ่ง, สับสน

Congratulations! r)khaw l)sa!-daeng khawm yin'-
dee f)duay ขอแสดงความยินดีด้วย

connect v. l)taw, l)tit! h)wai! ต่อ, ติดไว้

consider v. h)phi!-ja-h)ra!-na พิจารณา

consist of l)pra!-l)kawp f)duay ประกอบด้วย

constipated (bowels won't move) h)thawng
l)phook ท้องผูก

constitution n. h)rat-l)tha-tham!-ma!-noon รัฐ
ธรรมนูญ

construct v. f)sang, l)kaw f)sang สร้าง, ก่อสร้าง

consult v. l)preuk'-r)sa ปรึกษา

consultant (n., person) f)thee l)preuk!-r)sa
ที่ปรึกษา

contact v. l)tit!-l)taw ติดต่อ

content adj. phaw jai! พอใจ

continue v. l)taw pai!, tham! taw pai! ต่อไป,
ทำต่อไป

contract (n., document) r)san!-ya สัญญา

control v. f)khuap-khoom! ควบคุม

control birth khoom! kam!-l)nuht คุมกำเนิด

convenient adj. 1)sa!-1)duak สมควร

conversation n. kan r)son!-h)tha-na การสนทนา

cook (n., person) 1) (female) f)mae khrua

 2) (male) f)phaw khrua แม่ครัว, พ่อครัว

cook v. tham! ah-r)han ทำอาหาร

cool adj. yen! เย็น

cool v. (make cool) tham! f)hai! yen! ทำให้เย็น

cooperate v. f)ruam meu ร่วมมือ

cooperation n. khwam f)ruam meu ความร่วมมือ

coordinate v. 1)pra!-r)san ngan ประสานงาน

coordinates (mapping) 1)joot! h)phi!-1)kat จุดพิก

copper n. thawng daeng ทองแดง

copy n. (duplicate) r)sam!-nao! สำเนา

copy v. (make a copy of) tham! r)sam!-nao
 ทำสำเนา

cord n f)cheuak เชือก

corn n. f)khao f)phot ข้าวโพด

corner n. moom! มุม

corporal (mil.) 1)sip! tho สิบโท

 (lance corporal, PFC) 1)sip tree สิบตรี

corpse (body) 1)sop! ศพ

correct adj. 1)thook, 1)thook f)tawng ถูก, ถูกต้อง

correct v. f)kae, f)kae-r)khai! แก้, แก้ไข

correct time we-la trong! เวลาตรง

correspond (by letter) l)tit!-l)taw thang l)jot!-r)mai ติดต่อทางจดหมาย

cost (price) ra-kha ราคา

costly (expensive) phaeng แพง

cost of living f)kha khrawng f)cheep ค่าครองชีพ

cost of something f)kha.... ค่า.... (as in "cost of electricity" = f)kha fai!)

costs (expenses) f)kha h)chai! l)jai ค่าใช้จ่าย

cotton n. f)fai! ฝ้าย

cough v. ai! ไอ

count v. h)nap! นับ

counterfeit money nguhn plawm เงินปลอม

country (nation) l)pra!-f)thet ประเทศ
  (rural areas) f)ban f)nawk บ้านนอก

couple (a pair) f)khoo คู่

court (of law) r)san ศาล

cousins (relatives) f)look f)phee f)look h)nawng ลูกพี่ลูกน้อง

cover n. r)fa l)pit! ฝาปิด

cover v. l)pit!, khloom ปิด, คลุม

cow n. wua วัว

crab n. poo ปู

cramp (in the body) l)ta!-khew! ตะคิว

crane (lifting machine) f)pan!-l)jan, khre:
  (from Eng.) ปั้นจั่น, เครน

crash (auto crash) h)rot! chon! kan! รถยนต์ชน

crawl v. khlan คลาน

crazy adj. f)ba บ้า

cream (mixture, as in shaving cream) khree:
  (from Eng.) ครีม

cream (thick milk) nom! f)khon! นมข้น

cremate (a corpse) r)phao! l)sop! เผาศพ

criminal n. l)at-h)cha'-ya-kawn อาชญากร

crippled adj. h)phl!-kan พิการ

criticize v. (find fault) tam!-l)nih! ตำหนิ

crocodile n. jaw-h)ra!-f)kheh จรเข้

crops (n., agri.) f)pheut-r)phon! พืชผล

cross v. (as in cross the street) f)kham ข้าม

crossroads thang f)yaek ทางแยก

  3-way junction r)sam f)yaek สามแยก

  4-way junction l)see f)yaek สี่แยก

crowbar n. h)cha!-laeng ชะแลง

crowd, crowded khon! f)naen คนแน่น

cruel adj. tha-roon! ทารุณ

crush v. h)thap!, l)kha!-h)yee ทับ, ขยี้

crutches (aids for walking) h)mai yan h)rak!
　h)rae ไม้ค้ำรักแร้

cry (tears) h)rawng f)hai! ร้องไห้

cry out (shout) h)rawng, ta!-kon ร้อง, ตะโกน

cubic adj. (for volume) f)look l)bat ลูกบาศก์

cucumber n. taeng-kwa แตงกวา

cup n. f)thuay ถ้วย

cure (v. med.) h)rak!-r)sa r)hai รักษาหาย

currency (money) nguhn tra เงินตรา

current (electric) l)kra!-r)sae fai-h)fa กระแส
　ไฟฟ้า

curriculum (n., educ.) l)lak!-l)soot หลักสูตร

curry (food) kaeng แกง

curse v. l)da ด่า

curtain n. f)pha f)man ผ้าม่าน

curve n thang h)khong ทางโค้ง

cushion n. l)baw! เบาะ

custodian (janitor) phan-rong ภารโรง

custom n. tham!-niam ธรรมเนียม

customer n f)look h)kha ลูกค้า

customs (duties on imports) pha-r)see r)kha
　f)khao! ภาษีขาเข้า

cut (n., injury) l)bat r)phlae บาดแผล

cut v. l)tat! ตัด

cute adj. f)na h)rak!, f)na ehn-doo น่ารัก, น่าเอ็นดู

cylinder (of an engine) l)kra!-l)bawk l)soop
กระบอกสูบ

daily adj. l)pra!-jam! wan! ประจำวัน

dam n. l)kheuan เขื่อน

damaged adj. r)sia-r)hai เสียหาย

dance v. f)ten-ram! เต้นรำ

danger n. phai!, an!-l)ta!-rai ภัย, อันตราย

dark (for colors) l)kae แก่

dark adj. (no light) f)meut มืด

dark blue (color) r)see h)nam!-nguhn สีน้ำเงิน

date (of the month) wan!-f)thee วันที่

daughter n f)look-r)sao ลูกสาว

daughter-in-law f)look l)sa'-h)phai! ลูกสะใภ้

day n. wan! วัน

day after tomorrow h)ma!-reun-h)nee มะรืนนี้

day before yesterday f)meua wan seun เมื่อวานซืน

daytime, in the daytime we-la klang wan เวลา
กลางวัน

dead (no longer alive) tai h)laeo ตายแล้ว

deaf adj. r)hoo l)nuak หูหนวก

dear (expensive) phaeng แพง

dear (term of endearment) f)thee·h)rak! ที่รัก

debt n. f)nee·r)sin! หนี้สิน

decayed (teeth) fan! l)phoo ฟันผุ

deceive v. l)lawk luang หลอกลวง

December than!·wa·khom! ธันวาคม

decide v. l)tat!·r)sin! jai! ตัดสินใจ

deck·chair (canvas chair) f)kao!·f)ee f)pha·bai
เก้าอี้ผ้าใบ

decrease v. h)lot! long ลดลง

deep adj. h)leuk ลึก

defective (out of order, broken) r)sia, cham'·
h)root! เสีย, ชำรุด

defend v. f)pawng·kan! ป้องกัน
   (Ministry of Defence) l)kra!·suang l)ka!·la·
r)hom กระทรวงกลาโหม

degree n. (angular, temperature) ong!·r)sa องศา;
   (college, univer.) l)pa!·rin!·ya ปริญญา

delicious (in taste) l)ah!·l)rawy อร่อย

deliver v. l)song! pai! f)hai! ส่งไปให้

demand v. f)riak h)rawng เรียกร้อง

democracy n. pra!·cha·h)thi·pa!·tai! ประชาธิปไตย

dentist r)maw tham! fan! หมอทำฟัน

deny v. l)pa!·l)ti!·l)set ปฏิเสธ

depart (go out, leave) l)awk pai! ออกไป

depth n. khwam h)leuk! ความลึก

deputy commander (mil.) rawng f)phoo ban!-cha-kan รองผู้บัญชาการ

describe v. pan-na!-na พรรณนา, (explain) a!-thi-bai อธิบาย

desk n h)toh! โต๊ะ

dessert n. (sweets after meals) r)khawng r)wan ของหวาน

destroy v. tham! lai ทำลาย

detailed adj. h)la!-l)iat ละเอียด

details n. rai h)la!-l)iat รายละเอียด

detective n. h)nak! l)seup นักสืบ

detour n. thang f)awm ทางอ้อม

develop v. (build up) h)phat!-h)tha!-na พัฒนา

develop film (photography) h)lang fim! ล้างฟิล์ม

dial a telephone number r)moon r)mai f)lek tho-h)ra!-l)sap หมุนหมายเลขโทรศัพท์

diamond ring r)waen f)phet แหวนเพชร

diarrhea (n., med.) h)thawng duhn ท้องเดิน

dice (for playing games) f)look r)tao! ลูกเต๋า

dictionary n. h)dik!, h)dik!-chan!-nuh-f)ree, h)phot!-l)ja-na-h)noo-krom! ดิก, ดิกชันเนอรี, พจนานุกรม

die v. **tai** ตาย

diesel **dee-sen** ดีเซล

different (not the same) l)tang kan!, f)mai r)meuan kan! ต่างกัน, ไม่เหมือนกัน
(various kinds) l)tang l)tang ต่าง ๆ

difficult f)yak ยาก

difficult to find r)ha f)yak หายาก

dig v. l)khoot! ขุด

diligent adj. l)kha!-r)yan! ขยัน

dining room f)hawng ah-r)han ห้องอาหาร

dining table h)to! ah-r)han โต๊ะอาหาร

dinner (evening meal) ah-r)han f)kham! อาหาร ค่ำ

dipper (n., for water etc.) r)khan l)tak! h)nam! ขันตักน้ำ

direct adj. doy trong! โดยตรง

direction n. (way to go) h)thit thang ทิศทาง

director n. (chief) f)phoo am!-nuay kan ผู้อำนวยการ,
(company director) kam!-ma!-kan กรรมการ

dirty adj. l)sok!-l)ka!-l)prok! สกปรก

disagree v. f)mai r)hen! f)duay ไม่เห็นด้วย

disappear v. r)hai pai! หายไป

disappointed adj. l)phit! r)wang ผิดหวัง

disarm v. l)plot! ah-h)woot! ปลดอาวุธ

discharge (from employment) f)hai! l)awk ให้ออก

discount n. l)suan h)lot! ส่วนลด

discouraged adj. h)thaw jai! ท้อใจ

discover v. h)khon! h)phop! ค้นพบ

discuss v. r)ha-reu kan! หารือกัน

disease n. f)rok โรค

dish (for eating) jan จาน

dishes (in general, for eating) f)thuay cham
ถ้วยชาม

disinfect (kill germs) f)kha h)cheua f)rok
ฆ่าเชื้อโรค

dislike v. f)mai! chawp ไม่ชอบ

disobey v. f)mai! f)cheua fang! ไม่เชื่อฟัง

dispensary (drugstore) h)ran r)khai ya ร้านขายยา

display v. l)sa!-daang แสดง

dissatisfied adj. f)mai! phaw jai! ไม่พอใจ

dissolve v. h)la!-lai ละลาย

distance n. h)ra!-h)ya! thang ระยะทาง

distant (far away) l)hang klai ห่างไกล

distilled water h)nam! l)klan! น้ำกลั่น

distribute (give out) l)jaek แจก

district (subdiv. of changwat or province) am!-
phuh อำเภอ

district office f)thee f)wa kan am!-phuh ที่ว่าการ
อำเภอ

district officer (chief of amphoe) nai am!-phuh
นายอำเภอ

distrust v. f)mai! h)wai! jai! ไม่ไว้ใจ

disturb v. h)rop!-kuan รบกวน

ditch (small) khoo คู

dive into water dam! h)nam! ดำน้ำ

divide (arith.) r)han หาร, (into parts) l)baeng
l)suan แบ่งส่วน, (share) l)baeng kan! แบ่งกัน

division (mil. unit) kawng phon! l)yai! กองพลใหญ่

divorce v. l)ya kan! หย่ากัน

dizzy (feeling faint) f)na f)meut, wian r)hua
หน้ามืด, เวียนหัว

do (or make) tham! ทำ,

dock, docks t)tha reua ท่าเรือ

doctor (medical) r)maw, nai f)phaet หมอ,
นายแพทย์
(Ph. D.) dawk-tuh ดอกเตอร์ (Dr., ดร.)

document n. l)ek!-l)ka!-r)san เอกสาร

dodge v. (get out of way) l)lop', l)leek หลบ, หลีก

dog n. r)ma, l)soo!-h)nak! หมา, สุนัข

doll n. h)took!-l)ka!-ta ตุ๊กตา

dollar n. dawn, dawn-la, r)rian ดอล, ดอลล่าร์, เหรียญ

donate v. baw-h)rih!-l)jak บริจาค

Do not! Don't! l)ya อย่า

don't have (there is not) f)mai mee ไม่มี

don't know f)mai! h)roo, f)mai! f)sap ไม่รู้, ไม่
ทราบ

don't mention it (you're welcome) f)mai! pen!-
rai! ไม่เป็นไร

door n. l)pra!-too ประตู

doubt v. r)song!-r)sai! สงสัย

downhearted adj. f)kloom! jai! กลุ้มใจ

downstairs f)khang f)lang ข้างล่าง

downtown nai meuang ในเมือง

do work tham! ngan ทำงาน

dozen (12 of something) r)lo l)neung! โหลหนึ่ง

drag v. f)lak ลาก

drain n. thang h)ra!-bai ทางระบาย

drain v. h)ra!-bai ระบาย

draw a line l)kheet f)sen ขีดเส้น

drawer (of a desk, etc.) h)lin!-h)chak! ลิ้นชัก

draw pictures f)wat f)roop วาดรูป

dream r)fan! ฝัน

dream about r)fan! r)theung! ฝันถึง

dress (female clothing) l)kra!-prong กระโปรง

dress (put on clothing) l)taeng tua แต่งตัว

dressmaker (seamstress) f)chang l)tat! f)seua l)sa!-tree ช่างตัดเสื้อสตรี

drill (v., practice) l)feuk'-l)hat! ฝึกหัด

drink v. l)deum ดื่ม

drinks (refreshments) f)khreuang f)deum เครื่อง ดื่ม

drive (a vehicle) l)khap h)rot! ขับรถ

drive away (chase away) l)khap! f)lai! ขับไล่

driver (chauffeur) khon! l)khap! h)rot! คนขับรถ

driver's license bai! l)khap!-l)khee ใบขับขี่

drop (let fall) l)plawy t)hai! l)tok! ปล่อยให้ตก

drop (liquid) l)yot! หยด

drown v. jom! h)nam! tai จมน้ำตาย

drug addict f)phoo l)sep-l)tit! ผู้เสพติด

drugs (medicine) ya, (narcotics) ya l)sep!-tit! ยา, ยาเสพติด

drug store (pharmacy) h)ran r)khai ya ร้านขายยา

drum n. klawng กลอง

drunk (intoxicated) mao! เมา

drunkard khon! f)khee mao! คนขี้เมา

dry adj. f)haeng แห้ง

dry off (as with a towel) h)chet! เช็ด

dry-clean (clothing) h)sak! f)haeng ซักแห้ง

dry-cleaners h)ran h)sak! f)haeng ร้านซักแห้ง

dry season h)reu!-doo h)laeng ฤดูแล้ง

duck (animal) l)pet! เป็ด

duck (move to avoid something) l)lop! หลบ

due (time to pay) r)theung kam'-l)not! l)jai
ถึงกำหนดจ่าย

due to (owing to) f)neuang l)jak เนื่องจาก

dull (not sharp) f)theu, f)mai' khom! ทื่อ, ไม่คม

dumb (cannot speak) pen! bai! เป็นใบ้; (stupid)
f)ngo โง่

duplicate n. (copy) r)sam!-nao! สำเนา

duplicate v. (make a copy of) tham! r)sam!-
nao! ทำสำเนา
    (by machine) l)at! r)sam!-nao! อัดสำเนา

durable adj. thon!-than ทนทาน

durian (Thai fruit) h)thoo!-rian ทุเรียน

during h)ra!-l)wang ระหว่าง

dusk n. tawn f)kham! ตอนค่ำ

dust n. l)foon! ฝุ่น

dustpan n. f)thee koy r)phong! ที่โกยผง

duty n. (responsibility) f)na-f)thee หน้าที่

dye v. h)yawm ย้อม

dysentery (have dysentery) pen! l)bit! เป็นบิด ach l)tae h)la! แต่ละ

ach other f)seung! kan! h)lae! kan! ซึ่งกันและกัน

ear (of body) r)hoo หู

early (before the time) l)kawn weh-la ก่อนเวลา

earth (the world) f)lok โลก

case (convenience) khwam l)sa!-l)duak ความ สะดวก

east (direction) l)ta!-wan! l)awk ตะวันออก

easy adj. f)ngai ง่าย

easy to do (convenient) l)sa!-l)duak สะดวก

easy to see (clear) h)chat:-jen ชัดเจน

easy to understand f)khao! jai! f)ngai เข้าใจง่าย

eat v. kin! f)khao, than ah-r)han กินข้าว, ทาน อาหาร

economical (saving, not wasteful) l)pra! l)yat! ประหยัด

edge n. (as edge of window) l)khawp, rim! ขอบ, ริม

education n. kan l)seuk!-r)sa การศึกษา

efficient adj. mee l)pra!-l)sit!-h)thi!-f)phap มีประสิทธิภาพ

egg n. l)khai! ไข่; (fried eggs) l)khai! dao ไข่ดาว

egg omelette l)khai jeeo ไข่เจียว

eggplant (veg.) h)ma!-r)kheua มะเขือ

eight (8) l)paet แปด (๘)

eighteen (18) l)sip!-l)paet สิบแปด (๑๘)

eighty (80) l)paet-l)sip! แปดสิบ (๘๐)

either (or) r)reu, ...r)reu...f)kaw f)dai หรือ, ...หรือ...ก็ได้

elbow (of body) f)khaw l)sawk ข้อศอก

election n. kan f)leuak f)tang! การเลือกตั้ง

electric, electrical fai! h)fa ไฟฟ้า

electrical circuit wong! jawn วงจร

electric bill f)kha fai!-h)fa ค่าไฟฟ้า

electrician f)chang fai! ช่างไฟ

electricity fai!, fai! h)fa ไฟ, ไฟฟ้า

electric lights fai! ไฟ; (light bulb) l)lawt fai! หลอดไฟ

elephant h)chang ช้าง

elevation (altitude) khwam r)soong ความสูง

elevator (lift) lift (from Eng.), f)khreuang lift ลิฟท์, เครื่องลิฟท์

eleven (11) l)sip!-l)et! สิบเอ็ด (๑๑)

embarrassed adj. r)khuay r)khuhn ขวยเขิน

embassy n. l)sa!-r)than f)thoot สถานทูต

embezzle v. h)yak!-f)yawk nguhn ยักยอกเงิน

embrace (hug) l)kawt กอด

emergency l)het l)chook!-r)chuhn เหตุฉุกเฉิน

emphasize v. h)nen, h)yam! เน้น, ย้ำ

employ (hire a person) f)jang จ้าง

employee f)look f)jang, h)pha!-h)nak -ngan
ลูกจ้าง, พนักงาน

employer nai f)jang นายจ้าง

empty adj. f)wang l)plao! ว่างเปล่า

encouraged adj, mee kam!-lang! jai! f)kheun!
มีกำลังใจขึ้น

end (of something) tawn h)thai ตอนท้าย

end v. l)jop! จบ

ended (finished) l)jop! h)laeo จบแล้ว

end of the month f)sin! deuan สิ้นเดือน

enemy (in war) f)kha h)seuk ข้าศึก

energy n. raeng, kam!-lang! แรง, กำลัง

engagement (to marry) kan f)man! การหมั้น

engine n. f)khreuang yon! เครื่องยนต์

engineer n. h)wit!-l)sa!-h)wa!-kawn วิศวกร

engineers (mil.) h)tha!-r)han f)chang ทหารช่าง

England ang!-l)krit! อังกฤษ

English (language) pha-r)sa ang!-l)krit! ภาษา
อังกฤษ

enjoyable adj. 1)sa!-1)nook! สนุก

enough phiang phaw เพียงพอ
  (that's enough) phaw h)laeo พอแล้ว

enquire v. 1)sawp r)tham สอบถาม

ensign (navy) reua tree เรือตรี

enter (come inside) f)khao! ma เข้ามา; (go
  inside) f)khao! pai! เข้าไป

entrance (the way in) thang f)khao! ทางเข้า

entrance fee f)kha 1)phan 1)pra!-too ค่าผ่านประตู

entrust (to another's care) 1)fak h)wai! ฝากไว้

envelope (for letters) sawng 1)jot!-r)mai ซอง
  จดหมาย

envious adj. 1)it!-r)cha อิจฉา
  (jealous, in love) r)heung! หึง

equal to (something else) f)thao! 1)kap! เท่ากับ

equipment n. 1)oop!-1)pa!-kawn อุปกรณ์

erase v. h)lop! 1)awk ลบออก

eraser n. yang h)lop! ยางลบ

escape v. (run away) f)wing! r)nee วิ่งหนี; (try to
  escape and succeed) r)nee pai! f)dai หนีไปได้

escort (mil. guards) h)tha!-r)han khoom! ทหารคุม
  (bodyguard) f)phoo ah-h)rak!-r)kha ผู้อารักขา

especially doy 1)chal-h)phaw! โดยเฉพาะ

espionage n. ja-h)ra!-kam! จารกรรม

establish v. l)jat! f)tang! จัดตั้ง

estimate v. l)pra!-man ao! ประมาณเอา

Europe, European h)yoo!-f)rop ยุโรป

evade v. l)leek f)liang หลีกเลี่ยง

even (tie score) l)sa!-r)muh kan! เสมอกัน;
(smooth, level) f)rap f)riap ราบเรียบ

even if r)theung! l)mae f)wa ถึงแม้ว่า

evening r)hua f)kham! หัวค่ำ

ever (in a question) khuhy [as in "have you
ever gone?" = khoon! khuhy pai! r)mai!] เคย

every adj. h)thook! (as in "every day" =
h)thook! wan!) ทุก

everybody, everyone h)thook! khon! ทุกคน

every day h)thook! wan! ทุกวัน

everything h)thook! l)yang ทุกอย่าง

everywhere f)thua pai!, h)thook! l)haeng ทั่วไป,
ทุกแห่ง

exactly (right, correct) l)thook f)tawng ถูกต้อง

examine v. l)truat doo ตรวจดู

example n. tua l)yang ตัวอย่าง

exams n. kan l)sawp การสอบ

excellent (very good) dee f)mak ดีมาก

except (prep., conj.) h)wen l)tae, f)nawk l)jak
เว้นแต่, นอกจาก

exchange v. f)laek l)plian แลกเปลี่ยน

exchange money (foreign currency) f)laek l)plia: nguhn tra แลกเปลี่ยนเงินตรา

exchange rate (for money) l)at!-l)tra f)laek l)plian nguhn tra อัตราแลกเปลี่ยนเงินตรา

excited adj. l)teun-f)ten ตื่นเต้น

exciting adj. f)na l)teun-f)ten น่าตื่นเต้น

excrement (human) l)oot!-ja-h)ra!, (vulgar) f)khee อุจจาระ, ขี้

excuse n. f)khaw f)kae tua ข้อแก้ตัว

excuse v. (pardon someone) l)ah'-phai! f)ha อภัยให้

Excuse me! r)khaw f)thot ขอโทษ

exercise v. (take exercise) l)awk kam'-lang ออกกำลัง

exhaust pipe (of a vehicle) f)thaw ai! r)sia ท่อไอเสีย

exit n. (way out) thang l)awk ทางออก

expect v. f)khat f)wa คาดว่า

expenses (costs incurred) f)kha h)chai! l)jai ค่าใช้จ่าย

expensive (dear) phaeng แพง

experienced adj cham'-nan ชำนาญ

expert adj. cham!-nan ชำนาญ

expire (as a license) l)mot! ah-h)yoo! หมดอายุ

explain v. l)ah!-h)thi!-bai อธิบาย

explode v. h)ra!-l)buht ระเบิด

exports n. r)sin!-h)kha r)kha l)awk สินค้าขาออก

express train h)rot! l)duan รถด่วน

exterminate v. kam!-l)jat! กำจัด

extinguish v. (put out, as a fire) l)dap! ดับ

eye n. ta ตา

eye-glasses n. f)waen ta แว่นตา

face (of a person) bai! f)na ใบหน้า

face powder (for ladies) f)paeng l)phat! f)na แป้งผัดหน้า

facilitate (make convenient) am'-nuay khwam l)sa!-l)duak อำนวยความสะดวก

factory n. rong ngan โรงงาน

facts (the facts about something) f)khaw h)thet!-jing! ข้อเท็จจริง

fade (of colors) r)see l)tok! สีตก

fail (not be successful) f)mai! r)sam!-l)ret ไม่สำเร็จ

fail an exam l)sawp l)tok! สอบตก

faint (v., med.) pen! lom!, l)sa!-l)lop! เป็นลม, สลบ

fair n. ngan งาน

faithful adj. f)seu-l)sat! ซื่อสัตย์

fall v. l)tok! ตก

fall down l)hok! h)lom! หกล้ม

false (not true) f)mai! jing! ไม่จริง; (not genuine) plawm ปลอม

family n. f)khrawp khrua ครอบครัว

famous adj. mee f)cheu r)siang มีชื่อเสียง

fan n. (for air-circulation) h)phat!-lom! พัดลม

far, far away klai!, l)hang klai! ไกล, ห่างไกล

fare (for travel) f)kha doy-r)san ค่าโดยสาร

farm n. (rice) na นา; (not rice) f)rai! ไร่

farmer n. (rice) chao na ชาวนา; (not rice) chao f)rai! ชาวไร่

fast adj. reh!-o เร็ว

fasten v. l)tit! ติด; l)pit ปิด

faster (than something else) reh!-o l)kwa เร็วกว่า (go faster) reh!-o f)khao! เร็วเข้า

fat adj. f)uan อ้วน

father n. f)phaw, khoon! f)phaw พ่อ, คุณพ่อ

father-in-law (of man) f)phaw ta พ่อตา, (of woman) f)phaw r)phua

faucet n. h)kawk h)nam! ก๊อกน้ำ

fault (error, wrongdoing) khwam l)phit! ความผิด

fear v. klua กลัว

feather n. r)khon! h)nok! ขนนก

February koom!-pha-phan! กุมภาพันธ์

feel (have feelings) h)roo-l)seuk! รู้สึก

fees n. f)kha tham!-niam ค่าธรรมเนียม
   (school fees) f)kha thuhm ค่าเทอม

female r)ying! หญิง; (for animals only) tua
   mia ตัวเมีย

fence (n., enclosure) h)rua รั้ว

fertilizer n. r)pooy! ปุ๋ย

feverish adj. pen! f)khai! เป็นไข้

few (not many) h)nawy น้อย; (a few, two or
   three) r)sawng r)sam สองสาม

fiancé fiancée f)khoo f)man! คู่หมั้น

field n. l)sa!-r)nam สนาม; (rice field) f)thoong
   na ทุ่งนา

field marshal (mil.) jawm phon! จอมพล

fierce adj. l)doo! h)rai ดุร้าย

fifteen (15) l)sip!-f)ha สิบห้า (๑๕)

fifty (50) f)ha-l)sip! ห้าสิบ (๕๐)

fight l)taw r)soo kan! การต่อสู้กัน; (v.)
   l)taw r)soo kan! ต่อสู้กัน

file n. (tool) ta!-bai! ตะไบ, (folder) h)faem แฟ้ม

fill up l)sai! f)hai! tem! ใส่ให้เต็ม

film n. (motion picture) r)nang!, f)phap!-h)pha!-yon! หนัง, ภาพยนตร์
(photographic) feem l)thai f)roop ฟีล์มถ่ายรูป

filter v. krawng กรอง

finally (at last) nai! f)thee l)soot! ในที่สุด

final one (last one) an! l)soot! h)thai อันสุดท้าย

find v. h)phop! พบ

fine adj. (very good) dee f)mak ดีมาก; (well, in good health) l)sa!-bai dee สบายดี

fine (for an offense) f)kha l)prap! ค่าปรับ

finger (of hand) h)new meu นิ้วมือ

fingernail h)lep meu เล็บมือ

fingerprints n. lai meu phim! ลายมือพิมพ์

finish (stop) f)luhk, l)jop! เลิก, จบ; (make complete) tham! f)hai! l)set ทำให้เสร็จ

finished adj. l)set h)laeo เสร็จแล้ว; (all gone) l)mot! h)laeo หมดแล้ว; (stopped) l)jop! h)laeo จบแล้ว

Fire! (shouted warning) fai! f)mai! ไฟไหม้

fire (a gun) ying! peun ยิงปืน; (discharge from work) f)hai! l)awk ให้ออก

Fire Dept. kawng l)dap! phluhng กองดับเพลิง

first f)raek แรก; (at first) thee f)raek ที่แรก; (No. 1) f)thee l)neung! ที่หนึ่ง; (before something else) l)kawn ก่อน

first aid (med.) l)pa!-r)thom! h)pha!-ya-ban ปฐมพยาบาล

first-class (1st-class, first-grade) h)chan! f)thee l)neung! ชั้นที่หนึ่ง

first floor (1st storey) h)chan! f)thee l)neung! ชั้นที่หนึ่ง

first lt. (army) h)rawy tho; (AF, flying officer) reua ah-l)kat tho; (police 1st lt., police lt.) h)rawy tam!-l)ruat tho ร้อยโท, เรืออากาศโท, ร้อยตำรวจโท

first name (of a person) f)cheu ชื่อ

first time thee f)raek, h)khrang! f)raek ที่แรก, ครั้งแรก

fish (animal) pla ปลา; (v.) l)tok! pla ตกปลา

fish sauce, fish soy h)nam! pla น้ำปลา

fit (be good fit, as clothing) r)suam phaw dee สวมพอดี

five (5) f)ha ห้า (๕)

fix (attach) l)tit! h)wai! ติดไว้; (specify time) k3m³-l)not! weh-lah กำหนดเวลา; (make secure) l)tɪt! f)hai! f)naen ติดให้แน่น; (repair) f)sawm ซ่อม; (troublesome situation) l)deuat h)rawn เดือดร้อน

flag n. thong! ธง

flashlight n. fai! r)chai ไฟฉาย

flat adj. baen แบน; (level) f)rap f)riap ราบเรียบ; (apartment) flaet แฟลต; (flat tire) yang baen ยางแบน

flea (insect) tua l)mat! ตัวหมัด

flexible adj. l)awn tua อ่อนตัว

flight (in general) kan bin! การบิน; (a flight, by an airplane) f)theeo bin! เที่ยวบิน

flight-lt. (AF capt.) reua ah-l)kat l)ek เรืออากาศ เอก

flint (for cigarette-lighter) l)tban fai! h)chaek ถ่านไฟแช็ค

float v. lawy ลอย

flooded adj. h)nam! f)thuam น้ำท่วม

floor n h)pheun พื้น; (storey) h)chan! ชั้น

floormat f)pha h)chet! h)thao! ผ้าเช็ดเท้า

floor show kan l)sa!-daeng flaw cho การแสดง ฟลอร์โชว์

flour n. f)paeng แป้ง

flow v. r)lai! ไหล

flower n. l)dawk h)mai คอกไม้

flu (influenza) f)khai! l)wat! l)yai! ไข้หวัดใหญ่

fly (insect) ma-laeng-wan! แมลงวัน

fly v. bin! บิน

flying officer (AF 1st lt.) reua ah-l)kat tho เรือ อากาศโท

foggy adj. mee l)mawk มีหมอก

fold v. h)phap! พับ

follow v. tam pai! ตามไป

food n. ah-r)han อาหาร

food-poisoning ah-r)han pen! h)phit! อาหารเป็นพิษ

fool (play trick on) l)lawk f)len หลอกเล่น; (stupid person) khon! f)ngo คนโง่

foolish adj. f)ngo โง่

foot (measurement) h)new f)foot นิ้วฟุต; (of body) h)thao! เท้า; (for animals) teen ตีน

football (soccer) h)foot!-bawn ฟุตบอลล์

footprint rawy h)thao! รอยเท้า

for r)sam!-l)rap!, f)pheua สำหรับ, เพื่อ

forbid, forbidden f)ham ห้าม

force v. bang!-h)khap! บังคับ

foreign adj. 1)tang 1)pra!-f)thet ต่างประเทศ

foreigner chao 1)tang 1)pra!-f)thet ชาวต่างประเทศ;
(fair-skinned) 1)fa!-1)rang! ฝรั่ง

foreign language pha-r)sa 1)tang 1)pra!-f)thet
ภาษาต่างประเทศ

forests 1)pa h)mai! ป่าไม้; (jungles) 1)pa dong!
ป่าดง

forever (from now on) 1)ta!-1)lawt pai! ตลอดไป

for example f)chen, tua 1)yang เช่น, ตัวอย่าง

forget v. leum ลืม

forgetful adj. f)khee leum ขี้ลืม

forgive v. 1)ah!-phai f)hai อภัยให้

fork (for eating) f)sawm ส้อม

for lease, for rent f)hai f)chao! ให้เช่า

form (shape) f)roop f)rang รูปร่าง; (printed
form) 1)baep fawm แบบฟอร์ม

formerly (in the past) f)meua kawn เมื่อก่อน

for sale 1)ja! r)khai จะขาย

fortune-teller r)maw doo หมอดู

forty (40) 1)see-1)sip! สี่สิบ (๔๐)

four (4) สี่ (๔)

fourteen (14) 1)sip!-1)see สิบสี่ (๑๔)

France, French 1)fa'-l)rang!-l)set ฝรั่งเศส; (French language) pha-r)sa 1)fa!-l)rang!-l)set ภาษา ฝรั่งเศส

free (no charge) free ฟรี; (not busy) f)wang ว่าง; (liberate) l)plawy ปล่อย

free time (spare time) we-la f)wang เวลาว่าง

fresh (not stale) l)sot! สด

Friday wan! l)sook! วันศุกร์

fried (for food) f)thawt ทอด; (fried eggs) l)khai dao ไข่ดาว; (fried rice, a delicious Thai dish) f)khao l)phat! ข้าวผัด

friend f)pheuan เพื่อน

frightened adj. l)tok! jai! ตกใจ

from l)jak จาก

front (in front) f)khang f)na ข้างหน้า

frozen pen! h)ŋam! r)khaeng! เป็นน้ำแข็ง

fruit r)phon!-h)la!-h)mai! ผลไม้; (fruit juice) h)ŋam! r)phon!-h)la!-h)mai น้ำผลไม้

fry (food) f)thawt ทอด; (frying-pan) l)ka'-h)tha! กะทะ

fuel n. h)cheua-phluhng เชื้อเพลิง

full adj. tem! h)laeo เต็มแล้ว; (after eating) l)im! h)laeo อิ่มแล้ว

furniture (for home) f)khreuang reuan, fuh-ni-juh เครื่องเรือน, เฟอร์นิเจอร์

fuse (for detonation) h)cha!-nuan ชนวน; (electrical) few! ฟิวส์

future n. ah-na-khot! อนาคต; (in the future) nai ah-na-khot! ในอนาคต

gamble v. f)len kan h)pha!-nan! เล่นการพนัน

garage (for repairs) l)oo h)rot! อู่รถ; (for parking) rong h)rot! โรงรถ

garbage n. l)kha!-l)ya! ขยะ; (garbage-can) r)thang! l)kha!-ya! ถังขยะ

garden n. r)suan สวน; (gardener) khon! r)suan คนสวน

garlic n. l)kra!-thiam กระเทียม

gas (for cooking) h)kaes, h)kaet แก๊ส

gasoline (petrol) h)nam!-man! น้ำมัน

general (in general) doy f)thua pai! โดยทั่วไป

general (n., mil.) nai phon!, (AF) nai phon! ah-l)kat, (police) nai phon! tam!-l)ruat นายพล, นายพลอากาศ, นายพลตำรวจ

generous (free-hearted) h)nam!-jai dee น้ำใจดี

genuine (real, not fake) r)khawng h)thae ของแท้

German, Germany yuh-h)ra!-man! เยอรมัน; (language) pha-r)sa yuh-h)ra!-man! ภาษาเยอรมัน

germs n. h)cheua f)rok เชื้อโรค

get v. f)dai! ได้

ghost n. r)phee ผี

gift n. r)khawng-r)khwan! ของขวัญ

girl n. l)dek! r)ying เด็กหญิง

girlfriend (sweetheart) faen, f)khoo h)rak! แฟน, คู่รัก

give v. f)hai! ให้; (give back) kheun f)hai! คืนให้; (give up, surrender) yawm h)phae ยอมแพ้

glad yin!-dee ยินดี

glass (for drinking) f)thuay f)kaeo, ถ้วยแก้ว; (glass in general) f)kaeo แก้ว

glasses (for eyes) f)waen ta แว่นตา

gloves n. r)thoong! meu ถุงมือ

glue n. kao กาว

go v. pai! ไป; (go back) l)klap! pai! กลับไป; (go inside) f)khao pai! เข้าไป; (go out) l)awk pai!, ออกไป; (go to bed) pai! nawn ไปนอน

gold n. thawng ทอง

golf (the game) h)kawf กอล์ฟ; (golf course) l)sa!-r)nam h)kawf สนามกอล์ฟ

gonorrhea (the "clap") f)rok r)nawng nai! โรค หนองใน

good adj. dee ดี

Goodbye. Good evening. Good morning. Good night.
l)sa!-l)wat!-dee สวัสดี

government h)rat!-l)tha!-ban รัฐบาล

grade n. (level, rank) h)chan!, ชั้น; (marks on exams, etc.) h)kha!-naen คะแนน

graduate from r)sam!-ret! l)jak.... สำเร็จจาก....

grandchild r)lan หลาน

grandfather (maternal) ta ตา, (paternal) l)poo ปู่

grandmother (maternal) yat ยาย; (paternal) f)ya ย่า

grape n. l)ah!-l)ngoon! องุ่น

grass f)ya หญ้า

grave (for burial) r)loom! r)fang! l)sop! หลุมฝังศพ

gravel n. f)kawn l)kruat ก้อนกรวด

gray, grey (color) r)see thao! สีเทา

grease (for cooking) h)nam!-man! r)moo, น้ำมันหมู; (for lubrication) h)nam'-man! ja-h)ra!-bee, น้ำมันจารบี; (lubricate a vehicle) l)at! l)cheet อัดฉีด

green (color) r)see r)kheeo, สีเขียว; (green light) fai! f)kheeo ไฟเขียว

ground (earth, land) h)pheun-din! พื้นดิน; (soil, dirt) din daen ดินแดน; (by land) thang l)bok!

ทางบก; (wire for grounding) r)sai din! สายดิน;
(ground floor) h)chan! f)lang ชั้นล่าง

ground forces (mil.) h)tha!-r)han l)bok! ทหารบก

group (category) jam!-f)phuak จำพวก, (of people
l)kloom! กลุ่ม, (of things) f)phuak พวก

group-capt. (AF col.) na-wa ah-l)kat l)ek นาวา
อากาศเอก

grow (become bigger) toh f)kbeun! โตขึ้น

guard n. khon! yam คนยาม; (mil. guard) h)tha!-
r)han yam ทหารยาม

guerrilla (bandit, outlaw, terrorist) jon', f)phoo
l)kaw kan h)rai โจร, ผู้ก่อการร้าย
(communist terrorist) f)phoo l)kaw kan
h)rai khawm-mew-nit ผู้ก่อการร้ายคอมมิวนิสต์

guess v. dao! ao! เดาเอา

guest n. l)khaek แขก

guide n. f)phoo nam! thang ผู้นำทาง

guilty mee khwam l)phit มีความผิด

gulf n. l)ao อ่าว, Gulf of Thailand l)ao thai!
อ่าวไทย

gum (chewing gum) n. l)mak l)fa!-f)rang หมาก
ฝรั่ง; (gums of mouth) l)ngeuak เหงือก

gun (in general) peun ปืน; (gunpowder) din!
peun ดินปืน

had (See HAVE.)

hair (animals) r)khon! l)sat! ขนสัตว์; (people, body) r)khon! ขน; (people, on head only) r)phom ผม; (hairbrush) praeng praeng r)phom! แปรงแปรงผม; (haircut) l)tat! r)phom! ตัดผม

half (one half) f)kreung l)neung! ครึ่งหนึ่ง

Halt! (Stop!) l)yoot! หยุด

ham n. r)moo haem หมูแฮม

hammer n. h)khawn ค้อน

hand n. meu มือ

handbag (lady's handbag) l)kra!-r)pao! r)theu กระเป๋าถือ

handkerchief f)pha h)chet f)na ผ้าเช็ดหน้า

handle (for holding) f)thee meu l)jap! ที่มือจับ

handsome (for men) l)law, f)roop l)law หล่อ, รูปหล่อ

handwriting n. lai meu ลายมือ

hang v. r)khwaen แขวน

hangar (for airplanes) rong l)kep! f)khreuang-bin! โรงเก็บเครื่องบิน

hanger (for clothing) h)mai! r)khwaen f)seua ไม้แขวนเสื้อ

happen v. l)kuht f)kheun! เกิดขึ้น

happiness n. khwam l)sook! ความสุข

happy adj. dee jai! ดีใจ

hard adj. (not soft) r)khaeng! แข็ง; (difficult) f)yak ยาก; adv. (very much) l)nak! หนัก

has (See HAVE.)

hat n. l)muak หมวก

hate v. l)kliat เกลียด

have, has, had (there is, there are) mee มี

he (or him) r)khao! เขา, (respectful) f)than ท่าน

head (of a person) r)hua, r)see-l)sa! หัว, ศีรษะ

headache l)puat r)hua ปวดหัว

headlights (of a vehicle) fai! f)na h)rot! ไฟหน้ารถ

healthy mee l)sook!-l)kha!-f)pbap dee มีสุขภาพดี

bear v. f)dai! yin! ได้ยิน

heart n. r)hua jai! หัวใจ

heat n. khwam h)rawn ความร้อน; (v.) tham! f)hai! h)rawn ทำให้ร้อน

heavy adj. l)nak! หนัก

height n. khwam r)soong ความสูง

Hello. hal-r)lo, l)sa!-l)wat!-dee ฮัลโหล, สวัสดี

help v. f)chuay ช่วย

Help ! (cry for help, in emergency) f)chuay f)duay ช่วยด้วย

hepatitis (n., med) f)rok l)tap l)ak!-l)sep โรคตับอักเสบ

her pron. (same as she), (belonging to her) r)khawng r)khao! ของเขา

here f)thee f)nee นี่

hers (belonging to her) r)khawng r)khao! ของเขา

hide v. f)sawn h)wai! ซ่อนไว้

high adj. r)soong สูง; (higher) r)soong l)kwa สูงกว่า

h_ghway thang r)luang l)phaen din! ทางหลวงแผ่นดิน

hill n. r)khao! เขา

him (same as he)

hinge n. ban h)phap! บานพับ

hire v. (for employment) f)jang จ้าง

his (belonging to him) r)khawng r)khao ของเขา

hit v. tee ตี

hold v. (in the hands) r)theu h)wai! ถือไว้

hole n. roo รู

holiday wan! l)yoot! วันหยุด

home f)ban บ้าน

homesick adj. h)khit! r)theung! f)ban คิดถึงบ้าน

honest adj. f)seu trong! ซื่อตรง

hooked (fastened together) l)keeo l)yoo เกี่ยวอยู่

hope v. r)wang! f)wa หวังว่า; (hopeless) f)mai! mee r)wang! ไม่มีหวัง

horn (of vehicle) trae h)rot! แตรรถ

horse (animal) h)ma ม้า; (horsepower) raeng h)ma แรงม้า

horse racing kan l)khaeng h)ma การแข่งม้า

hose (rubber hose) f)thaw yang ท่อยาง

hospital rong pha!-ya-ban โรงพยาบาล

host, hostess (especially for ceremonies, such as weddings) !)jao f)phap เจ้าภาพ

hot (temperature) h)rawn ร้อน, (in taste) l)phet! เผ็ด

hotel rong-raem, ho-ten! โรงแรม, โฮเต็ล

hot season (March-May in Thailand) f)na h)rawn, reu!-doo h)rawn หน้าร้อน, ฤดูร้อน

hot-water bottle (thermos) l)kra!-l)tik! h)nam! กระติกน้ำ

hour (60 minutes) f)chua-mong ชั่วโมง

house f)ban บ้าน

houseboy (servant) r)bawy, l)dek! h)rap! h)chai! บ๋อย, เด็กรับใช้

house for rent f)ban f)hai! f)chao! บ้านให้เช่า

house number f)lek f)thee f)ban เลขที่บ้าน

housewife f)mae f)ban แม่บ้าน

how? (in what way?) l)yang!-rai? อย่างไร; (to what extent) ....f)thao!-rai! ....เท่าไร

How are you? l)sa!-bai dee r)reu? สบายดีหรือ

how long? (length) yao f)thao!-rai? ยาวเท่าไร; (time) nan f)thao!-rai! นานเท่าไร

how many? l)kee...., ...f)thao!-rai! กี่...., ...เท่าไร

how much? (money) f)thao!-rai! เท่าไร

how old? ah-r)yoo! f)thao!-rai! อายุเท่าไร

How old are you (is he, is she, etc.)? ah-h)yoo! f)thao!-rai! อายุเท่าไร

hug (embrace tightly) l)kawt กอด

humid adj. h)cheun l)chae! ชื้นแฉะ

hundred (100) h)rawy ร้อย, l)neung! h)rawy หนึ่งร้อย (๑๐๐)

hungry adj. r)hew, r)hew f)khao หิว, หิวข้าว

hunt (for something) r)ha, h)khon! r)ha หา, ค้นหา

Hurry! reh-o reh-o เร็วๆ

hurt (injured) adj. l)jep!, l)bat l)jep! เจ็บ, บาดเจ็บ

husband n. r)phua, r)sa-mee, faen ผัว, สามี, แฟน

I (or me) (males) r)phom! ผม; (females) r)chan! ฉัน

ice n. h)nam!-r)khaeng! น้ำแข็ง; ice-cream (same as English)

idea n. khwam h)khit! ความคิด

idiom n. r)sam!-nuan สำนวน

if f)tha ถ้า

ill (not well) f)mai! sa'-bai ไม่สบาย

illegal l)phit! l)kot!-r)mai ผิดกฎหมาย

imagine v. f)wat f)phap nai! jai! วาดภาพในใจ

imitate v. (copy) lian l)baep เลียนแบบ

immediately doy thar! thee โดยทันที

Immigration Division (Police Dept.) kawng l)truat khon f)khao! meuang กองตรวจคนเข้าเมือง

important adj. r)sam!-khan! สำคัญ

impossible pen! pai! f)mai! f)dai! เป็นไปไม่ได้

improve v. l)prap! proong! ปรับปรุง

in nai! ใน

in advance f)luang f)na ล่วงหน้า

in a hurry f)reep h)rawn รีบร้อน

in a moment l)pra!-r)deeo ประเดี๋ยว

inch (1/12 of foot) h)new! h)foot! นิ้วฟุต

including adj., ruam h)thang! รวมทั้ง

income tax pha-r)see nguhn f)dai! ภาษีเงินได้

increase (become bigger) l)yai f)kheun! ใหญ่ขึ้น; (make bigger) tham! f)hai! l)yai! f)kheun! ทำให้ใหญ่ขึ้น; (increase price) f)kheun! ra-kha ขึ้นราคา; (increase salary) f)phuhm nguhn-deuan เพิ่มเงินเดือน

India(n) in-dia อินเดีย; (Amer. Indian) in-dian daeng อินเดียนแดง

indifferent (impassive) r)chuhy r)chuhy เฉยๆ

indigestion n. ab-r)han f)mai f)yawy อาหารไม่ย่อย

industry n. l)oot!-r)sa l)ha!-kam! อุตสาหกรรม

inexpensive (not costly) f)mai phaeng ไม่แพง

infantry (n., mil.) f)tha!-r)ban f)rap ทหารราบ

infected (with germs) l)ak!-l)sep, l)tit! h)cheua f)rok ลักเสบ, ติดเชื้อโรค

infiltrate v. f)saek seum! แทรกซึม

inflammable adj. wai! fai! ไวไฟ

influence n. am!-f)nat, l)it!-h)thi!-phon! อำนาจ, อิทธิพล

influenza (the flu) f)khai! l)wat! l)yai! ไข้หวัดใหญ่

inform v. f)jaeng แจ้ง

information (details) rai h)la!-l)iat รายละเอียด; (news) l)khao ข่าว

in front (of) f)na, f)khang f)na หน้า, ข้างหน้า

in general doy f)thua pai โดยทั่วไป

injection (of medicine) (kan) l)cheet ya (การ) ฉีดยา

injured adj. l)bat l)jep! บาดเจ็บ

ink (for writing) h)nam! l)meuk! น้ำหมึก

innertube (of a tire) yang nai! ยางใน

innocent (not guilty) f)mai! mee khwam l)phit!
ไม่มีความผิด; (pure) baw-h)ri!-l)soot! บริสุทธิ์

inoculate (for disease-prevention) l)cheet ya
f)pawng-kan ฉีดยาป้องกัน

in order (one by one) tam lam!-l)dap! ตามลำดับ;
(in good order) f)riap h)rawy เรียบร้อย

in order to f)pheua, r)sam!-l)rap! เพื่อ, สำหรับ

inquire l)sawp r)tham สอบถาม

insane (crazy, mad) f)ba บ้า

insect n. tua ma-laeng ตัวแมลง

insecticide n. ya f)kha ma-laeng ยาฆ่าแมลง

insert v. l)sawt f)khao! pai! สอดเข้าไป

inside f)khang-nai! ข้างใน

insignia of rank f)khreuang h)yot! เครื่องยศ

insist v. yeun yan!, h)yam! ยืนยัน, ย้ำ

insomnia nawn f)mai! l)lap! นอนไม่หลับ

inspect v. l)truat doo ตรวจดู

install (as machinery, etc.) l)tit! f)tang! ติดตั้ง

installment plan (hire-purchase) h)seu nguhn
l)phawn ซื้อเงินผ่อน

instance (example) tua l)yang ตัวอย่าง
(for instance, for example) h)yok! tua l)yang
ยกตัวอย่าง, tua-l)yang f)chen ตัวอย่างเช่น

instead of thaen f)thee แทนที่

instruct (teach) r)sawn สอน; (train) l)feuk ฝึก

instruments n. f)khreuang h)chai! เครื่องใช้

insult v. doo l)thook ดูถูก

insure v. (take out insurance) l)pra!-kan! phai
ประกันภัย

(life insurance) l)pra!-kan! chee-h)wit ประกัน
ชีวิต

intelligence (n., mil.) kan l)khao การข่าว

intelligent adj. l)sa! l)ti pan-ya dee สติปัญญาดี

interest (n., on money owed) l)dawk f)bia
ดอกเบี้ย

interested adj. r)son!-jai! สนใจ

interesting adj. f)na r)son jai! น่าสนใจ

interpreter (n., person) f)lam ล่าม

interrogate v. h)sak! r)tham ซักถาม

interview v. r)sam!-f)phat สัมภาษณ์

into (go into) f)khao! pai เข้าไป; (come into)
f)khao! ma เข้ามา

intoxicated (drunk) mao! f)lao! เมาเหล้า

introduce (someone to somebody) h)nae! nam!
แนะนำ

invade v. l)book! h)rook! บุกรุก

invader n. 1)fai h)rook!-ran ผ้ายรุกราน

invest (v., fin.) long! thoon! ลงทุน

investigate v. 1)seup r)suan, 1)sawp r)suan
สืบสวน, สอบสวน

investment (n., fin.) kan long! thoon! การลงทุน

invite v. chuhn เชิญ

invited guest 1)khaek f)phoo h)rap! chuhn แขก
ผู้รับเชิญ

involved adj. 1)keeo f)khawng เกี่ยวข้อง

iron (n., for ironing clothes) tao! f)reet f)pha
เตารีดผ้า
   (the metal) 1)lek! เหล็ก

iron clothes f)reet f)pha รีดผ้า

irrigation n. kan chon! 1)pra!-than การชลประทาน

irritate v. h)rop!-kuan รบกวน

irritated adj. ram!-khan รำคาญ

irritating adj. f)na ram!-khan น่ารำคาญ

is (See BE.)

island n. 1)kaw! เกาะ

Isn't that right? f)chai! r)mai! ใช่ไหม?

issue v. (as a permit, etc.) 1)awk f)hai! ออกให้

Is that all right? (Okay?) f)dai! r)mai! ได้ไหม?

Is that right? f)chai! r)mai! ใช่ไหม?

it (pron.) man! มัน

itch v. khan! คัน

item n. (as in a list) rai-kan รายการ

it's a pity (showing regret) f)na r)sia dai, น่าเสียดาย; (showing pity) f)na r)song!-r)san น่าสงสาร

it's up to you (as you like) h)laeo l)tae khoon! แล้วแต่คุณ

jack (as a car-jack) f)mae-raeng แม่แรง

jacket n. f)seua r)nao เสื้อหนาว

jail n. (gaol) h)khook!, ta-rang คุก, ตาราง

jail (lock up, put in jail) r)khang! h)wai! ขังไว้

jam n. (fruit preserves) yaem แยม

January h)mok!-l)ka!-ra-khom! มกราคม

Japan, Japanese f)yee-l)poon! ญี่ปุ่น (country of Japan) l)pra!-f)thet f)yee-l)poon! ประเทศญี่ปุ่น (Japanese language) pha-r)sa f)yee-l)poon! ภาษาญี่ปุ่น (Japanese people) chao f)yee-l)poon! ชาวญี่ปุ่น

jaundice (disease) f)rok dee f)san โรคดีซ่าน

jealous (envious) l)it!-r)cha อิจฉา; (romantically) r)heung! หึง

jellyfish n. maeng-l)ka!-f)phroon! แมงกะพรุน

Jesus, Jesus Christ h)phra! yeh-soo พระเยซู

jet, jet plane f)khreuang-bin! ai! f)phon! เครื่องบิน
ไอพ่น

Jew, Jewish yew (pronounced as English word
"you") ยิว

jewelry shop h)ran r)khai f)khreuang f)phet
phlawy ร้านขายเครื่องเพชรพลอย

job (work) ngan งาน

join, join in (participate) f)khao! f)ruam เข้าร่วม

joke (tell jokes, speak jokingly) f)phoot f)len,
f)phoot l)ta!-l)lok พูดเล่น, พูดตลก

judge n. (in court) f)phoo h)phi!-f)phak-r)sa
ผู้พิพากษา

(umpire, referee) f)phoo l)tat!-r)sin! ผู้ตัดสิน

juice (any liquid juice) h)nam!........ น้ำ........

(fruit juice) h)nam! r)phon!-h)la!-h)mai!
น้ำผลไม้

July ka-ra-ka-da-khom! กรกฎาคม

jump v. l)kra!-l)dot กระโดด

June mi!-thoo!-na-yon! มิถุนายน

jungle n. l)pa dong', l)pa h)rok! ป่าดง, ป่ารก

JUSMAG (Joint United States Military Advisory
Group) l)nuay jas-maek หน่วยจัสแม็ก

just (fair) pen! tham เป็นธรรม; h)yoot!-l)ti!-tham!
ยุติธรรม

(only) phiang, f)thao! h)nan! เพียง, เท่านั้น

just a minute l)pra!-r)deeo ประเดี๋ยว

just now (just a moment ago) f)meua f)kee
l.)nee เมื่อกี้นี้

keep v. l)kep, l)kep! h)wai เก็บ, เก็บไว้

kerosene n. h)nam!-man! h)kat น้ำมันก๊าด

kettle (for boiling water, etc.) ka, ka h)nam!
กา, กาน้ำ

key (for a lock) f)look koon!-jae ลูกกุญแจ

Khmer (Cambodia, Cambodian) l)kha!-r)men,
kam!-phoo-cha เขมร, กัมพูชา

kick v. l)teh! เตะ

kidneys (of the body) tai! ไต

kill v. f)kha ฆ่า

kill germs (disinfect) f)kha h)cheua-f)rok ฆ่า
เชื้อโรค

kilo, kilogram (2.2 pounds) l)kee!-lo, l)kee!-lo-
kram! กิโล, กิโลกรัม

kilo, kilometre (0.62 miles) l)kee!-lo, l)kee!-lo-
f)met กิโล, กิโลเมตร

kind adj. (toward others) jai! dee, mee h)nam!
jai! dee ใจดี, มีน้ำใจดี

kind n. (type, species) h)cha!-h)nit! ชนิด

kindergarten rong-rian ah-noo-ban โรงเรียนอนุบาล

king n. h)phra!-f)jao! l)phaen-din! พระเจ้าแผ่นดิน

king cobra (snake) ngoo jong!-ahng งูจงอาง

King of Thailand nai! r)luang, h)phra l)bat r)som!-l)det! h)phra! f)jao! l)yoo r)hua ใน หลวง, พระบาทสมเด็จพระเจ้าอยู่หัว

kiss (n., v.) l)joop จูบ

kitchen (room of house or outside of house) khrua, f)hawng khrua ครัว, ห้องครัว

kitten n. f)look maeo ลูกแมว

knee (of the leg) r)hua l)khao! หัวเข่า

knife f)meet มีด

knock at a door h)khaw! l)pra!-too เคาะประตู

know (someone or a place) h)roo-l)jak รู้จัก (know something, have knowledge) h)roo, f)sap รู้, ทราบ

know how tham! f)dai!, tham! pen! ทำได้, ทำเป็น

knowledge n. khwam h)roo ความรู้

knuckles (of fingers) f)khaw h)new-meu ข้อนิ้วมือ

Korea, Korean kao!-r)lee เกาหลี (country of Korea) l)pra!-f)thet kao!-r)lee ประเทศเกาหลี

(Korean language) pha-r)sa kao!-r)lee ภาษา
เกาหลี

(Korean people) chao kao!-r)lee ชาวเกาหลี

krait (banded krait snake) ngoo r)sam l)liam
งูสามเหลี่ยม

labor, labour n. raeng ngau แรงงาน

(Dept. of Labour) krom! raeng ngan กรมแรงงาน

laborer, labourer kam!-h)ma!-kawn กรรมกร

lack (be short of, need) l)khat, l)khat khlaen
ขาด, ขาดแคลน

ladder n. ban!-dai! l)kra!-dai! บันได, กระได

lady n. l)soo!-f)phap l)sa!-tree สุภาพสตรี

lake l)sa! h)nam!, r)nawng h)nam! สระน้ำ, หนอง
น้ำ

lamp n. l)ta!-kiang ตะเกียง

lance corporal (1-stripe NCO, PFC) l)sip! tree
สิบตรี

land n. (in general) f)thee-din! ที่ดิน

(country, kingdom) meuang, l)phaen-din!
เมือง, แผ่นดิน

(Dept. of Land) krom! f)thee-din! กรมที่ดิน

(land, as opposed to water) l)bok!, thang
l)bok! บก, ทางบก

land (v., as an airplane) long!, long! l)sa!-r)nam
  bin! ลง, ลงสนามบิน

landing (for boats, ships) f)tha, f)tha reua
  ท่า, ท่าเรือ

landing field for airplanes) l)sa!-r)nam bin!
  สนามบิน

landlord f)jao!-r)khawng f)ban เจ้าของบ้าน,
  f)jao!-r)khawng f)thee เจ้าของที่

lane (soi, small street) sawy, l)trawk ซอย, ตรอก

language n. pha-r)sa ภาษา

Laos, Laotian lao ลาว
  (the country) l)pra!-f)thet lao ประเทศลาว
  (the language) pha-r)sa lao ภาษาลาว
  (the people) khon! lao, chao lao คนลาว, ชาวลาว

lard (for cooking) h)nam!-man! r)moo น้ำมันหมู

large (big) l)yai!, toh, l)yai! toh ใหญ่, โต, ใหญ่โต

last adj. f)thee h)laeo ที่แล้ว [as in "last week"
  = l)ah!-h)thit f)thee h)laeo อาทิตย์ที่แล้ว]
  (last one, final one) ....l)soot! h)thai ....สุดท้าย
  [as in "an! l)soot! h)thai" = the last one]

last (endure) thon!-than ทนทาน

last name (family name, surname) nam l)sa!-
  koon! นามสกุล

last night f)meua kheun เมื่อคืน

late (at night) l)deuk!, tawn l)deuk! ดึก, ตอนดึก
  (late in the afternoon) yehn, tawn yehn เย็น, ตอนเย็น
  (late in the morning) r)sai, r)sai r)sai สาย, สายๆ

late (not on time) r)sai, f)mai! than! สาย, ไม่ทัน

later (after, afterwards) nai phai r)lang! ในภายหลัง
  (another time, after now) thee r)lang! ทีหลัง
  (later than someone or something else) h)cha l)kwa ช้ากว่า

laugh v. r)hua-h)raw! หัวเราะ

lavatory n. (bathroom, rest room) f)hawng h)nam! ห้องน้ำ

law n. l)kot!-r)mai กฎหมาย

lawn (of a home, etc.) l)sa!-r)nam f)ya สนามหญ้า

lawyer n. h)tha!-nai khwam ทนายความ

laxative (n., medicine) ya l)thai ยาถ่าย

lay (lay something down) wang, wang long วาง, วางลง

lazy adj. l)kiat-h)khran, f)khee l)kiat เกียจคร้าน, ขี้เกียจ

lead n. (the metal) l)ta!-l)kua ตะกั่ว

lead v. (take or escort someone somewhere)
nam pai!, pha pai! นำไป, พาไป
(towards the speaker) nam ma, pha ma นำมา,
พามา

leader (person) f)phoo nam! ผู้นำ

leaf (of a tree) bai! h)mai! ใบไม้

leak n. l)joot! f)rua, f)thee f)rua จุดรั่ว, ที่รั่ว

leak v. f)rua!, f)rua l)awk รั่ว, รั่วออก

learn v. rian เรียน

lease (let out, lease) f)hai! f)chao˙ ให้เช่า
(take on lease) f)chao เช่า

least n. (the least) l)suan h)nawy ส่วนน้อย; (at
least) l)yang h)nawy อย่างน้อย

leather n. r)nang! l)sat! หนังสัตว์

leave (go out and away) l)awk pai! ออกไป

Leave! (Go away!) h)pai! ไป

leave (vacation from work) la h)phak!, la l)yoot˙
ลาพัก, ลาหยุด

leech (blood-sucking insect) f)thak, pling!
ทาก, ปลิง

left, lefthand side h)sai, h)sai meu, f)khang h)sai
ซ้าย, ซ้ายมือ, ข้างซ้าย

left over (remaining) r)leua เหลือ

leftovers (of food) ah-r)han r)leua, l)set! ah-r)ban อาหารเหลือ, เศษอาหาร

leg (of body) r)kha ขา

legal adj. tam l)kot!-r)mai ตามกฎหมาย

lemon, lime n. h)ma!-nao มะนาว

lemonade, limeade h)nam! h)ma!-nao น้ำมะนาว

lend (let someone borrow) f)hai! yeum ให้ยืม

length n. khwam yao ความยาว

leprosy (n., med.) f)rok h)reuan โรคเรื้อน

less, less than h)nawy l)kwa น้อยกว่า

lesson n. l)bot! rian บทเรียน

let v. (allow) f)hai!, a-noo-f)yat f)hai! ให้ อนุญาตให้

let go (release) l)plawy ปล่อย

Let me (do this or that) r)khaw.. ..... ขอ.........

letter (correspondence) l)jot!-r)mai จดหมาย; (o alphabet) tua r)nang-r)seu ตัวหนังสือ

lettuce (veg.) l)phak!-l)kat r)hawm ผักกาดหอม

level (in surface) f)rap f)riap ราบเรียบ (a certain level) h)ra!-l)dap! ระดับ

library n. f)hawng l)sa!-l)moot! ห้องสมุด

license n. bai: a-noo-f)yat ใบอนุญาต

license plate (for a motor vehicle) h)tha!-bian h)rot! ทะเบียนรถ

lick (with the tongue) lia เลีย

lid n. r)fa, r)fa l)pit! ฝา, ฝาปิด

lie (n., v.) ko-l)hok! โกหก

lie down nawn long! นอนลง

lieutenant (army, 2nd lt., sub-lt.) h)rawy tree ร้อยตรี

    (lt., 1st lt., senior lt.) h)rawy tho ร้อยโท

    (air force, 2nd lt., pilot officer) reua ah-l)kat tree เรืออากาศตรี

    (1st lt., flying officer) reua ah-l)kat tho เรืออากาศโท

    (flight-lt., AF capt.) reua ah-kat l)ek เรืออากาศเอก

    (navy, lt., sub-lt.) reua tho เรือโท

    (lt., senior grade, senior lt.) reua l)ek เรือเอก

    (police, 2nd lt., sub-lt.) h)rawy tam!-l)ruat tree ร้อยตำรวจตรี

    (1st lt., lt.) h)rawy tam!-l)ruat tho ร้อยตำรวจโท

lieutenant-colonel (army) phan! tho พันโท

    (air force, wing-commander) na-wa ah-l)kat tho นาวาอากาศโท

(police) phan! tam!-l)ruat tho พันตำรวจโท

lieutenant-commander (navy) na-wa tree นาวาตรี

lieutenant-general (army) phon tho พลโท

(air force, air-marshal)   phon! ah-l)kat tho
พลอากาศโท

(marines) phon tho l)fai! na-wi-ka-yo-thin!
พลโทลำนาวิกโยธิน

(police) phon! tam!-l)ruat tho พลตำรวจโท

life n. chee-h)wit! ชีวิต

life insurance l)pra!-kan! chee-h)wit! ประกันชีวิต

lift (elevator) lift!, f)khreuang lift! ลิฟท์, เครื่อง
ลิฟท์

lift, lift up v h)yok!, h)yok! f)kheun! ยก, ยกขึ้น

light adj. (for color) l)awn; อ่อน; (not dark)
l)sa -l)wang ส่วาง; (weight, not heavy) bao เบา

light n. (beam or ray) r)saeng fai! แสงไฟ; (lamp
for lighting) khom fai! โคมไฟ; (light-bulb)
l)lawt fai! หลอดไฟ

light v. (ignite) l)joot', l)joot fai! จุด, จุดไฟ

light blue, light-blue color r)see h)fa สีฟ้า

lightning h)fa f)laep ฟ้าแลบ; (lightning bolt,
which strikes something) h)fa l)pha ฟ้าผ่า

like (like something else, for example) f)chen
เช่น; (similar, alike) r)meuan, meuan kan!
เหมือน, เหมือนกัน

like v. f)chawp ชอบ

lime (fruit) h)ma!-nao มะนาว; (limeade) h)nam
h)ma!-nao น้ำมะนาว

lime (material) poon r)khao ปูนขาว

limit, limits n. l)khawp l)khet ขอบเขต

limit (v.) jam!-l)kat จำกัด

limited company   baw-h)rih!-l)sat jam!-l)kat!
บริษัทจำกัด

line n. f)sen เส้น; (short line, hyphen) l)kheet
f)san! ขีดสั้น; (long line, dash) l)kheet yao
ขีดยาว
(draw a line) l)kheet f)sen, f)lak f)sen
ขีดเส้น, ลากเส้น

line is busy (on phone) r)sai f)mai f)wang
สายไม่ว่าง

lips (of mouth) rim! r)fee l)pak ริมฝีปาก

liquor (bev:) f)lao! เหล้า

list   (of items)   rai-kan รายการ;   (of names)
rai-f)cheu รายชื่อ

listen, listen to v. fang ฟัง

liter, litre (1,000 c.c.) h)lit!, h)leet! ลิตร

little (not much) f)mai f)mak, h)nawy ไม่มาก,
น้อย; (a little bit) h)nit l)nawy นิดหน่อย;
(small) h)lek!, h)lek! h)leki เล็ก, เล็กๆ

little by little (gradually) f)khawy f)khawy
ค่อยๆ

live (be alive) l)yoo, mee chee-h)wit! l)yoo
อยู่, มีชีวิตอยู่; (live in a place) l)yoo, ah-r)sai!
l)yoo อยู่, อาศัยอยู่

liver (body organ) l)tap! ตับ; (beef liver)
l)tap! h)neua ตับเนื้อ; (pork liver) l)tap! r)moo
ตับหมู

living room (front room, parlor) h)hawng h)rap!
l)khaek ห้องรับแขก

lizard (large house lizard) h)took!-kae ตุ๊กแก;
(small house lizard) f)jing!-l)jok! จิ้งจก

load, load on v. ban!-h)thook บรรทุก

loaf of bread l)kha!-r)nom!-pang! pawn l)neung!
ขนมปังปอนด์หนึ่ง

loan n. (of money) nguhn yeum, nguhn f)koo
เงินยืม, เงินกู้

lobster (seafood) f)koong กุ้ง

located (at) f)tang! l)yoo [f)thee] ตั้งอยู่ (ที่)

lock n. (padlock) koon!-jae กุญแจ; (v.) l)sai!
koon!-jae ใส่กุญแจ

lonely, lonesome r)ngao!, h)wa l)weh เหงา, ว้าเหว่

long (in size) yao ยาว; (in time) nan นาน

long-distance (telephone) tho-ra-l)sap! thang klai! โทรศัพท์ทางไกล

look, look at v., doo; mawng doo ดู, มองดู

look after (care for) doo-lae ดูแล; (look after a child) h)liang l)dek! เลี้ยงเด็ก

look for (search for) r)ha, h)khon! r)ha หา, ค้นหา

look like r)meuan, doo r)meuan เหมือน, ดูเหมือน

loose adj r)luam หลวม

lorry (truck) h)rot! ban!-h)thook! รถบรรทุก

lose (be defeated) h)phae, r)sia แพ้, เสีย; (lose something) ....r)hai ....หาย, (lose one's way) r)long! thang หลงทาง

lottery (ticket) lawt-tuh-f)ree ลอตเตอรี่, l)sa!-l)lak kin-l)baeng สลากกินแบ่ง

loud adj. (in sound) dang!, r)siang dang ดัง, เสียงดัง

loudspeaker n. f)khreuang l)kha!-r)yai r)siang เครื่องขยายเสียง

lovable, lovely adj. f)na h)rak! น่ารัก

love v. h)rak! รัก

low adj. l)tam! ต่ำ; (low-class) h)chan· l)tam! ชั้นต่ำ

loyal adj. f)seu l)sat! ซื่อสัตย์

lubricate (a vehicle) l)at! l)cheet อัดจืด

luck f)chok โชค; (lucky, good luck) f)chok dee โชคดี; (unlucky, bad luck) f)chok f)mai! dee, f)chok h)rai โชคไม่ดี โชคร้าย

luggage n. l)kra!·r)pao duhn thang กระเป๋าเดินทาง

lump (as of sugar) f)kawn ก้อน

lunch (mid-day meal) ah·r)han klang·wan อาหารกลางวัน

lungs (of the body) l)pawt ปอด

ma'am, Ma'am (spoken by males) h)khrap!, khoon! h)khrap' ครับ, คุณครับ
(spoken by females) h)kha!, khoon! h)kha! คะ, คุณคะ

machine (in general) f)khreuang เครื่อง

machinegun (weapon) peun kon! ปืนกล; (sub-machineguṇ) peun kon! meu ปืนกลมือ

mad (crazy, insane) f)ba บ้า

Madam, Madame khoon!·nai คุณนาย

magnet n. f)mae l)lek! แม่เหล็ก

maid (female servant) r)ying! h)rap! h)chai! หญิงรับใช้

mail n. prai!-l)sa!-nee phan ไปรษณีย์ภัณฑ์; (air mail) prai!-l)sa!-nee ah-l)kat ไปรษณีย์อากาศ

mail v. (send a letter) l)sohng! l)jot!-r)mai ส่งจดหมาย

main adj. (most important) f)thee r)sam!-khan ที่สำคัญ

maintain (care for, as machinery) bam!-roong! h)rak!-r)sa บำรุงรักษา

major (mil. rank) (AF, squadron-leader) na-wa ah-l)kat tree นาวาอากาศตรี; (army) phan! tree พันตรี; (police) phan! tam!-l)ruat tree พันตำรวจตรี

major-general (mil. rank) (AF, air vice-marshal) phon! ah-l)kat tree พลอากาศตรี; (army) phon! tree พลตรี; (police) phon! tam!-l)ruat tree พลตำรวจตรี

make (or do) tham! ทำ

malaria (n., med.) h)ma-leh-ria, f)khai! l)jap!-l)san มาเลเรีย, ไข้จับสั่น

Malay (language) pha-r)sa h)ma!-la-yoo ภาษามลายู; (people) chao h)ma!-la-yoo ชาวมลายู

Malaysia, Malaysian h)ma-leh-sia มาเลเซีย

male (for humans) chai, f)phoo chai ชาย, ผู้ชาย; (animals) tua f)phoo ตัวผู้

man n. chai, f)phoo chai, khon f)phoo **chai**
ชาย, ผู้ชาย, คนผู้ชาย

manager n. f)phoo l)jat!-kan ผู้จัดการ

Mandarin (standard Chinese) pha-r)sa (jeen)
klang ภาษา(จีน)กลาง

maneuvers (n., mil.) kan h)sawm h)rop! การ
ซ้อมรบ

mango (fruit) h)ma!-f)muang มะม่วง

manicure n., v. l)taeng h)lep แต่งเล็บ

manners (conduct) ma-h)ra!-f)yat มารยาท; (bad
manners) ma-h)ra!-f)yat f)mai dee มารยาท
ไม่ดี; (good manners) ma-h)ra!-f)yat dee
มารยาทดี

manufacture (produce) l)pha!-l)lit! ผลิต

many adj. f)mak, r)lai มาก, หลาย

map n. r)phaen-f)thee แผนที่

March (month) mee-na-khom! มีนาคม

marihuana, marijuana kan!-cha กัญชา

Marines, Marine Corps na-h)wik!-l)ka!-yo-thin!
นาวิกโยธิน

marker n. f)khreuang-r)mai เครื่องหมาย

market n. l)ta!-l)lat ตลาด

married (already married) l)taeng ngan h)laeo
แต่งงานแล้ว

marry (get married) l)taeng ngan แต่งงาน

marshal (field marshal) jawm phon! จอมพล;
(marshal of the air force) jawm phon! ah-
l)kat จอมพลอากาศ

martial (law l)kot! ai-h)ya!-kan l)seuk! กฎอัยการศึก

massage v. f)nuat นวด; (massage girl) r)ying!
f)nuat หญิงนวด; (masseur, masseuse) r)maw
f)nuat หมอนวด,

master-sergeant (AF) phan!-l)ja ah-l)kat l)ek
พันจ่าอากาศเอก; (army) l)ja l)sip l)ek จ่าสิบเอก;
(police. top police NCO rank) l)ja nai l)sip!
tam!-l)ruat จ่านายสิบตำรวจ

mat (floor covering) l)seua เสื่อ

match, matches (for lighting) h)mai! l)kheet
(fai) ไม้ขีด (ไฟ)

material (in general) h)wat!-l)sa!-l)doo! วัสดุ

mathematics kha!-h)nit!-l)ta!-l)sat คณิตศาสตร์

matter (be important) r)sam!-khan! สำคัญ; (it
doesn't matter) f)mai! pen!-rai! ไม่เป็นไร

mattress n. f)thee nawn ที่นอน

May (month) h)phreut!-l)sa!-pha-khom! พฤษภาคม

may (possibility) l)at l)ja! อาจจะ; (permission)
f)dai! ได้

maybe bang thee บางที

me (See "I".)

meal (a meal of food) ah-r)han h)meu ()neung อาหารมื้อหนึ่ง

mean (bad, evil) adj. jai! h)rai ใจร้าย

mean v. (have a certain meaning) r)mai khwam f)wa หมายความว่า

meaning n. khwam r)mai ความหมาย

measure v. (length) h)wat! วัด, (volume) tuang ตวง

meat n. h)neua เนื้อ; (beef) h)neua wua เนื้อวัว; (pork) h)neua r)moo เนื้อหมู

mechanic n. f)chang kon! ช่างกล; (auto) f)chang h)fit! ช่างฟิต

medicine n. (for illness) ya ยา

medium adj. (average) pan klang ปานกลาง

meet v. (first time) h)roo-l)jak! kan! รู้จักกัน; (meet by accident) h)phop! kan! doy bang!-uhn พบกันโดยบังเอิญ; (meet by appointment) h)phop kan! tam h)nat! พบกันตามนัด

meeting n. (conference, etc.) kan l)pra!-choom! การประชุม

Mekong (river) f)mae-h)nam! r)khong แม่น้ำโขง;
(whisky) [f)lao!] f)mae-r)khong (เหล้า) แม่โขง

melt v. h)la:-lai ละลาย

member (n., person) l)sa!-ma-h)chik! สมาชิก

memorize (learn by heart) f)thawng jam! ท่องจำ

mend v. (clothing) h)yep! f)pha l)khat เย็บผ้าขาด;
(in general) f)sawm saem ซ่อมแซม

men's room, men's rest room f)hawng h)nam! chai
ห้องน้ำชาย

mention (refer to) l)klao r)theung! กล่าวถึง

menu (in restaurant) rai-kan ah-r.)han รายการ
อาหาร

merciful adj. mee khwam pra-nee มีความปรานี

merciless adj. l)hot h)rai โหดร้าย

message n. r)san, l)khao, l)khao r)san สาร, ข่าว,
ข่าวสาร; (leave a message, on phone) l)sang!
h)wai! สั่งไว้

metal (in general) lo-l)ha! โลหะ

meter, metre (measurement) f)met เมตร, (taxi-
meter) mee-f)tuh มิเตอร์

method n. thang, wi-thee tham! ทาง, วิธีทำ

middle klang กลาง; (in the middle) trong! klang
ตรงกลาง

midnight (24.00 hours) f)thiang kheun เที่ยงคืน

might (may, possibility) v. l)at l)ja! อาจจะ

mildew n., v. f)kheun! ra ขึ้นรา

mile (measurement) mai! ไมล์

military adj. h)tha!-r)han, thang h)tha!-r)han ทหาร, ทางทหาร

military occupational specialty (MOS) cham!-nan kan h)tha!-r)han ชำนาญการทหาร

military officer (in general) nai h)tha!-r)han นายทหาร; (commissioned) nai h)tha!-r)han h)chan! r)san!-ya-l)bat! นายทหารชั้นสัญญาบัตร (NCO) nai h)tha!-r)han h)chan! l)pra!-thuat นายทหารชั้นประทวน

military police (MP) r)sa-h)ra!-h)wat! h)tha!-r)han สารวัตรทหาร

military unit l)nuay h)tha!-r)han หน่วยทหาร

milk n. nom!, h)nam!-nom! นม, น้ำนม; (fresh milk) nom! l)sot! นมสด

million (1,000,000) h)lan ล้าน, h)lan l)neung ล้านหนึ่ง (๑,๐๐๐,๐๐๐)

millionaire (wealthy person) l)set-r)thee เศรษฐี

mind n (of a person) l)jit! jai! จิตใจ

mind v. (object to) rang!-l)kiat รังเกียจ: (Never mind.) f)mai! pen'-rai! ไม่เป็นไร

mine (belonging to me) (males) r)khawng r)phom! ของผม, (females) r)khawng r)chan! ของฉัน

mine (explosive) h)ra!-l)but, f)thoon! h)ra!-l)but ระเบิด, ทุ่นระเบิด
(place for mining) r)meuang f)rae เหมืองแร่

mineral(s) n. f)rae แร่

minister (of govt.) h)rat!-l)tha!-mon!-tree รัฐมนตรี

ministry (of govt.) l)kra!-suang กระทรวง

minor wife mia h)nawy เมียน้อย

minus (opposite of plus) h)lop! ลบ

minute (of time) na-thee นาที

mirror n. l)kra!-l)jok [l)sawng f)na] กระจก (ส่องหน้า)

mischievous (for children) son! ซน

miscount v. h)nap! l)phit! นับผิด

Miss (females 15 or over) nang-r)sao นางสาว

miss (be absent) l)khat, f)mai ma ขาด, ไม่มา; (make a mistake) l)phit! ผิด; (miss trains, etc.) l)tok! h)rot! ตกรถ; (not hit a target) f)mai! l)thook ไม่ถูก; (think about) h)khit! r)theung! คิดถึง

missionary n. mit-chan-nuh-ree, f)phoo [r)maw]
r)sawn l)sat-l)sa!-r)na   มิสชันเนอรี, ผู้ (หมอ)
สอนศาสนา

mistake n. l)phit!, khwam l)phit!   ผิด, ความผิด

mistaken adj. l)phit!, f)mai l)thook   ผิด, ไม่ถูก

Mister (Mr.) nai   นาย

misunderstand v. f)khao! jai l)phit!   เข้าใจผิด

mix v. l)pha!-r)som!   ผสม

mixed up (in a mess) f)yoong!, l)sap! r)son!   ยุ่ง, สับสน

model n. l)baep แบบ; (for autos, etc.) f)roon!
รุ่น; (fashion model) nang l)baep   นางแบบ

modern adj. than! l)sa!-r)mai!   ทันสมัย

mold, mould n. (fungus) ra รา; (matrix) f)mae
phim!   แม่พิมพ์

mold, mould v. (mold dough) f)nuat นวด; (mold
into form) f)pan!   ปั้น

moldy, mouldy adj. f)kheun! ra   ขึ้นรา

mole (on the body) r)fai!   ไฝ

moment (just a moment) r)deeo deeo   เดี๋ยวเดียว

Monday wan! jan!   วันจันทร์

money n. nguhn, l)sa!-tang   เงิน, สตางค์

money-changer khon! f)laek l)plian nguhn tra
คนแลกเปลี่ยนเงินตรา

money-lender khon! l)awk ng_uhn f)koo คนออก
เงินกู้

money-order tha-na-h)nat! ธนาณัติ

monk (Buddhist monk) h)phra! พระ

monkey (animal) ling! ลิง

month deuan เดือน ((*Note*. "The month of...." =
deuan + name of month, as "the month of
May" = deuan h)phreut!-l)sa!-pha.khom.)

monthly l)pra!-jam! deuan, rai deuan ประจำเดือน,
รายเดือน; (menstrual period) l)pra!-jam! deuan
ประจำเดือน

mood (of a person) ah-rom! อารมณ์

moon (the moon) h)phra!-jan! พระจันทร์

mop (for housecleaning) h)mai r)thoo f)ban
ไม้ถูบ้าน

mop v. (mop a floor) r)thoo f)ban ถูบ้าน

more (additional) f)mak f)kheun! มากขึ้น; (more
than) f)mak l)kwa มากกว่า; (some more) l)eek
l)nawy อีกหน่อย

morning (in the morning) tawn h)chao! ตอนเช้า;
(this morning) h)chao! h)nce เช้านี้

mortar (mil. weapon) peun h)khrok! ปืนครก;
(pounding device) h)khrok ครก

mosquito (insect) yoong! ยุง

mosquito-net h)moong! มุ้ง

most (superlative) ....f)thee l)scot!, i)mak
f)thee l)soot ....ที่สุด, มากที่สุด; (greater part)
l)suan l)yai: ส่วนใหญ่

mothballs f)look r)mehn ลูกเหม็น

mother f)mae แม่

mother in-law (mother of husband) f)mae
r)phua, f)mae r)sa-mee แม่ผัว, แม่สามี; (mother
of wife) f)mae-yai แม่ยาย

motion picture (cinema, film) r)nang!, f)phap-
h)pha!-yon! หนัง, ภาพยนตร์

motion-picture theatre (for showing films) rong
r)nang! โรงหนัง

motor n. f)khreuang yon! เครื่องยนต์

motor-car (automobile) h)rot! yon! รถยนต์

motorcycle l)jak-h)ra'-yan yon!, maw-tuh-sai
จักรยานยนต์, มอเตอร์ไซค์

motor lorry (truck) h)rot! ban-h)thook! รถบรรทุก

motor mechanic f)chang h)fit, f)chang f)khreuang
yon! ช่างฟิต, ช่างเครื่องยนต์

motor vehicle (in general) h)rot! yon! รถยนต์

mount, mountain phoo-r)khao! ภูเขา

mouse (rat) r)noo หนู

mousetrap l)kap! l)dak! r)noo กับดักหนู

moustache, mustache n. 1)nuat หนวด

mouth (of the body, of a river etc.) 1)pak ปาก

move v. (in general) f)leuan, f)khleuan r)wai! เลื่อน, เคลื่อนไหว; (move forward, as a vehicle) duhn f)na เดินหน้า; (move one's place of residence) h)yai f)ban ย้ายบ้าน

movie (cinema, film) r)nang!, f)phap-h)pha!-yon! หนัง, ภาพยนตร์

movie star da-ra r)nang! ดาราหนัง

Mr. (Mister) nai นาย

Mrs. nang นาง

much f)mak, f)mak f)mak มาก, มากๆ

muddy adj. pen! khlon, pen! tom! เป็นโคลน, เป็นตม

muffler (of a vehicle) f)thaw ai! r)sia ท่อไอเสีย

multiply (arith.) khoon คูณ

mumps (illness) khang thoom คางทูม

murder n. f)khat-1)ta!-kam!, kan f)kha khon! โทษ ฆาตกรรม, การฆ่าคนตาย

muscle (of the body) f)klam h)neua กล้ามเนื้อ

museum phi!-h)phit!-h)tha!-phan! พิพิธภัณฑ์; (the National Museum of Thailand) phi!-h)phit!-h)tha!-phan! 1)sa!-r)than 1)haeng f)chat พิพิธภัณฑ์สถานแห่งชาติ

mushrooms n. 1)het! เห็ด

music n. don)-tree ดนตรี

musician n. h)nak! don!-tree นักดนตรี

Muslim (Islamite) chao moos-lim ชาวมุสลิม

must (helping v.) f)tawng, jam!-pen! ต้อง, จำเป็น

mustard mas-1)tad, h)nam! f)jim! .mas-1)tad
มัสตาด, น้ำจิ้มมัสตาด

mutual, mutually f)seung! kan! h)lae! kan! ซึ่งกัน
และกัน

muzzle (of a weapon) l)pak l)kra!-1)bawk peun
ปากกระบอกปืน

my, mine (belonging to me) (female) r)khawng!
r)chan! ของฉัน; (males) r)khawng r)phom!
ของผม

myself (female) r)chan: ehng ฉันเอง; (male)
r)phom' ehng ผมเอง

nail (for driving with hammer) l)ta!-poo ตะปู

nail-file (for fingernails) l)ta!-bai! h)lep!
ตะไบเล็บ

naked (no clothes on) pleuay kai เปลือยกาย

name n. (first name) f)cheu ชื่อ; (last name)
nam l)sa!-koon! นามสกุล; (first and last name)
f)cheu h)lae! nam l)sa!-koon! ชื่อและนามสกุล

name-card (business card) nam-l)bat! นามบัตร

napkin n. f)pha h)chet! meu ผ้าเช็ดมือ

narrow (of space) f)khaep แคบ

narrow-minded jai f)khaep ใจแคบ

nation n. l)pra!-f)thet f)chat ประเทศชาติ

national (of a nation) l)haeng f)chat แห่งชาติ;
(person of a certain nation) khon! r)san!-
f)chat.... (name of country).... คนสัญชาติ....

nationality (of a person) r)san!-f)chat สัญชาติ

native adj. h)pheun meuang พื้นเมือง

natural (of nature) tam tham!-ma!-f)chat ตาม
ธรรมชาติ

nausea n. f)khleun r)bian คลื่นเหียน

naval (partaining to navy) h)tha! r)han reua,
thang h)tha!-r)han reua ทหารเรือ, ทางทหารเรือ

naval base r)than h)thap reua ฐานทัพเรือ

naval officer nai h)tha!-r)han reua นายทหารเรือ

naval personnel (in general) h)tha!-r)han reua
ทหารเรือ

navigate v. (airplanes) duhn ah-l)kat เดินอากาศ;
(ships) duhn reua เดินเรือ

navy, RTN kawng h)thap! reua กองทัพเรือ

near, nearby f)klai! f)klai! ใกล้ ๆ

nearly (almost) l)keuap เกือบ

necessary adj. jam!-pen' จำเป็น

neck (of body) khaw คอ

necklace n. f)sawy khaw สร้อยคอ

necktie n. f)pha l)phook khaw, nek-thai! ผ้าผูก
คอ, เน็คไท

need v. f)tawng-kan ต้องการ

needle n. r)khem! h)yep! f)pha เข็มเย็บผ้า

negative (opposite of positive) h)lop! ลบ; (of
photograph) fim! ฟิล์ม

neglect v. h)la! h)thing! ละทิ้ง

negotiate v. jeh-h)ra!-ja เจรจา

neighbor, neighbour f)pheuan f)ban เพื่อนบ้าน

nephew r)lan cbai หลานชาย

nerves (of the body) l)pra!-l)sat ประสาท

nervous adj. l)tok! jai! f)ngai, l)pra!-l)sat
l)awn ตกใจง่าย ประสาทอ่อน

net n. ta-l)khai, f)rang r)hae ตาข่าย, ร่างแห

neutral adj pen! klang เป็นกลาง

never (not ever) f)mai! khuhy ไม่เคย

Never mind. f)mai! pen!-rai! ไม่เป็นไร

new adj. l)mai ใหม่

news n. l)khao ข่าว

newspaper r)nang!-r)seu-phim! หนังสือพิมพ์

New Year's Day wan! pee l)mai! วันปีใหม่

next.... ....f)na ....หน้า [as in "next week" = ah-h)thit! f)na]; (next in a series) l)that! pai ถัดไป

Next Stop! (said when one is riding a bus and wants to get off at next stop) l)jawt f)pai จอดบ้าย

next time khrao f)na คราวหน้า

next to (adjoining) l)tit! l)kap ติดกับ

next week ah-h)thit f)na อาทิตย์หน้า

nice (good) dee ดี

nickname f)cheu f)lehn ชื่อเล่น

niece r)lan r)sao หลานสาว

night n. kheun คืน

night club (same as English) ไนท์คลับ

nightmare (bad dream) r)fan h)rai ฝันร้าย

nighttime weh-la klang kheun เวลากลางคืน

nine (9) f)kao! เก้า (๙)

nineteen (19) l)sip!-f)kao! สิบเก้า (๑๙)

ninety (90) f)kao!-l)sip! เก้าสิบ (๙๐)

no adj. f)mai! mee ไม่มี (as in "no money" = f)mai! mee nguhn); (cannot) f)mai! f)dai! ไม่ได้; (do not want) f)mai! ao! ไม่เอา; (that's not right) f)mai! f)chai! ไม่ใช่

nobody f)mai! mee khrai! ไม่มีใคร

noise n. r)siang l)nuak r)hoo เสียงหนวกหู

noisy adj. l)nuak r)hoo หนวกหู

no more f)mai mee l)eek ไม่มีอีก; (don't want any more) f)mai! ao! l)eek ไม่เอาอีก; (not again) f)mai! l)eek ไม่อีก

non-commissioned officer (NCO) (mil., in general) nai l)sip!, nai h)tha-r)han h)chan: l)pra!- thuan, นายสิบ, นายทหารชั้นประทวน

none f)mai mee luhy ไม่มีเลย

noodles (Chinese noodles) r)kuay-r)teeo [usually pronounced quickly as "kwit-r)teeo"] ก๋วยเตี๋ยว

noon (12.00 noon) f)thiang เที่ยง

No parking ! f)ham l)jawt h)rot! ห้ามจอดรถ

normal adj. tham!-h)ma!-da, l)pok!-l)ka'-l)ti! ธรรมดา, ปกติ

normally adv. tam tham!-h)ma!-da, doy l)pok! l)ka'-l)ti! ตามธรรมดา, โดยปกติ

north (direction) r)neua!, h)thit! r)neua เหนือ, ทิศเหนือ; (region) f)phak r)neua ภาคเหนือ

northeast; (direction) l)ta!-wan l)awk r)chiang r)neua ตะวันออกเฉียงเหนือ (region) ee-r)san,f)phak ee-r)san อีสาน, ภาคอีสาน

nose (of body) l)ja!-l)mook จมูก

No smoking! f)ham l)soop boo-l)ree ห้ามสูบบุหรี่

not f)mai! ไม่; (not so, not true) f)mai! f)chai! ไม่ใช่ (*Notes.* Before a noun or pronoun, "not" is usually "f)mai! f)chai!", as in "f)mai! f)chai! r)khao!"=not him.)

note n. (short letter) l)jot!-r)mai f)san! f)san! จดหมายสั้น ๆ

note, note down v. l)jot!, l)jot! h)wai! จด, จดไว้,

note, notice (observe) r)sang!-l)ket สังเกต

notebook n. l)sa!-l)moot! h)not! สมุดโน๊ต

not good f)mai! dee ไม่ดี

nothing l)plao!, f)mai mee l)ah!-rai! เปล่า, ไม่มีอะไร; (empty) f)wang l)plao! ว่างเปล่า; (zero) r)soon ศูนย์

notice (observe) v. r)sang!-l)ket สังเกต

notify v. f)jaeng, f)jaeng f)hai! f)sap แจ้ง, แจ้งให้ทราบ

not in (not present) f)mai! l)yoo ไม่อยู่

not much (little, only a little) h)nawy, h)nit! l)nawy, h)lek! h)nawy น้อย, นิดหน่อย, เล็กน้อย

not necessary f)mai! jam!-pen!, f)mai! f)tawng ไม่จำเป็น, ไม่ต้อง

not often f)mai! l)bawy ไม่บ่อย

not so (not true, not correct) f)mai! f)chai!, l)plao: ไม่ใช่, เปล่า

not very far f)mai! klai! f)mak ไม่ไกลมาก

not very much f)mai! f)mak ไม่มาก

not very well (rather ill) f)mai! f)khawy l)sa!-bai ไม่ค่อยสบาย; (not good results) f)mai! f)khawy dee ไม่ค่อยดี

not well (ill, sick) f)mai l)sa!-bai, l)puay ไม่สบาย, ป่วย

not yet yang!, yang! f)mai.... ยัง, ยังไม่.... (as in "yang! f)mai! ma" = not yet come)

November (month) h)preut!-l)sa!-l)ji-ka-yon! พฤศจิกายน

now (at this time) we-la h)nee เวลานี้; (Right now!) r)deeo h)nee เดี๋ยวนี้

nowadays l)sa!-r)mai! nee สมัยนี้

numb (in feeling) cha, l)nep-cha ชา, เหน็บชา

number (as 1, 2, etc.) f)lek, r)mai-f)lek เลข, หมายเลข; (street number, house number) f)lek-f)thee f)ban เลขที่บ้าน; (telephone number) buh tho-ra!-l)sap!, r)mai-f)lek tho-ra!-l)sap! เบอร์โทรศัพท์, หมายเลขโทรศัพท์

number (ordinal number, as No. 1, No. 2, 1st, 2nd, etc.) f)thee.... ที่.... [as in "No. 2" = f)thee r)sawng]

nun (Buddhist) chee ชี; (Catholic) f)mae chee, "sis-tuh" แม่ชี, ซิสเตอร์

nurse n. nang pha!-ya-ban นางพยาบาล

nut (for eating) l)thua ถั่ว; (of a bolt) h)nawt!, h)nawt tua-mia น็อต, น็อตตัวเมีย

oatmeal (breakfast cereal) f)khao h)ot ข้าวโอ๊ต

obey v. f)cheua fang! เชื่อฟัง

object n. (thing in general) l)sing!-r)khawng สิ่งของ

object v. l)khat! f)khawng ขัดข้อง; (object to something, have an aversion to) rang!-l)kiat รังเกียจ

objective (purpose) wat!-l)thoo!-l)pra!-r)song! วัตถุประสงค์

obligation n. (commitment) phan!-h)tha!-ka'-ra!-nee พันธกรณี; (necessity) khwam jam!-pen ความจำเป็น

observe v. r)sang!-l)ket สังเกต

observer n. f)phoo r)sang!-l)ket kan ผู้สังเกตการณ์

obstruct v. 1)khat! r)khwang ขัดขวาง

obtain v. f)dai! ma ได้มา

occasion (opportunity) oh-1)kat โอกาส; (time) khrao คราว

occupation n. ah-f)cheep อาชีพ

occupy v. (occupy premises) ah-r)sai 1)yoo อาศัยอยู่; (take control) h)yeut!-khrawng ยึดครอง

ocean n h)ma!-r)ha 1)sa!-1)moot! มหาสมุทร

o'clock (24-hour official system) na-h)li!-ka นาฬิกา, (colloquial system) mong โมง

October (month) too-la-khom! ตุลาคม

odor n 1)klin! กลิ่น; (bad odor) 1)klin! r)mehn กลิ่นเหม็น; (good odor) 1)klin! r)hawm กลิ่นหอม; (very bad odor) r)mehn 1)boot เหม็นบูด

of (belonging to) r)khawng ของ; (of a certain place) 1)haeng แห่ง

of course (certainly) f)nae nawn แน่นอน

offer v. 1)sa!-r)nuh เสนอ

office (place of working) r)sam'-h)nak!-ngan, awf-fit สำนักงาน, ออฟฟิศ; (position, post) tam!-1)naeng ตำแหน่ง

office clerk l)sa!·r)mian เสมียน

officer (govt. official) f)jao!·f)na·f)thee เจ้าหน้าที่;
(mil. officer) nai h)tha!·r)han นายทหาร;
(police officer) nai tam!·l)ruat นายตำรวจ

office receptionist h)pha!·h)nak!·ngan f)tawn-
h)rap! พนักงานต้อนรับ

official adj. thang kan ทางการ

official n. (govt. official) f)jao!·f)na·f)thee
เจ้าหน้าที่

official business f)rat-h)cha!·kan ราชการ

offspring (of animals) f)look ลูก

often l)bawy, l)bawy l)bawy บ่อย, บ่อยๆ

oil n. h)nam!·man! น้ำมัน; (motor oil) h)nam!·
man! f)khreuang น้ำมันเครื่อง

oil v. l)sai! h)nam!·man!, l)yawt h)nam!·man!
ใส่น้ำมัน, หยอดน้ำมัน

O.K., okay (all right, agreed) l)tok!·long!, oh-
kheh ตกลง, โอ.เค.

old adj. (people) l)kae แก่; (things) l)kao! เก่า

omelette (egg) l)khai! jeeo ไข่เจียว

omit (cut out) l)tat! l)awk ตัดออก

der

(...eek) nai! ใน; (on top) bon! บน;

(..., as radio) l)puht เปิด; (continue on)

... pai! ต่อไป

...e (one time) l)neung! h)khrang! หนึ่งครั้ง

once again l)eek h)khrang! l)neung! อีกครั้งหนึ่ง

one (or "a, an") l)neung! หนึ่ง

one half f)khreung! l)neung! ครึ่งหนึ่ง

one more time l)eek thee, l)eek h)khrang!
l)neung! อีกที, อีกครั้งหนึ่ง

oneself eng, tua eng, ton! eng เอง, ตัวเอง, ตนเอง

one time (once) l)neung h)khrang! หนึ่งครั้ง

one-way street l)tha!-r)non! wan!-weh ถนนวันเวย์

onion n. r)hua r)bawm หัวหอม

only f)thao!-h)nan! เท่านั้น

on time than weh-lah ทันเวลา

on top, on top of bon!, f)khang bon! บน, ข้างบน

open, opened adj. l)puht i)yoo เปิดอยู่

open v. l)puht เปิด

open-end wrench koon!-jae l)pak tai กุญแจปากตาย

opener (can-opener) f)thee l)puht l)kra!-
r)pawng ที่เปิดกระป๋อง

operation (n., med., surgery) kan l)pha l)tat!
การผ่าตัด

operations (n., mil.) h)yoot!-h)tha!-kan ยุทธกร

operator (telephone) h)pha!-h)nak-ngan h)ra)
tho-h)ra!-l)sap! พนักงานรับโทรศัพท์

opinion n. khwam r)hen ความเห็น

opium n. ya l)fin ฝิ่น

opportunity n. oh-l)kat โอกาส

oppose v. h)khat! h)khan, f)mai r)hen f)duay
ค้ดค้าน, ไม่เห็นด้วย

opposite adj. trong! f)kham ตรงข้าม

oppress v. l)kot! l)khee กดขี่

or r)reu หรือ [Note. r)reu is also often used at
the end of a sentence, to show a question.]

orange (fruit) f)som! ส้ม; (orange color) r)see
f)som! สีส้ม

orange juice h)nam! f)som! น้ำส้ม

orchard (fruit) r)suan สวน

orchestra (band) wong! don!-tree วงดนตรี

orchid (flower) l)dawk f)kluay h)mai! ดอกกล้วยไม้

order n. (command) kham! l)sang! คำสั่ง;
(orderliness) pen! h)ra-l)biap เป็นระเบียบ; (in
order, progressive arrangement) tam lam!-
l)dap! ตามลำดับ

order v. (command) l)sang! kan สั่งการ; (order
food, as in restaurant) l)sang! ah-r)han สั่งอาหาร;
(order or buy something) l)sang! r)khawng
สั่งของ

orderly (in good order) f)riap h)rawy เรียบร้อย

ordinary adj. tham!-h)ma!-da ธรรมดา

ordnance (n , mil.) r)san!-pha-h)woot! สรรพาวุธ

ore n. r)sin! f)rae สินแร่

organ (of body) ah!-wai!-ya!-wa! อวัยวะ

organization n. (organized body) ong-kan องค์การ

organize v. (set up) l)jat! f)tang! จัดตั้ง

....or not? (used at end of questions) ....r)reu
f)mai!, ...r)reu l)plao! ....หรือไม่, ...หรือเปล่า

....or not yet? (used at end of questions) ....r)reu
yang! ....หรือยัง

orphan f)look kam!-h)phra ลูกกำพร้า

other, others l)eun, l)eun l)eun อื่น, อื่นๆ

ought, ought to (should) khuan, khuan l)ja! ควร,
ควรจะ

ounce (measurement) awn ออนซ์

our, ours r)khawng rao! ของเรา

out, outside f)khang f)nawk ข้างนอก

outdoors (in the open) klang f)jaeng กลางแจ้ง

outlaw (bandit) jon, f)phoo h)rai โจร, ผู้ร้าย

out of date (expired) l)mot! ah-h)yoo! หมดอายุ;
(old-fashioned) h)la l)sa!-r)mai ล้าสมัย

out of order (broken) r)sia, cham!-h)root! เสีย,
ชำรุด

oven (for cooking) tao! l)op! เตาอบ

over (above) r)neua เหนือ; (finished) l)set!
h)laeo เสร็จแล้ว; (more than) kuhn kwa.... เกิน
กว่า....; (more than enough) f)mak pai! มากไป

over and over (again and again) f)sam! f)sam!
ซ้ำ ๆ

overdose (as of medicine) kin! kuhn l)kha!-l)nat
กินเกินขนาด

overhaul (a vehicle engine) h)yok! f)khreuang
ยกเครื่อง

overlook v. (not notice) mawng f)kham pai!
มองข้ามไป

oversleep v. nawn l)teun f)mai! than! นอนตื่นไม่ทัน

over there h)non โน่น

overturn v. (as a car) f)khwam! คว่ำ

owe money (have debts) pen! f)nee เป็นหนี้

own (be owner of) pen! f)jao!-r)khawng เป็น
เจ้าของ

owner (n., person) f)jao!-r)khawng เจ้าของ

ox (animal) wua tua f)phoo วัวตัวผู้

oxcart n. kwian เกวียน

oxtail soup h)soop! r)hang wua ซุปหางวัว

oxygen n. awk-see-f)yehn ออกซิเย่น

oyster n. (seafood) r)hawy nang-rom! หอยนางรม

pack, package n. sawng, l)haw ซอง, ห่อ

pack v. (belongings) l)kep! r)khawng เก็บของ;
(put in packages etc.) ban!-l)joo! บรรจุ

paddle n. (for boat) h)mai! phai reua ไม้พายเรือ

paddle v. (a boat) phai reua พายเรือ

paddy (rice paddy) f)khao l)pleuak ข้าวเปลือก

paddy-field (for rice) f)thoong na ทุ่งนา

padlock n. l)dawk koon!-jae ดอกกุญแจ

page (for book etc.) f)na หน้า

pagoda (Buddhist architecture) jeh-dee เจดีย์

pail (bucket) r)thang! ถัง

pain v. (hurt) l)jep!, l)puat เจ็บ, ปวด

paint n. r)see สี

paint v. tha r)see ทาสี; (paint pictures) f)wat
f)roop วาดรูป

painter n. (houses, etc.) f)chang tha r)see ช่างทาสี; (artist) f)chang f)wat f)roop ช่างวาดรูป

painting n. (artistic) f)roop r)khian รูปเขียน; (work of painting, as of house) kan tha r)see การทาสี

pair (2 of something) f)khoo คู่

pajamas h)choot! nawn ชุดนอน

palace n. wang! วัง

pale adj (for colors) l)awn อ่อน; (for complexion) f)seet ซีด

pan (skillet, for frying) l)kra!-h)tha! กระทะ

pants (trousers) kang-keng กางเกง

papaya (fruit) ma!-la!-kaw มะละกอ

paper l)kra!-l)dat กระดาษ

paper-clip n. f)luat l)siap l)kra!-l)dat ลวดเสียบกระดาษ

parachute n. f)rom! choo f)cheep ร่มชูชีพ

parachute v. l)dot f)rom! โดดร่ม

parade v. r)suan l)sa!-r)nam สวนสนาม

paralyzed adj. (med.) pen! am!-h)ma!-f)phat เป็นอัมพาต

parcel post h)phat!-l)sa!-l)doo! prai!-l)sa!-nee พัสดุไปรษณีย์

Pardon me. r)khaw f)thot, r)khaw l)ah!-phai! ขอโทษ, ขออภัย; (meaning 'please say it again") l)ah!-rai! h)na! อะไรนะ

parents (father and mother) f)phaw f)mae, l)bi!-da man'-da พ่อแม่, บิดามารดา

park n. r)suan สวน

park v. l)jawt จอด

parking place f)thee l)jawt h)rot! ที่จอดรถ

parrot (bird) h)nok: f)kaeo นกแก้ว

part (of something) l)suan ส่วน

participate (take part) f)khao! f)ruam เข้าร่วม

partner n. - (comr.) f)hoon! l)suan หุ้นส่วน; (general) f)khoo คู่; (slang for "bargirl") phaht-nuh พาร์ทเนอร์

party n. (leg.) l)fai ฝ่าย; (gathering for pleasure) ngan h)liang, pah-f)tee งานเลี้ยง, ปาร์ตี้; (political) h)phak! kan-meuang พรรคการเมือง

pass (mountain) f)chawng r)khao! ช่องเขา

pass v. l)phan ผ่าน; (pass an exam) l)sawp f)dai! สอบได้; (pass by vehicle) saeng แซง; (pass something at table) l)song ส่ง

passenger n. f)phoo doy-r)san ผู้โดยสาร

pass out (faint) pen! lom! เป็นลม

passport r)nang!-r)seu duhn thang, phahs-pawt
หนังสือเดินทาง, พาส์ปอร์ต

pass through (go through) l)phan pai!, h)tha!-
h)loo! pai! ผ่านไป, ทะลุไป

paste n. kao กาว; v. l)pit!, l)tit! kao ปิด, ติดกาว

pat v. (slap gently) l)top! bao! bao! ตบเบาๆ

path, pathway (for walking) thang duhn ทางเดิน

patient adj. jai! yehn! ใจเย็น

patient (n., of doctor) khon! f)khai! คนไข้

patrol (n., mil.) l)nuay f)lat l)tra!-wehn หน่วย
ลาดตระเวน

pawn v. (at pawn shop) jam!-nam! จำนำ

pawnshop n. rong h)rap! jam!-nam! โรงรับจำนำ

pay (a debt or bill) l)jai nguhn, cham!-h)ra!-
nguhn จ่ายเงิน, ชำระเงิน

pay attention ao! jai! l)sai! เอาใจใส่

pay back (reimburse) h)chai! nguhn kheun
ใช้เงินคืน

peace (opposite of war) r)san!-l)ti!-f)phap,
khwam l)sa!-l)ngop! l)seuk! สันติภาพ, ความสงบศึก

Peace Corps (U.S.) l)nuay r)san!l)ti!-f)phap
หน่วยสันติภาพ

Peace Corps member ah-r)sa l)sa!-l)mak! อาสาสมัคร

peaceful adj. l)sa!-l)ngop! สงบ

peak (top of mountain) f)yawt r)khao! ยอดเขา

peanut n. l)thua h)li'-r)song! ถั่วลิสง

peanut butter nuhy l)thua [h)li!'-r)song!] เนยถั่ว(ลิสง)

pearl n. l)khai-h)mook! ไข่มุก

pedal a bicycle (ride a bicycle) l)theep h)rot!,
   l)khee h)rot! ถีบรถ, ขี่รถ

peddle (sell on streets) f)reh r)khai, l)hap
   f)reh r)khai เร่ขาย, หาบเร่ขาย

pedestrian n. f)phoo duhn h)thao! ผู้เดินเท้า

peek, peep (look at surreptitiously) l)aep doo
   แอบดู

peel, peeling (of fruit etc.) l)pleuak เปลือก

peel v. (as fruit) l)pawk l)pleuak ปอกเปลือก

pen n. (for writing) l)pak-ka ปากกา; (ballpoint
   pen) l)pak-ka f)look-f)leun ปากกาลูกลื่น;
   (fountain pen) l)pak-ka l)meuk! seum! ปากกา
   หมึกซึม

pen n. (for pigs and fowl) h)lao! เล้า

pencil n. din!-r)saw ดินสอ

pension n. (money) nguhn bam!-nan เงินบำนาญ

people n. (in general) khon! คน; (general public) l)pra!-cha-chon! ประชาชน; (people of a certain country) chao....(name of country) ชาว....

pepper n. h)phrik! thai! พริกไทย

per h)la!, l)taw ละ, ต่อ (*Notes.* "h)la" comes after noun; "l)taw" comes before noun)

per cent h)rawy h)la!...., puh sehn ร้อยละ...., เปอร์เซ็นต์

perforate (punch a hole) l)jaw! roo เจาะรู

perfume n. h)nam! r)hawm น้ำหอม

perhaps (maybe) bang thee บางที

per hour l)taw f)chua-mong ต่อชั่วโมง

permanent adj. r)tha-wawn ถาวร

permanent wave (for ladies' hair) l)dat! r)phom!, set! r)phom! ดัดผม, เซ็ทผม

permit n. bai! ah!-noo!-f)yat ใบอนุญาต

permit v. ah!-noo -f)yat อนุญาต

perpendicular adj. f)tang! l)chak ตั้งฉาก

person n. khon!, f)phoo คน, ผู้

personal adj. l)suan tua ส่วนตัว

personnel n. (general) book-kha-la-kawn บุคลากร; (mil.) kam!-lang! phon! กำลังพล

perspiration (sweat) l)ngeua เหงื่อ

perspire v. l)ngeua l)awk เหงื่อออก

[*Note.* "l)ngeua" is popularly pronounced "l)heua".]

pet (n., animal) l)sat! h)liang สัตว์เลี้ยง

pet v. f)loop, f)loop khlam! ลูบ, ลูบคลำ

petrol (gasoline) h)nam!-man! น้ำมัน

petty-officer (navy) (general) phan! l)ja พันจ่า;
   (CPO) phan! l)ja l)ek พันจ่าเอก; (1st-class)
   phan! l)ja tho พันจ่าโท, (2nd-class) phan l)ja
   tree พันจ่าตรี; (3rd-class) l)ja l)ek จ่าเอก

pharmacist (n., person) pheh-l)sat!-h)cha!-kawn
   เภสัชกร

pharmacy (drug store) h)ran r)khai ya ร้านขายยา

phonograph n. l)heep r)siang, l)pik!-h)ap!
   หีบเสียง, ปิ๊กอั๊พ

phonograph record l)phaen r)siang แผ่นเสียง

photo, photograph n. f)roop l)thai รูปถ่าย

photograph v. l)thai f)roop, l)thai f)phap ถ่ายรูป,
   ถ่ายภาพ

photographer f)chang l)thai f)roop ช่างถ่ายรูป

physical (exam) (kan) l)truat f)rang-kai (การ)
   ตรวจร่างกาย

piano n. pian-no เปียนโน

pick (at something, as a sore) l)kae! แกะ

pick (flowers) l)det! l)dawk h)mai! เด็ดดอกไม้

pickle n. l)phak! dawng ผักดอง

pickled adj. (of food) dawng ดอง

pick out (select) f)leuak ao! เลือกเอา

pick someone's pocket or purse h)luang l)kra!-r)pao! ล้วงกระเป๋า

pick up (collect and put away) l)kep!, l)kep! h)wai! เก็บ, เก็บไว้

pick up someone (usually in a vehicle) h)rap! รับ; (come to pick up) ma h)rap! มารับ; (go to pick up) pai! h)rap! ไปรับ

picnic (Same as in English)

picture n. (photo) f)roop l)thai รูปถ่าย; (painting) f)roop f)wat r)khian รูปวาดเขียน

piece n. (of something) h)chin ชิ้น

pier n. f)tha reua ท่าเรือ

pierce v. (as by a thorn) tam! ตำ; (make a hole in something) l)jaw! roo เจาะรู

pig (animal) r)moo หมู

pigeon (bird) h)nok! h)phi!-f)rap นกพิราบ

pile (of something) kawng.... กอง....

pile up v. kawng h)wai! กองไว้

pill (of medicine) ya h)met! ยาเม็ด

pillow n. r)mawn หมอน

pillow-case n. l)plawk r)mawn ปลอกหมอน

pilot n. (aviator) h)nak! bin! นักบิน; (ships)
f)phoo nam! f)rawng ผู้นำร่อง

pilot v. (a plane) l)khap! f)khɪeuang-bin!
ขับเครื่องบิน; (a ship) nam! f)rawng นำร่อง

pilot officer (RTAF, AF 2nd lt.) reua ab-l)kat
tree เรืออากาศตรี

pimples (on face) r)siu สิว

pin n. r)khem! l)moot! เข็มหมุด; (safety pin)
r)khem! l)moot f)sawn plai เข็มหมุดซ่อนปลาย

pin v. l)klat! h)wai!, l)siap h)wai! กลัดไว้, เสียบไว้

pinch (with fingers) l)yik! หยิก

pineapple (fruit) l)sap!-l)pa!-h)rot! สับปะรด

ping-pong (table tennis) ping!-pawng ปิงปอง

pink (color) r)see chom!-phoo สีชมพู

pipe n. (in general) f)thaw ท่อ; (for smoking)
f)klawng กล้อง; (rubber hose) f)thaw yang
ท่อยาง; (water pipe) f)thaw h)nam! ท่อน้ำ

pistol (weapon) peun h)phok! ปืนพก

pit (hole) r)loom! หลุม

pitiful adj. f)na r)song!-r)san น่าสงสาร

pity v. r)song!-r)san สงสาร

place n. 1)haeng, 1)sa!-r)than-f)thee แห่ง, สถานที่

place v. (put in a place) wang h)wai! วางไว้

plain adj. (clear, easy to see) h)chat! jehn
ชัดเจน; (ordinary) tham!-h)ma!-da ธรรมดา

plain n. (flat place) f)thee f)rap ที่ราบ

plan n. r)phaen kan แผนการ

plane n. (airplane) f)khreuang-bin' เครื่องบิน;
(carpenter's) r)sai! l)kop! ไสกบ

plank n. (of wood) h)mai! l)kra!-dan ไม้กระดาน

plant n. (agricultural) f)ton!, f)pheut phan! ต้น,
พืชพันธุ์; (industrial plant) rong ngan โรงงาน

plant v. (cultivate) h)phaw! l)plook เพาะปลูก

plantation n. f)rai!, r)suan ไร่, สวน

plaster (for plastering work) poon l)chap ปูนฉาบ

plaster v. (as a wall, etc.) l)chap poon ฉาบปูน

plastic n. (as in English) ปลาสติก

plate n. (for eating) jahn จาน

platform n. (at railway station) chan cha-la ชาน
ชาลา; (stage) weh-thee เวที

platoon (n., mil.) l)muat หมวด

play n. (drama) h)la!-khawn ละคร

play v. f)lehn เล่น

play cards v. f)lehn f)phai! เล่นไพ่

pleasant (refreshing) f)cheun jai! ชื่นใจ

please (polite request) l)prot, ka-roo-na โปรด,
    กรุณา; please (do this or that) f)chuay.... ช่วย....

pleased (glad, happy) yin!-dee ยินดี

pliers n. kheem คีม

plumber n. f)chang f)thaw ช่างท่อ

plus (arithmetic) l)buak f)duay บวกด้วย

plywood n. h)mai l)aht ไม้อัด

p.m. (after 12 noon) r)lang! f)thiang หลังเที่ยง

pneumonia n. l)pawt buam ปอดบวม

pocket n. l)kra!-r)pao! กระเป๋า

pocketbook n. (general, billfold or purse) l)kra!-
    r)pao! กระเป๋า

pocket-knife n. f)meet h)phap มีดพับ

point, point at v. h)chee ชี้

poison ya h)phit! ยาพิษ

poisonous adj. pen! h)phit! เป็นพิษ

pole, post n r)sao! เสา

police, policeman n. tam!-l)ruat ตำรวจ

polish v. l)khat!, r)thoo ขัด, ถู

polite adj. l)soo!-f)phap สุภาพ

politely adj. l)yang l)soo!-f)phap อย่างสุภาพ

political adj. thang kan meuang ทางการเมือง

politician n. h)nak! kan meuang นักการเมือง

politics n. kan meuang การเมือง

pomelo (fruit similar to grapefruit) f)som! oh
ส้มโอ

pond, pool (of water) l)sa! h)nam! สระน้ำ

poor adj. (in poverty) f)yak jon! ยากจน; (pitiful)
f)na r)song!-r)san น่าสงสาร

popular adj. h)ni!-yom! นิยม

population n. l)pra!-cha-kawn ประชากร

pork (meat) h)neua r)moo เนื้อหมู

port n. (for shipping) f)tha reua ท่าเรือ

porter (for carrying things) khon r)khon!
r)khawng คนขนของ

portion (part) l)suan ส่วน

position n. (in govt., in business, etc.) tam!-
l)naeng ตำแหน่ง

positive (opposite of negative) l)buak บวก;
(without doubt) l)yang f)nae nawn อย่างแน่นอน

possible adj. pen! pai! f)dai! เป็นไปได้

post, pole n. r)sao! เสา; (post or stake used as
marker) l)lak! หลัก

postage n. f)kha l)song! ค่าส่ง

postage stamps 1)sa!-taem, prai!-1)sa!-nee-ya-kawn แสตมป์, ไปรษณียากร

postal cheque (check) h)chek! prai!-1)sa!-nee เช็กไปรษณีย์

postal money order h)tha!-na-h)nat! ธนาณัติ

post-box (mailbox) f)too 1)jot!-r)mai ตู้จดหมาย

postcard post-kahd, prai!-1)sa!-nee-h)ya!-1)bat! โปสท์การ์ด, ไปรษณียบัตร

postdated cheque (check) h)chek! loŋ! wan!-f)thee f)luaŋ f)na เช็กลงวันที่ล่วงหน้า

postman (mailman) khon! prai!-1)sa!-nee, 1)boo!-1)root! prai!-1)sa!-nee คนไปรษณีย์, บุรุษไปรษณีย์

post office prai!-1)sa!-nee, f)thee tham!-kan prai!-1)sa!-nee ไปรษณีย์, ที่ทำการไปรษณีย์; (GPO, New Road, Bangkok) prai!-1)sa!-nee klaŋ ไปรษณีย์กลาง

postpone v. f)leuan pai! เลื่อนไป

pot (for cooking, etc.) f)maw หม้อ

potato (Irish potato) man! 1)fa!-1)raŋ! มันฝรั่ง; (sweet potato) man! f)thet มันเทศ

potato chips man! f)thawt มันทอด

pound n. (pound sterling) pawn, nguhn pawn ปอนด์ เงินปอนด์; (weight, 16 ounces) pawn ปอนด์

pound v. (beat, as food in container) tam! ตำ; (crush) l)bot! บด; (hit with heavy object) h)thoop! ทุบ

pour (a liquid) theh, rin! เท, ริน

powder n. r)phong! ผง; (face-powder) f)paeng แป้ง; (gunpowder) din! peun ดินปืน

powder v. (the face) tha f)phaeng ทาแป้ง

powdered milk nom! r)phong! นมผง

power n. (authority, influence) am!-f)nat อำนาจ; (electric) kam!-lang! fai!-h)fa กำลังไฟฟ้า; (energy) kam!-lang!, raeng กำลัง, แรง; (exponential power, math.) kam!-lang! กำลัง [as in $3^3 = $ r)sam kam!-lang! r)sam]

powerful (strong) r)khaeng!-raeng แข็งแรง

power line (elect.) r)sai fai-h)fa สายไฟฟ้า; (high tension line) r)sai fai-h)fa raeng r)soong สายไฟฟ้าแรงสูง

power-of-attorney (leg. document) r)nang'-r)seu f)mawp am!-f)nat หนังสือมอบอำนาจ

practice v. l)feuk! l)hat! ฝึกหัด

praise v. chom!-chuhy, h)yck!-f)yawng ชมเชย, ยกย่อง

prawn (shrimp) f)koong! กุ้ง

pray v. (rel.) l)suat สวด

preach v. (rel.) f)thet-l)sa!-r)na เทศนา

precious stone f)phet phlawy เพชรพลอย

predict v. tham!-nai ทำนาย

predict the weather pha!-ya-kawn ah-l)kat พยากรณ์ อากาศ

prefer v. f)chawp f)mak l)kwa kan! ชอบมากกว่ากัน

pregnant adj. mee h)thawng มีท้อง

premier (prime minister) na-h)yok! h)rat!-l)tha!-mon!-tree นายกรัฐมนตรี

prepare v. triam เตรียม

prescription (for medicine) bai! l)sang! ya ใบสั่งยา

present adj. (not absent) l)yoo อยู่

present n. (gift) r)khawng r)khwan! ของขวัญ; (present time) l)pat!-l)joo!-ban! ปัจจุบัน

president (of a country) l)pra!-tha-na-h)thi!-baw dee ประธานาธิบดี; (of an association, etc.) na-h)yok! นายก

press n. (the press, journalists) ban!-da h)nak! r)nang!-r)seu-phim! บรรดานักหนังสือพิมพ์; (machinery for printing) f)thaen phim! แท่นพิมพ์

press v. 1)kot! กด

pressure n. khwam dan! ความดัน; (high blood-
  pressure) khwam dan! lo-l)hit! r)soeng ความ
  ดันโลหิตสูง; (low blood-pressure) khwam dan!
  lo-l)hit! l)tam! ความดันโลหิตต่ำ

pretty adj. r)suay สวย

prevent v. f)pawng-kan! ป้องกัน

price n. ra-kha ราคา

priest (Buddhist priest) h)phra! พระ; (Catholic)
  l)bat r)luang บาทหลวง

primary school rong-rian h)chan! l)pra!-r)thom!
  โรงเรียนชั้นประถม

prime minister (See premier.)

primer n. (fuse) h)cha!-nuan ชะนวน

prince n. f)jao!-h)fa chai เจ้าฟ้าชาย

princess f)jao-h)fa r)ying! เจ้าฟ้าหญิง

principal adj. (most important) f)thee r)sam!-
  khan! ที่สำคัญ; (n., headmaster) khroo l)yai!,
  ah-jahn l)yai! ครูใหญ่, อาจารย์ใหญ่

principle n. (fundamental holding) l)lak! หลัก

print v. (do printing work) phim! r)nang!-r)seu
  พิมพ์หนังสือ

printer n. f)chang phim! ช่างพิมพ์; (compositor, typesetter) f)chang riang ช่างเรียง

printing press n. rong phim! โรงพิมพ์

prison n. reuan jam! เรือนจำ

prisoner (convict) h)nak! f)thot นักโทษ

prisoner-of-war h)cha!-luhy l)seuk! เชลยศึก

private adj. l)cha!-h)phaw!, l)suan tua เฉพาะ, ส่วนตัว

private n. (AF) phon! h)tha! r)han ah-l)kat+ พลทหารอากาศ; (army) phon! h)tha!-r)han พล ทหาร; (PFC) l)ja l)sip! tree อ่าสิบตรี; (police pvt.) phon! tam!-l)ruat พลตำรวจ

private bath f)hawng-b)nam! l)suan tua ห้องน้ำ ส่วนตัว

private property h)sap!-r)sin l)suan l)book!-khon หรัพย์สินส่วนบุคคล

private school rong-rian (f)raht โรงเรียนราษฎร์

privilege (right) l)sit!, l)sit!-h)thi! สิทธิ, สิทธิ

prize (reward) rang-wan! รางวัล

probably (most likely) khong! l)ja! คงจะ

problem n pan!-r)ha ปัญหา

proclaim v. l)pra!-l)kat ประกาศ

produce (make) tham! f)kheun! ทำขึ้น; (manufacture) l)pha!-l)lit! ผลิต

profession (higher-level occupation) wi-cha
f)cheep วิชาชีพ

professor (in a university) l)sat-l)sa!-tra-jan
ศาสตราจารย์

profit n. kam!-rai! กำไร; v. f)dai! kam!-rai!
ได้กำไร

progress v. (advance) f)kao f)na ก้าวหน้า

prohibited (forbidden) f)ham ห้าม

project n. (program) khrong kan โครงการ

project v. (give off light) r)chai ฉาย; (project
films) r)chai r)nang! ฉายหนัง

projector (for films) f)khreuang r)chai r)nang!
เครื่องฉายหนัง

promise n. v. r)san!-ya สัญญา

promote v. (encourage, foster) l)song!-r)suhm
ส่งเสริม

promotion (higher position) f)leuan tam!-l)naeng
เลื่อนตำแหน่ง

pronounce (a word) l)awk r)siang ออกเสียง

proof (evidence) l)lak!-r)than หลักฐาน

proofread (printing) l)truat h)proof ตรวจปรู๊ฟ

proofs (printing) h)proof! ปรู๊ฟ

propaganda n. kan kho-sa-na chuan f)cheua การ
โฆษณาชวนเชื่อ

proper (suitable) r)som!-khuan สมควร

property n. h)sap!-r)sin! ทรัพย์สิน

propose (offer) l)sa!-r)nuh เสนอ

propose a price bid l)sa!-r)nuh ra-kha เสนอราคา

prosperous adj. l)ja!-ruhn เจริญ

prostitute n. so-peh-nee โสเภณี

protect v. f)pawng-kan! h)rak!-r)sa ป้องกันรักษา

protest v. l)pra!-h)thuang ประท้วง

protest demonstration (including protest marching)
kan duhn l)kha!-buan การเดินขบวน

proud adj. (feel proud of) phoom-jai! ภูมิใจ;
(arrogant) l)ying! หยิ่ง

prove (the truth of) h)phi!-l)soot พิสูจน์

province (changwat, of Thailand) jang'-wat!
จังหวัด

provinces (upcountry) l)tang jang!-l)wat! ต่างจังหวัด

psychological warfare r)song!-khram l)jit!-l)ta!-
h)wit-h)tha!-ya สงครามจิตวิทยา

public adj. r)sa-tha-h)ra!-h)na! สาธารณะ

public n. (the public) l)pra!-cha-chon! ประชาชน

publicity (advertising) kan kho-sa-na, kan r)phuhy f)phræ การโฆษณา, การเผยแพร่

public relations kan l)pra!-cha r)sam!-phan! การประชาสัมพันธ์

public telephone tho-h)ra!-l)sap r)sa-tha-h)ra!-h)na! โทรศัพท์สาธารณะ

publish v. l)jat! phim! จัดพิมพ์

pull v. deung! ดึง

pulley n. f)look f)rawk ลูกรอก

pullman (sleeper car on train) h)rot nawn รถนอน

pull out (as a drawer, a knife etc.) h)chak! l)awk ma ชักออกมา

pulse n. (of the body) f)cheep-h)pha!-jawn ชีพจร

pump n. f)khreuang l)soop, h)pam! เครื่องสูบ, ปั๊มป์; (water-pump) f)khreuang l)soop h)nam! เครื่องสูบน้ำ

pump v. l)soop, l)soop h)nam! สูบ, สูบน้ำ

punch v. (hit with fist) l)tawy, h)chok l)tawy ต่อย, ชกต่อย

puncture n. (of auto tire) yang l)taek ยางแตก;
(blow-out) yang h)ra!-l)buht ยางระเบิด; (leak
in tire) yang f)rua ยางรั่ว

puncture v. (make a hole) l)jaw! roo เจาะรู

punish long! f)thot ลงโทษ

pup (small dog) f)look r)ma ลูกหมา

pupil n. (of the eye) f)look ta dam! ลูกตาดำ;
(student) h)nak!-rian นักเรียน

pure adj. (innocent, uncontaminated) baw-h)ri!-
l)soot! บริสุทธิ์

pure water h)nam! baw-h)ri!-l)soot! น้ำบริสุทธิ์

purple (color) r)see f)muang สีม่วง

purse (for keeping money, etc.) l)kra!-r)pao!
กระเป๋า

pus (n., med.) h)nam! r)nawng น้ำหนอง

push v. dan!, l)phlak! ดัน, ผลัก

put, put in, put on (in general) l)sai! ใส่; (place,
put down) wang long! วางลง

put away l)kep! h)wai! เก็บไว้

put on (apply, as a liquid, etc.) tha ทา; (as
clothing) l)sai! ใส่

put on backwards l)sai! l)klap! ใส่กลับ

put out (extinguish) l)dap! ดับ

put up with (endure, tolerate) l)ot!-thon! อดทน

puzzle n. pan!-r)ha ปัญหา

puzzled adj. (confused) ngong! งง

python ngoo r)leuam งูเหลือม

quack doctor (illegal medical doctor) r)maw l)theuan หมอเถื่อน

qualified mee khoon-na-r)som!-l)bat! มีคุณสมบัติ

quality n. khoon-na-f)phap คุณภาพ

quantity n. paw-ri-man ปริมาณ

quarrel v. h)tha!-h)law! kan! ทะเลาะกัน

quarter (1/4 of something) l)set l)neung l)suan l)see เศษหนึ่งส่วนสี่

quartermaster (mil.) pha-la-thi-kan พลาธิการ

quarter of an hour (15 minutes) l)sip!-f)ha na-thee สิบห้านาที

quarters (living quarters) f)thee h)phak! ที่พัก

Queen (the Queen) (popular, colloquial, respect-ful) h)phra! ra-h)chi!-nee พระราชินี

queer adj. (strange) l)plaek แปลก

quell adj. (suppress) h)ra!-h)ngap!, l)prap pram ระงับ, ปราบปราม

question n. kham! r)tham คำถาม

question v. r)tham ถาม; (interrogate) h)sak!
r)tham ซักถาม; (make an inquiry) l)sawp
r)tham สอบถาม; (question officially) l)sawp
r)suan, l)tai! r)suan สอบสวน, ไต่สวน

quick, quickly reh-o, reh-o reh-o เร็ว, เร็วๆ

quicker (faster) reh-o l)kwa เร็วกว่า

quickest possible reh-o f)thee l)soot! เร็วที่สุด

quiet adj. (peaceful) l)sa!-l)ngop! สงบ; (Be
quiet!) f)ngiap เงียบ

quit v. f)luhk เลิก; (quit work) luhk ngan เลิก
งาน; (resign) la l)awk ลาออก

quite adj. thee deeo ทีเดียว

rabbit (animal) l)kra!-l)tai กระต่าย

rabies (hydrophobia) f)rok klua h)nam!,
(colloq.) f)rok r)ma f)ba โรคกลัวน้ำ, โรคหมาบ้า

race n. (competition) kan l)khaeng การแข่ง;
(foot race) kan f)wing! l)khaeng การวิ่งแข่ง;
(horse race) kan l)khaeng h)ma การแข่งม้า;
(race of people) chon! f)chat, h)cheua f)chat
ชนชาติ, เชื้อชาติ

race v. (compete) l)khaeng kan แข่งกัน; (foot
race) f)wing! l)khaeng วิ่งแข่ง; (horse race)
l)khaeng h)ma แข่งม้า

racetrack (horse-racing) l)sa!-r)nam h)ma สนาม
ม้า

radio n. h)wit!-h)tha!-h)yoo! วิทยุ

radio broadcasting station l)sa!-r)tha-nee h)wit!-
h)tha!-h)yoo! l)kra!-l)jai r)siang สถานีวิทยุกระ
จายเสียง

radio program rai-kan h)wit!-h)tha!-h)yoo! รายการ
วิทยุ

radio tube l)lawt h)wit!-h)tha!-h)yoo! หลอดวิทยุ

radish (veg.) f)look daeng ลูกแดง; r)hua l)phak!-
l)kat daeng หัวผักกาดแดง

rag n. f)pha f)khee h)riu ผ้าขี้ริว

rai (Thai measurement of area = to 0.396
acres) f)rai! ไร่

rail, railing n rang, rao ราง, ราว

railroad, railway n. thang f)rot! fai! ทางรถไฟ

railroad crossing thang f)kham thang h)rot! fai!
ทางข้ามทางรถไฟ

railway train h)rot! fai! รถไฟ

rain n. h)nam r)fon! น้ำฝน

rain v. r)fon! f)tok! ฝนตก

rainbow n. h)roong! รุ้ง

raincoat n. f)seua r)fon! เสื้อฝน

rainstorm n. pha-h)yoo! r)fon! พายุฝน

rain tree (a beautiful tropical shade tree) f)ton! jam l)joo!-ree ต้นจามจุรี

rainy season (in Thailand) h)reu!-doo r)fon, f)na r)fon! ฤดูฝน, หน้าฝน

raise n. (increase in salary) nguhn deuan f)kheun! เงินเดือนขึ้น

raise v. (lift up) h)yok! f)kheun! ยกขึ้น; (raise children or animals) h)liang เลี้ยง

rake n. v. f)khrat คราด

rambutan (a Thai fruit) h)ngaw! เงาะ

ram wong (a popular Thai dance) rahm! wong! รำวง

rank (mil.) h)yot! ยศ; (relative position) h)chan! ชั้น

rank insignia (mil.) f)khreuang h)yot! เครื่องยศ

rape v. l)khom! r)kheun ข่มขืน

rare adj. (as meat) l)sook! l)sook! l)dip! l)dip! สุกๆ ดิบๆ (difficult to find) r)ha f)yak หายาก

rash (heat rash) pen! l)phot! เป็นผด

rat (mouse) r)noo หนู

rate n l)aht!-tra อัตรา

rate of exchange (for currency) l)aht!-tra f)laek l)plian อัตราแลกเปลี่ยน

rather (showing preference) f)mak l)kwa มากกว่า; (to a certain extent) f)khawn f)khang ค่อนข้าง

ration n. pan! l)suan ปันส่วน

rations n. (mil.) l)sa!-r)biang ah-r)han เสบียง อาหาร

rattan n. (wood used in making furniture) r)wai หวาย

raw adj. (not cooked) l)dip! ดิบ

raw materials h)wat!-l)thoo! l)dip! วัตถุดิบ

ray (of light, etc.) r)saeng แสง; (X-ray) eks-ray เอกซเรย์

razor (for shaving) f)meet kohn มีดโกน

razor blade bai! f)meet kohn ใบมีดโกน

reach v. r)theung! ถึง; (arrive at, coming) ma r)theung! มาถึง; (arrive at, going) pai! r)theung! ไปถึง

read v. l)ahn อ่าน

ready adj. (all prepared) h)phrawm พร้อม; (finished) l)set h)laeo เสร็จแล้ว

real adj. jing', h)thae จริง, แท้

really (actually, truly) jing! jing! จริงๆ; (Really?) jing! jing! r)reu? จริงๆหรือ

rear l)suan h)thai ส่วนท้าย

rear-admiral phon! reua tree พลเรือตรี

rear door (back door) l)pra!-too r)lang! ประตูหลัง;
   (back door of a house) l)pra!-too r)lang!
   f)ban ประตูหลังบ้าน

reason n. (cause) l)het r)phon!, f)ton! l)het
   เหตุผล, ต้นเหตุ

reasonable adj. tam l)het r)phon! ตามเหตุผล;
   (reasonable extent, reasonable amount) phaw
   r)som!-khuan พอสมควร

rebellion n. kan l)ka!-l)bot! การกบฏ

receipt (showing payment of money) bai l)set!
   ใบเสร็จ

receive v. h)rap! รับ; (accept) yawm h)rap!
   ยอมรับ

recently adv. f)meua reh-o reh-o h)nee เมื่อ
   เร็ว ๆ นี้

recharge a battery l)aht! f)maw fai! l)mai
   อัดหม้อไฟใหม่

recipe (for cooking) tam!-ra ah-r)ban ตำราอาหาร

recognize v. (accept truth of) h)rap! h)roo รับรู้;
   (remember) jahm! f)dai! จำได้

---

recommend v. (advise) h)nae! nahm! แนะนำ;
(propose, suggest) l)sa!-r)nuh, h)nae! nam!
เสนอ, แนะนำ; (recommend something or someone) h)rap! rawng รับรอง

record n. (phonograph) l)phaen r)siang แผ่นเสียง;
(sports record) l)sa!-l)thi!-l)ti! สถิติ; (written
record) ban!-h)theuk! บันทึก

record v. (written) ban!-h)theuk! h)wai! บันทึกไว้;
(record sound) ban!-h)theuk r)siang บันทึกเสียง

record-player (phonograph) l)heep r)siang,
l)pik!-l)ahp! หีบเสียง, ปิคอัพ

recover v. (as from an illness) r)hai หาย

rectum (of the body, bottom) f)kon! ก้น

red (color) r)see daeng สีแดง

Red Cross (Thai) l)sa!-pha ka f)chat Thai
สภากาชาดไทย

red light (traffic) fai! daeng ไฟแดง

reduce v. h)lot!, h)lot! long! ลด, ลดลง; (reduce
price) h)lot! ra-kha ลดราคา; (reduce weight)
h)lot! h)nam!-l)nak! ลดน้ำหนัก

reel (of something) h)muan ม้วน

refer to v. h)phoot r)theung พูดถึง

referee (judge, umpire, in sports) f)phoo l)tat!
. r)sin! ผู้ตัดสิน

refine v. l)klan! กลั่น

refinery (oil) rong l)klan! h)nam!-man! โรง
กลั่นน้ำมัน; (sugar) rong l)klan! h)nam!-tan
โรงกลั่นน้ำตาล

reflect (light) l)sa!-h)thawn r)saeng สะท้อนแสง;
(think about) h)ra!-h)leuk! r)theung!, r)sam!-
h)neuk! ระลึกถึง, ดำนึก

refreshing adj. l)sot! f)cheun สดชื่น

refreshments (for drinking) f)khreuang l)deum
เครื่องดื่ม

refrigerator n. f)too yehn! ตู้เย็น

refuse n. (trash) l)kha!-l)ya! ขยะ

refuse v. l)pa!-l)ti!-l)set ปฏิเสธ

regarding (concerning) l)keeo l)kap! เกี่ยวกับ

regiment (n. mil.) krom! h)tha!-r)han กรมทหาร

regimental combat team (RCT, mil.) krom! l)pba!-
r)som! กรมผสม

region (in general) l)khet เขต; (of Thailand)
f)phak ภาค; (Central Region) f)phak klang
ภาคกลาง; (Eastern Region) f)phak l)ta!-wan!
l)awk ภาคตะวันออก; (Northern Region) f)phak
r)neua ภาคเหนือ; (Northeastern Region)

f)phak l)ta!-wan! l)awk r)chiang r)neua or
f)phak ee-r)san ภาคตะวันออกเฉียงเหนือ, ภาคอีสาน;
(Southern Region) f)phak f)tai! ภาคใต้

register, registry (official written record) h)tha!-
bian ทะเบียน

register v. (as a letter, etc.) long! h)tha!-bian
l)jot! h)tha!-bian ลงทะเบียน, จดทะเบียน

registered letter l)jot!-r)mai long! h)tha!-bian
จดหมายลงทะเบียน

registrar (govt. official) nai h)tha!-bian นาย
ทะเบียน

regret v. r)sia dai, r)sia jai! เสียดาย, เสียใจ

regrettable adj. f)na r)sia dai น่าเสียดาย

regular adj. l)pra!-jam!, r)tha-wawn ประจำ, ถาวร;
(normal) l)pok!-l)ka!-l)ti!, tham'-ท)ma!-da
ปกติ, ธรรมดา

regularly adv. pen l) pra!-jam! เป็นประจำ

regulation n. l)kot!-kehn, h)ra!-l)biap, f)khaw
bang!-h)khap! กฎเกณฑ์, ระเบียบ, ข้อบังคับ

rehearse v. (practice) h)sawm ซ้อม

reimburse (compensate, pay back) h)chot!
h)chai!, h)chai! kheun ชดใช้, ใช้คืน

reinforce (make stronger) r)suhm kam!-lang!
เสริมกำลัง; (mil.) f)phuhm kam!-lang เพิ่มกำลัง

reinforced concrete n. khawn-l)kreet r)suhm
l)lek! คอนกรีตเสริมเหล็ก

reinforcements (mil.) kawng r)som!-h)thop
กองเสริมทบ

reins (for riding a horse) r)sai bang!-r)hian
สายบังเหียน

reject (refuse to receive) f)mai! yawm h)rap!
ไม่ยอมรับ

relate v. (narrate, tell) f)lao! f)hai! fang!
เล่าให้ฟัง

relating to (concerning) l)keeo l)kap! เกี่ยวกับ

relations, relatives (kinsfolk) f)yat f)phee
h)nawng ญาติพี่น้อง

relations (with others) khwam r)sam!-phan!
ความสัมพันธ์

relax v. (relax oneself) l)yawn jai! หย่อนใจ;
(relax regulations) l)phawn r)phan! ผ่อนผัน

release v. l)plawy ปล่อย

reliable adj. f)cheua r)theu f)dai! เชื่อถือได้

relieve v. (as pain) f)kae l)puat แก้ปวด

relieved (freed of worry) f)long jai! โล่งใจ

religion n. 1)sat-1)sa!-r)na ศาสนา; (Buddhism) 1)sat-1)sa!-r)na h)phoot! ศาสนาพุทธ; (Christianity) 1)sat-1)sa!-r)na h)khrit! ศาสนาคริสต์; (Islam) 1)sat-1)sa!-r)na 1)it!-1)sa!-lam ศาสนาอิสลาม; (Judaism) 1)sat-1)sa!-r)na yiu (yew); ศาสนายิว

rely on someone f)pheung! pha ah-r)sai! พึ่งพาอาศัย

remainder (that left over) f)thee r)leua ที่เหลือ

remain in a place 1)yoo 1)taw pai! อยู่ต่อไป

remaining adj. (be left) r)leua เหลือ

remake (redo) tham! 1)mai! ทำใหม่

remarry v. 1)taeng ngan 1)mai! แต่งงานใหม่

remember v. jahm! f)dai! จำได้

remind v. teuan jai! เตือนใจ; (warn) 1)tak! teuan ตักเตือน

remote adj. 1)hang klai ห่างไกล

remove v. (take out) ao! 1)awk เอาออก

rent, rental n. f)kha f)chao! ค่าเช่า

rent v. (to someone) f)hai! f)chao! ให้เช่า; (take on rent) f)chao! เช่า

reorganize v. 1)jat! h)ra!-1)biap 1)mai! จัดระเบียบใหม่

repair v. f)sawm saem ซ่อมแซม

repairman n. f)chang f)sawm ช่างซ่อม

repair shop h)ran f)sawm ร้านซ่อม; (garage for repairing vehicles) l)oo h)rot! อู่รถ

repay v. h)chai! kheun ใช้คืน

repeat v. (happen again) l)kuht f)kheun! l)mai! เกิดขึ้นใหม่; (say again) f)phoot h)sam!, f)phoot l)mai! พูดซ้ำ, พูดใหม่

repeatedly (again and again) h)sam! h)sam! ซ้ำ ๆ

replace v. l)plian thaen เปลี่ยนแทน

reply n. kham!)thap คำตอบ (v., answer) l)tawp ตอบ

report n., v. rai-ngan รายงาน; (file official report with police) f)jaeng khwam แจ้งความ

reporter (news) h)nak l)khao นักข่าว

represent v. (be representative of) pen! f)phoo thaen เป็นผู้แทน

representative n (in general) f)phoo thaen ผู้แทน

reputation n. f)cheu r)siang ชื่อเสียง

request v. r)khaw h)rawng ขอร้อง

required (necessary) jam!-pen! จำเป็น; (needed, wanted) f)tawng-kan ต้องการ -

rescue v. (save someone's life) f)chuay chee h)wit! ช่วยชีวิต

research n. kan h)khon!·h)khwa, kan h)wi!·jai! การค้นคว้า, การวิจัย

resemble (be similar to) h)khlai l)kap! คล้ายกับ

reserve v. (book in advance) jawng h)wai!, h)book! จองไว้, บุ๊ค

reserves (n., mil.) kawng r)noon! กองหนุน

residence (house) f)ban h)phak! บ้านพัก; (place of residence, address) tam!·bon! f)thee l)yoo ตำบลที่อยู่

resign v. la l)awk ลาออก

resist v. l)taw f)tan ต่อต้าน

resort n. f)thee l)tak ah·l)kat ที่ตากอากาศ

respect v. h)nap!·r)theu นับถือ

respecting (with respect to) l)keeo l)kap! เกี่ยวกับ

respectfully f)duay khwam h)nap!·r)theu ด้วย ความนับถือ

responsibility n. khwam h)rap! l)phit! f)chawp ความรับผิดชอบ

responsible (be responsible) h)rap! l)phit! f)chawp รับผิดชอบ

rest v. (get rest) h)phak! l)phawn พักผ่อน

restaurant n. phat!·ta·khan, h)ran ah·r)han ภัตตาคาร, ร้านอาหาร

rest room f)hawng h)nam! ห้องน้ำ; (ladies')
f)hawng h)nam r)ying ห้องน้ำหญิง; (men's)
f)hawng nam! chai ห้องน้ำชาย

results n. r)phon! ผล

retreat v. (fall back) r)thawy ถอย

return v. (come back) l)klap! ma กลับมา; (go
back) l)klap! pai! กลับไป; (return home)
l)klap! f)ban กลับบ้าน

reveal v. (disclose) l)puht r)phuhy เปิดเผย

revenue stamp (duty stamp, for documents,
receipts) ah-kawn l)sa!-taem อากรแสตมป์

review v. (criticize) wi!-jan วิจารณ์; (study)
h)thop'-thuan ทบทวน; (troops) l)truat phon!
ตรวจพล

revise v. f)kae r)khai! l)mai! แก้ไขใหม่

revoke v. (abolish, cancel) h)yok! f)luhk ยกเลิก

revolt, revolution n. kan l)pa'-l)ti!-h)wat! การปฏิวัติ

revolve v. r)moon! wian หมุนเวียน

reward n. rang-wan รางวัล

rhythm n. jang!-l)wa! จังหวะ

rib n. f)see-khrong ซี่โครง

ribbon n. h)rib!-f)bin!, bo ริบบิ้น, โบว์

rice n. f)khao ข้าว

rice-farm, rice-field n. na, f)thoong! na นา, ทุ่งนา

rice-farmer n. chao na ชาวนา

rice-mill n. rong r)see f)khao โรงสีข้าว

rich adj. (financially) ruay รอย; (of food)
mee man! f)mak มีมันมาก

ride v. (sit in a motor vehicle, etc.) f)nang!
h)rot! etc. นั่งรถ; (ride a bicycle) l)khee
l)jak!-l)kra!-yan ขี่จักรยาน; (ride horseback)
l)khee h)ma ขี่ม้า; (ride a motorcycle) l)khee
h)rot! maw-tuh-sai ขี่รถมอเตอร์ไซค์

rifle (weapon) peun h)lek! yao ปืนเล็กยาว

right adj. (correct) l)thook f)tawng ถูกต้อง;
(That's right.) f)chai! h)laeo ใช่แล้ว

right n. (right to do something) l)sit!, l)sit'-
h)thi! สิทธ, สิทธิ

right, right-hand side r)khwa, r)khwa meu ขวา,
ขวามือ

right angle (90°) n. moom! l)chak มุมฉาก

right now r)deeo h)nee เดี๋ยวนี้

rigid adj. (inflexible, unchanging) tai tua
ตายตัว; (strict) f)khem f)nguat เข้มงวด;
(sturdy) f)man!-khong มั่นคง

rim n. rim! ริม; (edge) l)khawp ขอบ

rind (of fruit) l)pleuak เปลือก

ring n. (for finger) r)waen แหวน; (circle)
wong! klom! วงกลม; (diamond ring) r)waen
f)phet แหวนเพชร

ring v. (as a bell) l)kot! l)kra!-l)ding!, l)kot!
l)awt กดกริ่ง, กดออด

riot n: kan l)ja!-la.jon! การจลาจล

rip v. l)cheek ฉีก

ripe adj. l)sook! h)laeo สุกแล้ว

rise v. f)kheun! ขึ้น

river n. f)mae h)nam! แม่น้ำ

road n. l)tha!-r)non! ถนน

rob v. f)plon! ปล้น

robber n. jon, h)nak! f)plon! โจร, นักปล้น

rock n. f)kawn r)hin! ก้อนหิน

roll, roll up, a roll of something h)muan ม้วน

roll (of bread) l)kha!-r)nom!-pang! klom! ขนม
ปังกลม

roll, roll along v. f)kling!, f)kling! pai! กลิ้ง, กลิ้งไป

roof (of a building) r)lang.kha หลังคา

room n. f)hawng ห้อง; (space) f)thee ที่

root n. (of plant or tree) f)rak h)mai! รากไม้;
(arithmetic root) f)rak ราก; (square root)
f)rak f)thee r)sawng รากที่สอง

rope n. f)cheuak เชือก

rose (flower) l)dawk l)koo!-l)lap ดอกกุหลาบ

roster (list of names) rai f)cheu รายชื่อ

rotate v. r)moon! wian หมุนเวียน

rotten adj. f)nao! เน่า

rough adj. (not smooth) l)yap l)yap หยาบๆ

round adj. (circular) k!om! klom! กลมๆ

round n. (of boxing) h)yok! ยก

round-trip pai! l)klap! ไปกลับ; (round-trip ticket)
r)tua pai! l)klap! ตั๋วไปกลับ

route n. thang duhn, thang pai! ทางเดิน, ทางไป;
(highway route) thang r)luang l)phaen din!
ทางหลวงแผ่นดิน

routine adj. pen! l)pra!-jam เป็นประจำ

row n. (a line) r)thaeo แถว

row a boat jaeo reua แจวเรือ

Royal Thai Air Force (RTAF) kawng h)thap! ah-
l)kat กองทัพอากาศ

Royal Thai Army (RTA) kawng h)thap! l)bok!
กองทัพบก

Royal Thai Marines krom! na-wik-ka-yo-thin กรม
นาวิกโยธิน

Royal Thai Navy (RTN) kawng h)thap! reua กอง
ทัพเรือ

rub v r)thoo ถู

rubber n. (eraser) yang h)lop! ยางลบ; (from
rubber trees) yang ยาง

rubber band n. r)nang! l)sa!-h)tik!, yang h)rat!
หนังสติ๊ก, ยางรัด

rubbish n. (trash) l)kha!-l)ya! ขยะ

rub on (apply, as a liniment) tha ทา

rub out (erase) h)lop! l)awk ลบออก

ruby (precious stone) h)thap!-thim! ทับทิม

rug n. phrom!, l)seua poo h)pheun พรม, เสื่อปูพื้น

ruin v. (destroy) tham! lai ทำลาย

rule n. l)kot! kehn กฎเกณฑ์

rule, rule over v. l)pok! khrawng ปกครอง

ruler n. (for measuring) h)mai! ban!-h)that!
ไม้บรรทัด

rumor, rumour l)khao leu ข่าวลือ

run v. f)wing วิ่ง; (as a motor or clock) duhn
เดิน; (flow, as water) r)lai! ไหล; (operate, as
a business) dam!-nuhn kan ดำเนินการ

run away (flee) f)wing! r)nee วิ่งหนี

run over (as a car) h)thap ทับ

rupee (currency) nguhn roo-pee เงินรูปี

rural areas chon!-h)na!-l)bot!,   f)ban f)nawk
ชนบท, บ้านนอก

rush v. (hurry) f)reep f)reng รีบเร่ง

rushed adj. (hurried, short of time) f)reep
h)rawn รีบร้อน

rusty adj. l)sa!-r)nim! f)kheun!, pen! l)sa!-
r)nim! สนิมขึ้น, เป็นสนิม

sack n. r)thoong! ถุง; (gunny sack) l)kra!-l)sawp
กระสอบ

sacred adj. l)sak!-l)sit! ศักดิ์สิทธิ์

sacrifice v. r)sia l)sa!-l)la! เสียสละ

sad adj. (depressed) f)kloom! jai! กลุ้มใจ; (discouraged) h)thaw jai! ท้อใจ; (mournful, due
to bereavement such as death, etc.) f)sao!
l)sok, pen! h)thook! เศร้าโศก, เป็นทุกข์

saddle n (for riding a horse) ahn h)ma อานม้า

safe adj. l)plawt phal! ปลอดภัย

safe n. (for storing valuables, etc.) f)too sehf
ตู้เซฟ

safety-pin r)khem! f)sawn plai เข็มซ่อนปลาย

sailboat reua bai! เรือใบ

sailor (merchant marine, etc.) l)ka!-la-r)see กลาสี; (naval) h)tha!-r)han reua ทหารเรือ

salad (food) l)sa!-l)lat!, yam! l)sa!-l)lat! สลัด, ย่ำสลัด

salary n. nguhn deuan เงินเดือน; (wages) f)kha f)jang ค่าจ้าง

sale n. (selling at reduced prices) h)lot! ra-kha ลดราคา

salesperson khon! r)khai คนขาย

saliva n. (spit) h)nam! lai น้ำลาย

salt n. kleua เกลือ; v. (put on salt) l)sai! kleua ใส่เกลือ

salty (in taste) khem เค็ม

salung (Thai coin, 25 satangs, 1/4 of one Thai baht) l)sa!-r)leung! สลึง

same (alike, the same) r)meuan kan! เหมือนกัน; (the same thing) ahn! deeo kan! อันเดียวกัน

samlor (3-wheeled tricycle-taxi) r)sam h)law สามล้อ

sample n. tua l)yang ตัวอย่าง

sand n. sai ทราย

sandals (open rubber sandals) rawng h)thao! l)tae! รองเท้าแตะ

sandfly (insect) h)rin! ริ้น

sandpaper n. l)kra!-l)dat sai กระดาษทราย

sandwich n. saen-wit! แซนด์วิช

Sanskrit (language) pha-r)sa r)san!-l)sa!-l)krit! ภาษาสันสกฤต

sapphire (precious stone) nin! นิล

satang (1/100 of Thai baht) l)sa!-tang สตางค์

satisfactory adj. phaw h)chai! พอใช้

satisfied adj. phaw jai! พอใจ

Saturday wan! r)sao! วันเสาร์

sauce (for seasoning) h)nam! h)sawt น้ำซอส; (fish sauce) h)nam! pla น้ำปลา

saucer (dish) jan rawng f)thuay จานรองถ้วย

sausage (meat) f)sai! l)krawk ไส้กรอก

savage (wild) l)pa l)theuan ป่าเถื่อน

savage n. (person) khon! l)pa l)theuan คน ป่าเถื่อน

save v. (be economical) l)pra!-l)yat! nguhn ประหยัดเงิน; (rescue) f)chuay chee-h)wit! ช่วยชีวิต; (save money) l)kep! nguhn h)wai! เก็บเงินไว้

saw n. (for metal) f)leuay l)tat! l)lek เลื่อยลัด เหล็ก; (for wood) f)leuay h)mai! เลื่อยไม้

saw n., v. f)leuay เลื่อย

sawmill n. rong f)leuay โรงเลื่อย

say v. (speak) f)wa, 1)phoot, f)phoot f)wa ว่า, พูด, พูดว่า; (tell) f)wa, l)bawk, l)bawk f)wa ว่า, บอก, บอกว่า

scales (for weighing) f)khreuang f)chang! เครื่องชั่ง

scar (on skin) r)phlae pen! แผลเป็น

scare v. (frighten) tham! f)hai! l)tok! jai! ทำให้ตกใจ

schedule n. ta-rang, kam!-l)not! ตาราง, กำหนด; (timetable) ta-rang we-la ตารางเวลา

scholarship n. thoon! kan l)seuk!-r)sa ทุนการศึกษา

school n. rong rian โรงเรียน

school vacation l)yoot! thuhm หยุดเทอม

science n. h)wit!-h)tha!-ya-l)sat วิทยาศาสตร์

scientist n. h)nak! h)wit!-h)tha!-ya-l)sat นัก วิทยาศาสตร์

scissors n. kan!-krai!, l)ta!-krai! กรรไกร, ตะไกร

scold v. l)doo!, f)wa ดุ, ว่า

score n. (mark in games) f)taem แต้ม; (mark on exams) h)kha!-naen คะแนน

scorpion (insect) h)ma!-laeng l)pawng แมลงป่อง

scour v. l)khat!, r)thoo ขัด, ถู

scouring powder ya l)kbat! ยาขัด

scrape v. l)khoot l)awk ขูดออก

scraps n. l)set l)set เศษ ๆ

scratch v. (scratch oneself) kao! เกา; (scratch someone, as in anger or as an animal) l)khuan ข่วน

scream v. h)rawng r)siang dang! ร้องเสียงดัง

screens (for windows) h)moong! f)luat มุ้งลวด

screw n. l)ta!-poo khuang, l)sa!-kroo ตะปูควง, สะกรู

screwdriver n. r)khai! khuang ไขควง

scrub v. r)thoo, l)khat! ถู, ขัด

sea n. h)tha!-leh ทะเล

seacoast n. chai l)fang! ชายฝั่ง

seal (for stamping) tra ตรา

seal v. (as a package) l)pit! h)wai! ปิดไว้; (officially, with a seal) l)pra!-h)thap! tra ประทับตรา

sea level h)ra!-l)dap! h)nam! h)tha!-leh ระดับน้ำ
ทะเล

sea mail (via sea mail) thang reua ทางเรือ

seaman (ordinary seaman, navy) phon! h)tha!-
r)han reua พลทหารเรือ; (seaman, 2nd-class)
l)ja tree จ่าตรี; (seaman, 1st-class) l)ja tho
จ่าโท; (sailor, merchant seaman) l)ka!-la-r)see
กะลาสี

search v. h)khon! r)ha ค้นหา

seashore n. chai h)tha!-lee ชายทะเล

seasick adj. mao! f)khleun เมาคลื่น

season n. (of year) h)reu!-doo ฤดู

season v. (season food) choo h)rot! ชูรส

seat (place to sit) f)thee f)nang! ที่นั่ง

SEATO (Southeast Asia Treaty Orgn.) r)saw.
paw aw. ส.ป.อ.

second (1/60 of minute) h)wi!-na-thee วินาที;
(No. 2) f)thee r)sawng ที่สอง

second-hand (used, not new) h)chai! h)laeo
ใช้แล้ว

second lieutenant (air force, pilot officer) reua
ah-l)kat tree เรืออากาศตรี; (army, sub-lt.)

h)rawy tree ร้อยตรี; (police, sub-lt.) h)rawy tam!-l)ruat tree ร้อยตำรวจตรี

secret adj. h)lap! ลับ; n. khwam h)lap! ความลับ

secretary (in office) leh-kha-noo-kan เลขานุการ

section n. l)suan, tawn ส่วน, ตอน; (of Thai-govt. dept.) l)pha!-l)naek แผนก

securities (n., comr., fin., stock, shares, bonds, etc.) l)lak! h)sap! หลักทรัพย์

see v. r)hen เห็น

see a doctor r)ha r)maw หาหมอ

see a movie (film) doo r)nang! ดูหนัง

see someone (by appointment, etc.) h)phop! พบ

see someone off (on a trip etc.) pai! l)song! ไปส่ง

seed n. (for planting) h)ma!-h)let! f)pheut เมล็ดพืช

seem v. doo r)meuan ดูเหมือน

seep, seep into v. seum! f)khao! ซึมเข้า; (seep out) seum! l)awk ซึมออก

seize v. (confiscate, take by force) h)yeut! ao! ยึดเอา; (take hold of firmly) l)jap! l)yang f)naen จับอย่างแน่น

seldom (not often) f)mai l)bawy ไม่บ่อย

select v. f)leuak ao! เลือกเอา

self, selves tua ehng, ton! ehng ตัวเอง, คนเอง

selfish adj. r)hen l)kae tua เห็นแก่ตัว

sell v. r)khai ขาย

seller n. f)phoo r)khai ผู้ขาย

send v. l)song! ส่ง

sentry (mil. guard) h)tha!-r)han yam ทหารยาม

separate v. (take apart) f)yaek l)awk แยกออก

September (month) kan!-ya-yon! กันยายน

sergeant (mil. & police, in general) l)sip! l)ek,
l)ja l)sip! l)ek สิบเอก, จ่าสิบเอก

(AF) M/Sgt. phan! l)ja ah-l)kat l)ek พันจ่า
อากาศเอก; (T/Sgt) phan! l)ja ah-l)kat tho
พันจ่าอากาศโท (S/Sgt.) phan! l)ja ah-l)kat
tree พันจ่าอากาศตรี; (Sgt.) l)ja ah-l)kat l)ek
จ่าอากาศเอก

(army) M/Sgt. l)ja l)sip! l)ek จ่าสิบเอก;
(T/Sgt.) l)ja l)sip! tho จ่าสิบโท; (S/Sgt.) l)ja
l)sip! tree จ่าสิบตรี; (Sgt.) l)sip! l)ek สิบเอก

(police) Sgt.-Major, highest Thai police NCO
rank l)ja nai l)sip! tam!-l)ruat จ่านายสิบตำรวจ;
(Sgt.) l)sip! tam!-l)ruat l)ek สิบตำรวจเอก

serious adj. (important) r)sam!-khan! สำคัญ; (major, severe) h)rai raeng ร้ายแรง; (not joking) f)phoot jing! พูดจริง; (severe, for conditions, wounds, etc.) r)sa-l)hat! สาหัส

serious condition (physical) ah-kan r)sa-l)hat! อาการสาหัส

servant n. khon! h)chai!, khon! ngan คนใช้, คนงาน

serve v. (in general) h)rap! h)cha! รับใช้; (serve drinks) l)jaek f)khreuang l)deum แจกเครื่องดื่ม; (serve food) suhf ah-r)han เสิร์ฟ อาหาร

service n. (doing something for someone) baw-h)ri-kan บริการ

set n. (of something) h)choot! ชุด

set v. (set a clock) f)tang! na-h)li!-ka ตั้งนาฬิกา; (set an alarm clock) f)tang! na-h)li!-ka f)riak l)plook ตั้งนาฬิกาเรียกปลุก; (set fire to) l)joot! fai! จุดไฟ; (set fire to deliberately, commit arson) wang phluhng วางเพลิง; (set free) l)plot! l)plawy ปลดปล่อย; (set something down) wang long! วางลง; (set the table, for a meal) l)jat! b)to! ah-r)han จัดโต๊ะอาหาร

settle v. (begin living in a place) f)tang! f)ban-
reuan l)yoo ตั้งบ้านเรือนอยู่; (conclude an
argument) h)yoot!-l)ti! ยุติ

set up (establish) f)tang! f)kheun! ตั้งขึ้น
(install) l)tit! f)tang! ติดตั้ง

seven (7) l)jet! เจ็ด ๗

seventeen (17) l)sip!-l)jet! สิบเจ็ด (๑๗)

seventy (70) l)jet!-l)sip! เจ็ดสิบ ๗๐

sew v. h)yep! เย็บ

sewage n. h)nam! r)so-f)khrok น้ำโสโครก

sewing machine l)jak h)yep! f)pha จักรเย็บผ้า

sex adj. thang f)phet, "sex" ทางเพศ, เซ็กส์

sex n. f)phet. เพศ; (female sex) f)phet r)ying!
เพศหญิง; (male sex) f)phet chai เพศชาย

sexy adj. mee "sex" f)mak, "sexy" มีเซ็กส์มาก;
(provocative) f)yua yuan ยั่วยวน

shack n (building) l)kra!-h)tawp กระต๊อบ

shade n. (of a tree, etc.) f)rom! ร่ม

shadow n. ngao! เงา

shake v. (shake up, with the hands) l)kha!-
l)vao! เขย่า; (tremble) l)san!, tua l)san! สั่น,
ตัวสั่น

shake hands (in Western way) l)jap! meu kan!,
"shake hands" จับมือกัน, เช็คแฮนด์

shall (will, going to) l)ja! จะ

shame n. khwam h)la!-ai ความละอาย

shampoo n. chaem-phoo, ya l)sa! r)phom! แชมพู, ยาสระผม

shampoo v (wash hair) l)sa! r)phom! สระผม

shape n. (of body, of object, etc.) f)roop f)rang รูปร่าง; (status, condition) l)sa!-f)phap สภาพ

share (n., fin., stock) f)hoon! l)suan หุ้นส่วน; (in general, a share of something) l)suan l)baeng ส่วนแบ่ง

share v. l)baeng kan! แบ่งกัน

shareholder (n., comr.) f)phoo r)theu f)hoon! ผู้ถือหุ้น

shark (fish) pha l)cha! r)lam ปลาฉลาม

sharp adj. (not dull) khom! คม; (regarding exact time) trong! ตรง

sharp-pointed r)laem แหลม

shave n., v. (the beard) kon l)nuat โกนหนวด

shaving cream khreem kon l)nuat ครีมโกนหนวด; (brushless shaving cream) khreem kon l)nuat h)cha!-h)nit! f)mai! f)tawng b)chai! praeng ครีมโกนหนวดชนิดไม่ต้องใช้แปรง

she (or her) l) (normal) r)khao! เขา; (respectful f)than ท่าน

shears (for cutting) kan!-krai! l)yai! กรรไกรใหญ่

shed (for livestock) rong wua khwai โรงวัวควาย; (for storing things) rong l)kep r)khawng โรงเก็บของ

sheet (for a bed) f)pha poo f)thee-nawn ผ้าปู ที่นอน; (sheet of something) l)phaen แผ่น

shelf n. f)hing! [h)chan!] wang r)khawng หิ้ง (ชั้น) วางของ

shell (seashell) r)hawy หอย

shield v. (protect) bang!, f)pawng kan! บัง, ป้องกัน

shin n. (of the leg) f)na f)khaeng หน้าแข้ง

shine v. (give off light) l)sawng r)saeng ส่องแสง; (polish) l)khat! ngao! ขัดเงา; (shine light on) l)sawng fai! ส่องไฟ; (shine shoes) l)khat! rawng·h)thao! ขัดรองเท้า

shiny adj. f)kheun! ngao! ขึ้นเงา

ship n. reua, lam! เรือ, ลำ

ship v. (send by ship) l)song! pai! thang reua ส่งไปทางเรือ

shirt n. f)seua เสื้อ

shirtsleeve n. r)khaen f)seua แขนเสื้อ

shoe n. rawng-h)thao รองเท้า

shoelaces, shoestrings n. f)cheuak rawng-h)thao! เชือกรองเท้า

shoe polish n. ya l)khat! rawng-h)thao ยาขัดรองเท้า

shoe repairman n. f)chang f)sawm rawng-h)thao! ช่างซ่อมรองเท้า

shoot v. (as a gun) ยิง

shop n. h)ran ร้าน

shop v. (go shopping) h)seu r)khawng ซื้อของ

short adj. (not long) h)san! สั้น; (not tall, of things) l)tam! ต่ำ; (not tall, persons) f)tia เตี้ย

shortening (lard, for cooking) h)nam!-man! r)moo น้ำมันหมู

shorthand n. cha'-wa!-f)lek ชวเลข

short pants n. kang-keng r)kha f)san! กางเกง ขาสั้น

shorts (for men and boys, underclothes) kang-keng nai! กางเกงใน

should v. (ought to) khuan ควร

shoulder (of human body or of land) l)lai! ไหล่

shout v. l)ta!-kon ตะโกน

shovel v. f)phlua พลั่ว

show n. (in general) kan l)sa!-daeng, chow การแสดง, โชว์

show v. l)sa!-daeng แสดง; (show how to do something) l)sa!-daeng f)hai! doo แสดงให้ดู; (Show me. Let me see.) r)khaw doo ขอดู

shower v. (take a showar-bath) l)ab h)nam! l)fak! bua อาบน้ำฝักบัว

shower slippers (rubber slippers with rubber straps on top) rawng h)thao! l)tae! รองเท้าแตะ

shrimp (seafood) f)koong! กุ้ง

shrink v. (as clothing) l)bot! หด

shut v. (close) l)pit! ปิด; (shut the door) l)pit! l)pra!-too ปิดประตู; (shut the windows) l)pit! f)na-l)tang ปิดหน้าต่าง

shy adj. (bashful) ai อาย

Siam (old name of Thailand) l)sa!-r)yam สยาม

Siamese (language) pha-r)sa Thai ภาษาไทย; (people) khon! Thai! คนไทย

sick adj. (not well) f)mai! l)sa!-bai ไม่สบาย; (ill) l)puay ป่วย; (sick and tired of something) l)beua l)nai เบื่อหน่าย

side n. (of a person) f)khang ข้าง; (of something) f)khang,h)dan ข้าง, ด้าน; (opposing sides, as in politics, etc.) l)fai ฝ่าย

sidewalk (footpath, pavement) thang duhn h)thao ทางเดินเท้า

sightsee v. f)thawng f)theeo ท่องเที่ยว

sign n. (advertisement) f)pai ป้าย; (symbol) f)khreuang-r)mai เครื่องหมาย

sign v. (sign one's name) sehn! f)cheu เซ็นชื่อ

signal n. r)san'-yan! สัญญาณ; v. l)song! r)san'-yan ส่งสัญญาณ

signature n. lai sehn, lai meu f)cheu ลายเซ็น, ลายมือชื่อ

Silence! (Be quiet!) f)ngiap เงียบ

silent adj. f)ngiap เงียบ

silk n. (silk cloth) f)pha r)mai! ผ้าไหม; (Thai silk) f)pha r)mai! thai! ผ้าไหมไทย

silver (the metal) nguhn เงิน; (the color) r)see nguhn สีเงิน

silverware f)khreuang nguhn เครื่องเงิน

similar adj. h)khlai h)khlai kan! คล้ายๆกัน (alike) r)meuan kan! เหมือนกัน

simultaneously (at the same time) h)phrawm kan! พร้อมกัน

sin n. l)bap kam! บาปกรรม

since (from a time in the past) f)tang! l)tae ตั้งแต่; (since it is that way) nai f)meua ในเมื่อ

sing v. h)rawng phlehng ร้องเพลง

singer n. h)nak! h)rawng นักร้อง

single adj. (only one) ....deeo ....เดียว; (unmarried) pen! l)sot เป็นโสด

single room (in a hotel) f)hawng l)deeo ห้องเดียว

sink n. (for washing dishes) l)ang h)lang cham อ่างล้างจาน

sink v. (go under the water) jom! h)nam! จมน้ำ

sir (or, yes sir) (spoken by females) h)kha! คะ; (spoken by males) h)khrap! ครับ

sister n. (elder sister) f)phee r)sao พี่สาว; (younger sister) h)nawng r)sao น้องสาว; (Catholic sister, nun) sis-tuh ซิสเตอร์

sister-in-law (wife of one's younger brother) h)nawng l)sa-h)phai! น้องสะใภ้; (wife of one's older brother) h)phee l)sa!-h)phai! พี่สะใภ้

sit v. f)nang! นั่ง; (sit down) f)nang! long นั่งลง; (Please sit down.) chuhn f)nang! เชิญนั่ง

six (6) l)hok! หก ๖

sixteen (16) l)sip!-l)hok! สิบหก ๑๖

sixty (60) l)hok!-l)sip! หกสิบ ๖๐

size n. 1)kha!-1)nat ขนาด

ski n., v. 1)sa!-kee สกี; (water-ski, water-skiing) 1)sa!-1)kee h)nam! สกีน้ำ

skid v. (slip, slide) f)leun ลื่น

skillet (frying pan) 1)kra!-h)tha! กระทะ

skillful, skilled adj. (clever at doing things) 1)keng เก่ง; (experienced) cham!-nan, mee r)fee meu dee ชำนาญ, มีฝีมือดี

skin (human skin) r)phew r)nang ผิวหนัง; (of a fruit) 1)pleuak เปลือก; (of an animal, hide) r)nang! หนัง

skirt n. (article of feminine clothing) 1)kra!-prong กระโปรง

sky n. (the sky) h)thawng h)fa ท้องฟ้า

sky-blue (color) r)see h)fa สีฟ้า

slack adj. (as a rope) 1)yawn หย่อน; (slack in standards, negligent) 1)yawn 1)sa!-1)mat!-1)tha!-f)phap หย่อนสมรรถภาพ

slap v. (with the hand) 1)top! ตบ

sleep v. nawn 1)lap! นอนหลับ

sleepy adj. f)nguang nawn ง่วงนอน

sleeve n. (of a mechanical device) f)thaw, 1)plawk หลอด, ปลอก (of a shirt or blouse) r)khaen f)seua แขนเสื้อ

slice (of something) h)chin! ชิ้น

slice v. l)han! หั่น

sling n. (of a weapon) r)sai l)sa!-phai peun
สายสะพายปืน

slip v. (slip and fall) f)leun h)lom! ลื่นล้ม

slip off, slip out l)loot! l)awk หลุดออก

slippers (rubber, with open tops & rubber straps
over top) rawng h)thao! l)tae! รองเท้าแตะ

slippery adj. f)leun ลื่น

slow adj. h)cha ช้า

slower, more slowly (slow down) h)cha l)nawy
ช้าหน่อย

small adj. h)lek! เล็ก

small arms (weapons) peun h)lek! ปืนเล็ก

smaller adj. h)lek! l)kwa เล็กกว่า

smallest adj. h)lek! f)thee l)soot! เล็กที่สุด

smallpox (disease) f)khai! thaw-h)ra!-h)phit!
ไข้ทรพิษ

smart adj. (in appearance) l)sa!-h)mat, l)sa!-
nga ngam สมารถ, สง่างาม; (in intelligence)
l)cha!-l)lat, l)lak! r)laem ฉลาด, หลักแหลม

smart v. (burn, be painful) l)saep แสบ

smashed adj. (smashed to pieces) l)taek pen!
h)chin! h)chin! แตกเป็นชิ้น ๆ

smell n. (odor) l)klin! กลิ่น

smell v. f)dai l)klin! ได้กลิ่น

smell of, sniff dom! doo ดมดู

smile n. rawy! h)yim! รอยยิ้ม; v. h)yim! ยิ้ม

smoke n. khwan! ควัน

smoke (cigarettes) l)soop! [l)boo!-l)ree] สูบ (บุหรี่)

smooth adj. f)rap f)riap ราบเรียบ

smuggle adj. r)nee pha-r)see หนีภาษี

smuggler n. khon h)lak! f)lawp r)nee pha-r)see
     คนลักลอบหนีภาษี

snake n. ngoo งู

sneeze v. jahm จาม

snow n. l)hi-h)ma! หิมะ, v. l)hi-h)ma! l)tok! หิมะตก

so (be true) jing! จริง; (That's not so.) f)mai!
     jing! ไม่จริง; (therefore) dang! h)nan! ดังนั้น

so, so much l)yang f)mak อย่างมาก

soak v. f)chae h)wai! แช่ไว้

soap n. l)sa!-l)boo สบู่

socks (for the feet) r)thoong! h)thao! ถุงเท้า

soda, soda water (for mixing drinks) so-da โซดา

soda crackers (saltines) l)kha!-r)nom!-pang!
     h)khem! ขนมปังเค็ม

soda straw (for sucking refreshments) l)iawt l)doot หลอดดูด

sofa n. (couch) so-fa โซฟา

soft adj. f)nim! นิ่ม

soft-boiled eggs l)khai! f)luak ไข่ลวก

soft-drinks (refreshments) f)khreuang l)deum เครื่องดื่ม

softly (gently) bao! bao! เบา ๆ

soi (lane, name used in Thailand for small branch roads) sawy ซอย

soil (earth) din! ดิน

soiled adj. f)peuan เปื้อน

solder v. l)bat!-kree บัดกรี

soldering iron n. r)hua h)raeng หัวแร้ง

soldering lead l)ta!-l)kua l)bat!-kree ตะกั่วบัดกรี

soldier h)tha!-r)han ทหาร

solid adj. f)man!-khong! มั่นคง

solve v. (a problem) f)kae pan!-r)ha แก้ปัญหา

some adj. bang บาง; adv., pron. (somewhat) f)bang บ้าง

some more l)eek l)nawy อีกหน่อย

someone (a certain person) khrai! khon l)neung! ใครคนหนึ่ง

someone, somebody (in general) khrai!, mee khon! ใคร, มีคน

someone else (other person or people) khon! l)eun คนอื่น; (one other person) l)eek khon! l)neung! อีกคนหนึ่ง

some other time (in the future) thee r)lang! ทีหลัง

something l)ah!-rai!, mee l)ah!-rai! อะไร, มีอะไร

something else l)yang l)eun อย่างอื่น

some things bang l)yang บางอย่าง

sometimes bang thee, bang h)khrang บางที, บางครั้ง

somewhere l)sak! l)haeng l)neung! ลักแห่งหนึ่ง

so much (a certain amount) f)thao! h)nan! เท่านั้น; (very much) f)mak, l)yang f)mak มาก, อย่างมาก

son n. f)look chai ลูกชาย

song n. phleng เพลง

son-in-law f)look r)khuhy ลูกเขย

soon adv. nai! f)mai! h)cha ในไม่ช้า

sore adj. (bruised) h)cham! ช้ำ; (hurtful) l)jep! เจ็บ; (stinging) l)saep แสบ; (tired) f)meuay เมื่อย

sore n. (sore place on body, wound) r)phlae แผล

sore threat l)jep! khaw เจ็บคอ

sorry (be sorry) r)sia jai เสียใจ

so-so (not so bad, not so good--colloq.) f)reuay f)reuay เรื่อยๆ

soul n. (spirit) duang win!-yan ควงวิญญาณ; (vague inner being) l)jit!-jai! จิตใจ

sound n. r)siang เสียง

soup n. h)soop! ซุป

sour (in taste) h)rot! f)preeo รสเปรี้ยว

south (direction) h)tit! f)tai! ทิศใต้; (the South, the Southern Region) f)phak f)tai! ภาคใต้

South America ah-meh-ri-ka f)tai! อเมริกาใต้

southeast (direction) h)thit! l)ta!-wan! l)awk r)chiang f)tai!, ah-kha-neh ทิศตะวันออกเฉียงใต้, อาคเนย์

southwest (direction) h)thit! l)ta!-wan! l)tok! r)chiang f)tai! ทิศตะวันตกเฉียงใต้

Soviet (the Soviet Union, Russia, USSR) l)sa!-l)ha!-r)phap so-wiat สหภาพโซเวียต

sow, sow seeds v. l)wan หว่าน

space n. (interval) h)ra! h)ya! l)hang รยยะห่าง;
(outer space) ah-wa-l)kat อวกาศ; (vacant
space) f)thee f)wang ที่ว่าง

spade n. (small, narrow tool) r)siam เสียม

Spain (country) l)pra!-f)thet l)sa!-pen ประเทศ
สเปญ

Spanish (language) pha-r)sa l)sa!-pen ภาษาสเปญ;
(people) chao l)sa!-pen ชาวสเปญ

spanner n. (a kind of wrench) koon!-jae f)leuan,
koon!-jae l)pak tai กุญแจเลื่อน, กุญแจปากตาย

spare adj. (extra, reserve) l)ah!-l)lai! อะไหล่;
(spare parts, for cars, etc.) f)khreuang l)ah!-
l)lai! เครื่องอะไหล่: (spare tire) yang l)ah-l)lai!
ยางอะไหล่

spark plug n. r)hua thian หัวเทียน

speak v. f)phoot พูด; (make a speech) l)klao-
kham! pra-r)sai กล่าวคำปราศรัย; (speak bluntly)
f)phoot trong! pai! trong! ma พูดตรงไปตรงมา;
(speak crudely, roughly) f)phoot l)yap,
f)phoot l)sa!-l)bot! พูดหยาบ, พูดสบถ; (speak
English) f)phoot ang!-krit! พูดอังกฤษ; (speak
jokingly) f)phoot f)lehn, f)phoot l)ta!-l)lok!

พูดเล่น พูดคลอ; (speak on phone) f)phoot tho-ra-l)sap! พูดโทรศัพท์; (speak Thai) ·f)phoot thai! พูดไทย

special adj. h)phi!-l)set พิเศษ

special colonel (equivalent to brig.-gen.) (army) phan!)ek [h)phi!-l)set] พันเอก (พิเศษ); (police) phan! tam!-l)ruat l)ek [h)phi!-l)set] พันตำรวจเอก (พิเศษ)

specifications (n., engr.) rai h)la!-l)iat รายละเอียด

specify v. (stipulate) kam!-l)not! กำหนด

spectacles (eyeglasses) f)waen ta แว่นตา

speed n. khwam reh-o ความเร็ว

spell v. (a word) l)sa!-l)kot! tua สะกดตัว

spend v. (money) h)chai! nguhn, r)sia nguhn ใช้เงิน, เสียเงิน; (time) h)chai! we-la, r)sia we-la ใช้เวลา, เสียเวลา

spices n (for flavoring foods) f)khreuang f)thet, f)khreuang choo h)rot! เครื่องเทศ, เครื่องชูรส

spider n. maeng-moom! แมงมุม

spider webs yai maeng-moom! ใยแมงมุม

spigot (faucet, water tap) h)kawk h)nam! ก๊อกน้ำ

spill v. (as a liquid) l)hok! หก

spin v. r)moon! wian หมุนเวียน

spinach n. l)phak! r)khom! ผักขม

spine (of body) l)kra!-l)dook r)san! r)lang! กระดูกสันหลัง

spit n. (saliva) h)nam! lai น้ำลาย

spit v. (expectorate) f)buan h)nam! lai บ้วนน้ำลาย

splint (for bandaging) l)feuak เฝือก

spoiled adj. r)sia เสีย; (rotten) f)nao! เน่า

sponge n. fawng h)nam! ฟองน้ำ

spool n. l)lawt, h)muan หลอด, ม้วน; (for film) l)lawt h)muan feem l)thai f)roop หลอดม้วนฟิล์มถ่ายรูป; (for thread) l)lawt f)dai หลอดด้าย

spoon (for eating) h)chawn ช้อน; (teaspoon) h)chawn cha ช้อนชา; (tablespoon) h)chawn khao, h)chawn h)to! ช้อนคาว, ช้อนโต๊ะ

sports (athletics) kee-la, kan kee-la กีฬา, การกีฬา; (the National Stadium, Bangkok) l)sa!-r)nam kee-la สนามกีฬา

spot n. (small dot, speck, etc.) l)joot! จุด

sprain n. (as of ankle) h)khlet! เคล็ด

spray v. l)cheet ฉีด; (spray-paint, v.) f)phon! r)see พ่นสี

spring n. (as of watch etc.) lan, sa-pring!, l)khot!
f)luat ลาน สปริง, หลวด; (natural spring) h)nam!
h)phoo! tham!-h)ma!-f)chat น้ำพุธรรมชาติ; (season of year) h)reu-doo bai!-h)mai! l)phli! ฤดู
ใบไม้ดิ

spy n. (espionage agent) ja-ra-boo-root, sa-pai
จารบุรุษ, สปาย; (v., do espionage work) l)seup
rat-cha-kan l)lap! สืบราชการลับ

spyglass (small telescope) f)klawng l)sawng
thang klai! กล้องส่องทางไกล

squad (mil., as of infantry) l)moo h)tha!-r)han
หมู่ทหาร

squadron (AF) r)foong bin! ฝูงบิน; (navy)
kawng reua h)rop! กองเรือรบ

squadron-leader (AF major) na-wa ah-l)kat tree
นาวาอากาศตรี

square (geometric figure) l)see l)liam l)jat!-
l)too!-h)rat! สี่เหลี่ยมจัตุรัส; (square measure)
ta-rang.... ตาราง....; (square root) f)rak f)thee
r)sawng รากที่สอง

squeeze, squeeze out l)beep, l)beep h)khan! บีบ,
บีบคั้น

squid (seafood) pla l)meuk! ปลาหมึก

stable (for horses) f)khawk h)ma คอกม้า

staff (personnel) ban!-da f)jao!-f)na-f)thee บรรดาเจ้าหน้าที่; (general staff, mil.) kawng r)seh-na-h)thi!-kan กองเสนาธิการ

stagger v. (as in walking) duhn so-seh เดินโซเซ

stained adj. (soiled) f)peuan เปื้อน

stairs, stairway ban!-dai!, l)kra!-dai บันได, กระได; (downstairs) h)chan! f)lang ชั้นล่าง; (upstairs) h)chan! bon! ชั้นบน

stamp n. (official stamp, for stamping or sealing) tra ตรา; (postage stamp) l)sa!.taem, prai!-l)sa!-nee-ya-kawn แสตมป์, ไปรษณียากร

stamp v. (affix an official stamp or seal) l)pra!-h)thap tra, l)pit! tra ประทับตรา, ปิดตรา; (put a postage stamp on) l)tit! l)sa!-taem, l)pit! l)sa!-taem ติดแสตมป์, ปิดแสตมป์

stand v. (be standing) yeun l)yoo ยืนอยู่; (endure) l)ot!-thon อดทน; (located at a certain place, as a building) f)tang! l)yoo ตั้งอยู่; (stand up, get up) h)look! f)kheun!, yeun f)kheun! ลุกขึ้น, ยืนขึ้น

staple n (staple food) ah-r)han l)lak! อาหารหลัก; (stapling material) r)khem h)yep! l)kra!-l)dat เข็มเย็บกระดาษ

staple v. (with a stapler) h)yep! l)kra!-l)dat,
l)tawk l)huang เย็บกระดาษ, ตอกห่วง

stapler n. (for stapling) f)khreuang h)yep!
l)kra!-l)dat เครื่องเย็บกระดาษ

star (in sky) dao ดาว; (film star) da-ra ดารา

starch v. (starch clothes) long! f)paeng ลงแป้ง

stare, stare at v. f)jawng doo จ้องดู

start v. (begin) f)ruhm เริ่ม; (start a car engine)
sa!-tat f)khreuang สตาร์ทเครื่อง; (start out)
l)awk pai! ออกไป

starve v. (go without food) l)ot! ah-r)han อด
อาหาร; (starve to death) l)ot tai อดตาย

state adj (of or pertaining to the state or the
govt.) r)luang หลวง; (status, condition) l)sa!-
f)phap สภาพ

state n. (political entity) h)rat! รัฐ; (USA state)
mon!-h)rat! มลรัฐ

state road or highway l)tha!-r)non! r)luang, thang
r)luang ถนนหลวง, ทางหลวง

station n. (in general) l)sa!-r)tha-nee สถานี;
(gas station) h)pam! h)nam!-nan! ปั๊มน้ำมัน;
(police station) l)sa!r)tha-nee tam!-l)ruat,

    rong h)phak! สถานีตำรวจ, โรงพัก; (railway station) l)sa!-r)tha-nee h)rot!-fai! สถานีรถไฟ

stationery (& other writing supplies) f)khreuang r)khian เครื่องเขียน

statue (in general) f)roop f)pan! รูปปั้น; (memorial statue) ah-noot-sa-wa-ree อนุสาวรีย์; (of Lord Buddha) h)phra! h)phoot!-h)tha!-f)roop พระพุทธรูป; (small Buddha medallion) h)phra! พระ

stay v. (be at a place) l)yoo อยู่; (remain) l)yoo l)taw อยู่ต่อ; (stay temporarily, as at hotel) h)phak! l)yoo พักอยู่

steak (meat) h)neua l)sa!-l)tek! เนื้อสเต๊ก

steal v. l)kha!-moy ขโมย

steam n. ai! h)nam! ไอน้ำ

steam v. (in cooking) f)neung! นึ่ง

steamer, steamship n. reua duhn h)tha!-leh เรือ เดินทะเล

steel (metal) l)lek! f)kla เหล็กกล้า

steering wheel (of a vehicle) phuang ma-lai! h)rot! พวงมาลัยรถ

step v. (as in walking) f)kao ก้าว; (step on something) l)yiap เหยียบ

stepchild n. f)look h)liang ลูกเลี้ยง

stepdaughter n. f)look-r)sao h)liang ลูกสาวเลี้ยง

stepfather n. f)phaw h)liang พ่อเลี้ยง

stepmother n. f)mae h)liang แม่เลี้ยง

steps (stairway) ban!-dai!, l)kra!-dai บันได, กระได

stepson n. f)look-chai h)liang ลูกชายเลี้ยง

step-up(-down) (n., eloct.) l)sa!-h)tep-h)ap! (dao)
สะเต็ปอัพ(ดาวน์), f)khreuang plaeng fai! f)kheun!
(long!) เครื่องแปลงไฟขึ้น(ลง)

sterilize v. (disinfect) f)kha h)cheua f)rok
ฆ่าเชื้อโรค; (make sterile, incapable of having
children) tham! r)man! ทำหมัน

stew (food dish) l)sa!-too สตู

stick v. (attach to something) l)pit! h)wai!,
l)tit! h)wai! ปิดไว้, ติดไว้

stick to (be persevering) f)phak phian พากเพียร

sticky adj. r)neeo เหนียว; (sticky rice, glutinous
rice) f)khao r)neeo ข้าวเหนียว

stiff adj. (from fatigue, etc.) f)meuay เมื่อย;
(difficult) f)yak ยาก; (hard, not soft) r)khaeng!
แข็ง

still adj. (quiet) f)ngiap เงียบ

still adv. yang! ยัง

stingy adj. (colloq.) f)khee r)neeo ขี้เหนียว

stir v. (as in cooking) khon! คน

stomach (of body) h)thawng ท้อง

stomachache l)puat h)thawng ปวดท้อง

stone n. f)kawn r)hin! ก้อนหิน

STOP! l)yoot! หยุด; (stop doing something)
f)lubk เลิก; (stop work) l)yoot! ngahn หยุดงาน

stopper n. l)jook! l)khuat จุกขวด

store (business shop) h)rahn ร้าน

store v. (keep) l)kep! h)wai! เก็บไว้

storeroom n. f)bawng l)kep! r)khawng ห้องเก็บของ

storm n. pha-h)yoo! พายุ; (rain storm) pha-
h)yoo! r)fon! พายุฝน; (wind storm) lom! pha-
h)yoo! ลมพายุ

story n. f)reuang rao เรื่องราว

stove n. (for cooking) tao! เตา; (electric stove)
tao! fai!-h)fa เตาไฟฟ้า; (gas stove) tao! h)kaet
เตาแก๊ส

straight trong! ตรง; (straight ahead) trong!
pai! ตรงไป

strange adj. l)plaek l)pra!-l)lat แปลกประหลาด

stranger n. khon! l)plaek f)na คนแปลกหน้า

stream (small waterway) h)nam! f)huay น้ำห้วย

street (in general) l)tha!-r)non! ถนน; (lane) ซอย, l)trawk ซอย, ตรอก; (highway) thang r)luang ทางหลวง

streetcar (tram) h)rot! rang รถราง

street number (house number) f)lek-f)thee r)khawng f)ban เลขที่ของบ้าน

strength n. kam!-lang!, raeng กำลัง, แรง

stretcher (for carrying ill) pleh r)ham khon l)puay เปลหามคนป่วย

strict adj. f)khreng h)khrat เคร่งครัด

strike (work stoppage) l)sa!-h)trai!, h)nat! h)thing! ngan สไตรค์, นัดหยุดงาน

strike v. (beat, hit) tee ตี

strike out (mark out) f)kha l)awk ฆ่าออก

string n. f)sehn f)cheuak เส้นเชือก

stripes (for NCO ranks) f)bang! บั้ง

strong (physically) r)khaeng! raeng แข็งแรง; (very pronounced, as an odor) raeng แรง; (with little dilution, as drinks) l)kae แก่

struggle v. l)taw f)soo ต่อสู้

stuck l)tit!, l)tit! h)wai! ติด, ติดไว้

student n. (in general) h)nak! rian นักเรียน; (college or univ.) h)nak! l)seuk!-r)sa นักศึกษา

study v. (in general) rian เรียน; (higher study) l)seuk!-r)sa ศึกษา

stupid adj. f)ngo โง่

style n. l)baep แบบ

stylish adj. (popular) h)ni!-yom! นิยม

subject n. (topic) f)reuang เรื่อง

sub-lieutenant (2nd lt., army) h)rawy tree ร้อยตรี; (2nd lt., air force, pilot officer) reua ah-l)kat tree เรืออากาศตรี; (2nd lt., police) h)rawy tam!-l)ruat tree ร้อยตำรวจตรี; (lt., j. g., navy) reua tho เรือโท

submarine reua dam! b)nam! เรือดำน้ำ

subscriber (to a periodical) l)sa!-ma-h)chik! สมาชิก

substitute, substitute for v. (person) tham! thaen ทำแทน; (thing) h)chai! thaen ใช้แทน

subtract v. h)lop! ลบ

successful adj. r)sam!-l)ret! สำเร็จ

such as (for example) f)chen เช่น

suck v. l)doot ดูด; (hold in mouth, as a cough drop) om! อม

suddenly adv. doy l)kral-than! r)han! โดยกระทันหัน

sue v. (in court) h)fawng ฟ้อง

suffer v. thaw-h)ra!-man ทรมาน

sugar n. h)nam!-tan น้ำตาล

sugarcane f)awy อ้อย

suggest v. h)nae! nam! แนะนำ

suggestion n. kham! h)nae! nam! คำแนะนำ

suicide v. (commit suicide) f)kha tua tai
ฆ่าตัวตาย

suit n. (business suit, men) h)choot! r)sa-kon!
ชุดสากล; (clothes, for women) l)kra!-prong
h)choot กระโปรงชุด; (set of something) h)choot
ชุด

suitable adj. l)maw!-r)som! เหมาะสม

suitcase (for travelling) l)kra!-r)pao duhn thang
กระเป๋าเดินทาง

summer (season) h)reu!-doo h)rawn; f)nah
h)rawn ฤดูร้อน, หน้าร้อน

sun (the sun) h)phra! ah-h)thit! พระอาทิตย์

Sunday wan! ah-h)thit วันอาทิตย์

sunglasses f)waen kan! l)daet แว่นกันแดด

supervise v. f)khuap khoom! ควบคุม

supplies n r)sam!-pha-h)ra!, f)khreuang h)chai!
สัมภาระ, เครื่องใช้

supply v. l)jat! r)ha f)hai   จัดหาให้

support v. (assist, back) l)sa!-l)nap! l)sa!-r)noon! สนับสนุน; (support dependents, as family etc.) h)liang doo เลี้ยงดู; (support something, as a heavy object) rawng h)rap! รองรับ

suppose v. r)som!-h)moot! f)wa สมมติว่า

suppress v. (cancel, put a stop to) h)ra!-h)ngap ระงับ; (repress, as a rebellion) l)prap pram ปราบปราม

supreme commander (mil.) f)phoo ban!-cha kan h)tha!-r)han r)soong l)soot สู้บัญชาการทหารสูงสุด

Supreme Command Headquarters kawng ban!-cha-kan h)tha!-r)han r)soong l)soot กองบัญชาการ ทหารสูงสุด

sure adj. f)nae jai!, f)nae nawn แน่ใจ, แน่นอน

surface n. r)phew h)pheun ผิวพื้น

surgeon (med.) f)phaet l)pha l)tat! แพทย์ผ่าตัด

surprised adj. l)plaek jai! แปลกใจ; (suddenly) l)tok! jai! ตกใจ

surrender v. yawm h)phae ยอมแพ้; (surrender to authorities, as an outlaw, terrorist) f)khao pai! f)mawp tua เข้าไปมอบตัว

surround v. h)lawm f)rawp ล้อมรอบ

survey v. r)sam!-l)ruat สำรวจ; (survey land)
rang! h)wat! f)thee-din! รังวัดที่ดิน

surveyor n. (of land) f)phoo rang! h)wat!
f)thee-din! ผู้รังวัดที่ดิน; (surveyor in general, as
social-science surveyor) h)nak! r)sam!-l)ruat
นักสำรวจ

survive v. f)rawt ma f)dai! รอดมาได้

suspect v. r)song!-r)sai สงสัย

suspicious adj. f)na r)song!-r)sai!, l)phit!
r)sang!-l)ket น่าสงสัย, ผิดสังเกต

swallow v. kleun กลืน

swamp n. r)nawng h)nam! หนองน้ำ

swear v. (speak vulgarly) f)phoot l)yap-khai
พูดหยาบคาย; (swear oneself legally) r)sa-ban
tua สาบานตัว

sweat v. (perspire) mee l)ngeua l)awk มีเหงื่อ
ออก

sweater n. f)seua f)yeut, sa-wet-f)tuh เสื้อยืด,
สเวตเตอร์

sweep v. (with a broom etc.) l)kwat กวาด

sweet adj. r)wan หวาน

sweetheart n. f)kooh h)rak! คู่รัก

sweets (candy, dessert, etc.) l)kha!-nom! ขนม

swelling n. (med.) ah-kan buam อาการบวม

swim v. f)wai h)nam! ว่ายน้ำ

swimming pool l)sa! f)wai h)nam! สระว่ายน้ำ

swimming suit (bathing suit) h)choot l)ap h)nam! ชุดอาบน้ำ

switch (n., elect.) sa!-wit! fai! สวิตช์ไฟ

swollen adj. buam บวม

sword n. l)dap, l)kra!-l)bee ดาบ, กระบี่

symbol n. r)san!-h)ya!-h)lak! สัญญลักษณ์

sympathize, sympathize with r)hen jai! เห็นใจ

symptom (n., med.) ah-kan อาการ

syphilis (n., med.) f)rok f)phoo-r)ying!, si-fi-lit โรคผู้หญิง, ซิฟิลิส

syringe n. l)kra!-l)bawk l)cheet กระบอกฉีด

system n. h)ra!-l)bop!, h)ra!-l)bawp ระบบ, ระบอบ

table n. h)toh! โต๊ะ

tablecloth n. f)pha poo h)toh! ผ้าปูโต๊ะ

tablespoon n. h)chawn khao ช้อนคาว

tablet (medicine) yä h)met! ยาเม็ด

tail n. r)hang หาง

tail light fai! h)thai h)rot! ไฟท้ายรถ

tailor n. f)chang l)tat! f)seua ช่างตัดเสื้อ

take v. (in general) ao! เอา

take a bath l)ap h)nam! อาบน้ำ

take a picture (make a photograph) l)thai f)roop
ถ่ายรูป

take a shower l)ap h)nam! l)fak! bua อาบน้ำฝักบัว

take a trip duhn thang เดินทาง

take a vacation pai l)tak ah-l)kat ไปตากอากาศ

take away ao! pai! เอาไป

take care of doo-lae ดูแล

take care of a baby or child h)liang l)dek! เลี้ยงเด็ก

take exercise l)awk kam!-lang! ออกกำลัง

take medicine than ya, kin! ya ทานยา, กินยา

takeoff (of an airplane) f)khreuang-bin!
f)kheun! เครื่องบินขึ้น

take off clothing l)thawt f)seua f)pha, f)kae
f)pha ถอดเสื้อผ้า, แก้ผ้า

take off one's shoes l)thawt rawng-h)thao! ถอด
รองเท้า; (Never mind taking off your shoes.)
f)mai! f)tawng l)thawt rawng-h)thao! ไม่ต้อง
ถอดรองเท้า

take off something l)thawt l)awk ถอดออก

take out something ao! l)awk เอาออก

take part in (participate) f)khao! f)ruam เข้าร่วม

take pictures (photograph) l)thai f)roop ถ่ายรูป

talk v. f)phoot, f)phoot kan! พูด, พูดกัน

talkative f)chang khooy ช่างคุย

talk back (dispute, argue) r)thiang kan! เถียงกัน

talk in one's sleep r)fan! h)la!-muh ฝันละเมอ

tall adj. r)soong สูง

tambon (subdiv. of amphoe) tam!-bon! ตำบล

tame adj. f)cheuang h)laeo เชื่องแล้ว

tangerine (fruit) f)som! r)kheeo r)wan ส้มเขียวหวาน

tank (mil.) h)rot! r)thang! รถถัง; (water tank) r)thang! l)kep! h)nam! ถังเก็บน้ำ

tap (water tap) h)kawk h)nam! ก๊อกน้ำ

tape (for measuring) r)sai r)wat! สายวัด; (for recording) f)thep ban!-f)theuk! r)siang เทปบันทึกเสียง

tape-recorder f)khreuang ban!-h)theuk! r)siang เครื่องบันทึกเสียง

target (for shooting at) f)pao! เป้า; (objective, aim) f)pao!-r)mai เป้าหมาย

target practice l)hat! ying! f)pao! หัดยิงเป้า

taste n. h)rot! รส; (popular taste, style) h)rot! h)ni!-yom! รสนิยม

taste v. (check the taste) chim! h)rot! ชิมรส;
  (have a certain taste) mee h)rot!.... มีรส....

tasteful adj. mee h)rot! f)chat มีรสชาติ

tasteless adj. l)jeut, f)mai mee h)rot! f)chat จืด, ไม่มีรสชาติ

taut adj. (tight, tense) teung! ตึง

tax, taxes pha-r)see ภาษี

taxicab h)thaek!-f)see แท็กซี่

T.B. (tuberculosis) thee. bee., wan!-h)na!-f)rok ที. บี., วัณโรค

tea n. (bev.) h)nam! cha น้ำชา

teach v. ,r)sawn สอน

teacher khroo, ah-jahn ครู, อาจารย์

teakettle n. ka h)nam! กาน้ำ

teakwood h)mai l)sak! ไม้สัก

team n. h)theem, h)choot ทีม, ชุด

tea party ngan h)liang h)nam! cha งานเลี้ยงน้ำชา

teapot ka h)nam! cha กาน้ำชา

tear n. (from eye) h)nam! ta น้ำตา

tear v. (rip) l)cheek ฉีก

tease v. h)law f)lehn ล้อเล่น

teaspoon n. h)chawn cha ช้อนชา

telegram n. tho-h)ra!-f)lek โทรเลข

telegram v. (send a telegram) l)song! tho-h)ra!-
f)lek ส่งโทรเลข

telephone n. tho-h)ra!-l)sap! โทรศัพท์

telephone v. (call on phone) (to a place) tho.
pai! โทร. ไป; (from a place) tho. ma โทร. มา

telephone directory l)sa!-l)moot! tho-h)ra!-l)sap!
สมุดโทรศัพท์

telephone extension (another phone on same
number) tho-h)ra!-l)sap! `f)phuang โทรศัพท์พ่วง;
(extension number on main number) r)mai-
f)lek l)taw tho-h)ra!-l)sap! หมายเลขต่อโทรศัพท์

telephone line r)sai tho-h)ra!-l)sap! สายโทรศัพท์

telephone number r)mai-f)lek tho-h)ra!-l)sap!,
buh tho-h)ra!-l)sap! หมายเลขโทรศัพท์, เบอร์โทรศัพท์

telescope n. f)klawng tho-h)ra!-h)that! กล้อง
โทรทัศน์; (small telescope, spyglass) f)klawng
l)sawng thang klai! กล้องส่องทางไกล

teletype n. tho-h)ra!-f)phim! โทรพิมพ์

television set, T.V. set, tho-h)ra!-h)that! โทรทัศน์

telex theh-lex เทเล็กซ์

tell v. l)bawk!, l)bawk f)wa บอก, บอกว่า

temperature n. khwam h)rawn, oon-l)ha!-phoom ความร้อน อุณหภูมิ; (have high temperature, be feverish) mee f)khai! r)soong มีไข้สูง; (take one's temperature) h)wat! l)pa!-l)rawt วัดปรอท

temple n. (Buddhist) h)wat! วัด; (of the head) l)kha!-l)map! ขมับ

temporary f)chua khrao ชั่วคราว

ten (10) l)sip! สิบ (๑๐)

tenant n. f)phoo f)chao! ผู้เช่า

tender adj. (easy to chew) f)nim!, f)noom!, l)peuay นิ่ม, นุ่ม, เปื่อย; (painful, sore) l)jep! เจ็บ

tennis (the game) tehn-nit! เทนนิส

tennis shoes rawng-h)thao! tehn-nit!, rawng-h)thao! f)pha bai! รองเท้าเทนนิส, รองเท้าผ้าใบ

tense adj. (of nerves, situations) teung! f)khriat ตึงเครียด

tent n. tehn, l)kra!-jom เต๊นท์, กระโจม

termite (insect) l)pluak ปลวก

terrorist n. f)phoo l)kaw kan h)rai ผู้ก่อการร้าย; (Communist terrorist) f)phoo l)kaw kan h)rai khawm-mew-nit ผู้ก่อการร้ายคอมมิวนิสต์

test v. h)thot! lawng doo ทดลองดู

tetanus (n., med.) f)rok l)bat-h)tha!-h)yak! โรคบาดทะยัก; (anti-tetanus injection) l)cheet

ya f)pawng-kan! l)bat-h)tha!-h)yak! ฉีดยา
ป้องกันบาดทะยัก

textbook n. tam!-ra ตำรา

Thai adj. thai! ไทย; (language) pha-r)sa thai!
ภาษาไทย; (people) khon! thai, chao thai!
คนไทย, ชาวไทย

Thailand l)pra!-f)thet thai ประเทศไทย

than conj. l)kwa กว่า [as in "more **than** ten
baht" = "f)mak l)kwa l)sip! baht") มากกว่า
สิบบาท; = l)sip! baht l)kwa สิบบาทกว่า]

Thank you. l)khawp khoon! ขอบคุณ

that adj. h)nan! นั้น; (further away) h)non โน้น

that pron. f)nan! นั้น (further away) f)non โน่น

that, that which (relative pron.) f)thee, f)seung!
ที่, ซึ่ง

that is to say (much-used Thai connective)
kheu, kheu f)wa คือ, คือว่า

that means.... r)mai khwam f)wa...., plae f)wa....
หมายความว่า...., แปลว่า....

that place (there) f)thee f)nan! ที่นั่น

That's all right. (Never mind.) f)mai! pen!-rai!
ไม่เป็นไร

That's bad. f)mai! dee ไม่ดี

That's enough. phaw h)laeo พอแล้ว

That's good. dee h)laeo ดีแล้ว

That's not right. f)mai! f)chai ไม่ใช่

That's right. f)chai! h)laeo, l)thook h)laeo ใช่แล้ว, ถูกแล้ว

That's wrong. f)mai! f)chai!, f)mai! l)thook, l)phit! h)laeo ไม่ใช่, ไม่ถูก, ผิดแล้ว

that way (in that way, like that) f)chehn h)nan!, l)yang h)nan! เช่นนั้น, อย่างนั้น; (that road, that direction) thang h)nan!, thang h)non ทางนั้น; ทางโน้น

the (usually not necessary in Thai but may be translated as "that", h)nan! นั้น)

theater, theatre (drama) rong h)la!-khawn โรง ละคร; (films) rong r)nang!, rong f)phaph-h)pha!-yon! โรงหนัง, โรงภาพยนตร์

their, theirs r)khawng r)khao!, r)khawng r)khao! h)thang!-r)lai ของเขา, ของเขาทั้งหลาย

them (see THEY)

then (at that time) we-la h)nan! เวลานั้น; (connective) h)laeo, h)laeo f)kaw! แล้ว, แล้วก็

there (at that place) f)thee f)nan! ที่นั่น

therefore h)phraw! l)cha!-h)nan! เพราะฉะนั้น

there is, there are mee, mee l)yoo มี, มีอยู่

There isn't (aren't) any. f)mai! mee ไม่มี

There isn't any trouble (no problem, etc.) f)mai! mee f)reuang ไม่มีเรื่อง

There's nothing. There isn't anything. f)mai! mee l)ah!-rai! ไม่มีอะไร

thermometer n. l)pa!-l)rawt ปรอท

thermos bottle l)kra!-l)tik! h)nam! กระติกน้ำ

these (things) l)lao! h)nee เหล่านี้

they (them) r)khao!, r)khao! h)thang!-r)lai เขา, เขาทั้งหลาย; (2 persons) r)khao! h)thang! r)sawng เขาทั้งสอง

thick adj. (concentrated, liquids) f)khon! ข้น; (opposite of "thin") r)na หนา

thief n. l)kha!-moy ขโมย

thigh (of body) r)kha l)awn ขาอ่อน

thin adj. (for persons & animals) r)phawm ผอม; (things) bang บาง

thing n. l)sing! r)khawng สิ่งของ; (a few things) r)sawng r)sam l)yang สองสามอย่าง; (things, possessions) r)khawng ของ

think v. h)khit! คิด

think about h)khit! r)theung คิดถึง

third (⅓) l)set! l)neung l)suan r)sam เศษหนึ่ง ส่วนสาม

thirsty adj. r)hew h)nam! หิวน้ำ

thirteen (13) l)sip!-r)sam สิบสาม (๑๓)

thirty (30) r)sam-l)sip! สามสิบ (๓๐)

this adj. h)nee นี้

this pron. f)nee นี่

this place (here) f)thee f)nee ที่นี่

this way (in this manner) f)chen h)nee, l)yang
h)nee เช่นนี้, อย่างนี้; (this road, this direction)
thang h)nee ทางนี้

thorough adj. (complete) l)yang r)som!-boon
อย่างสมบูรณ์; (detailed) l)yang h)la!-l)iat อย่าง
ละเอียด

those l)lao! h)nan! เหล่านั้น

thought (idea) khwam h)khit! ความคิด

thousand (1,000) phan! พัน, l)neung phan
หนึ่งพัน (๑,๐๐๐)

thread (for sewing) f)dai ด้าย

threaded screw n. l)ta!-poo khuang ตะปูควง

threaten v. l)khoo ขู่

three (3) r)sam สาม (๓)

throat (of the body) lam! khaw ลำคอ; (have a
sore throat) l)jep! khaw เจ็บคอ

through, thru (no stopping enroute) l)ta!-l)lawt
ตลอด; (penetrating, coming out other side)

h)tha!-h)loo! หรอ; (through with something,
to be over) l)phan pai! h)laeo, f)luhk h)laeo
ผ่านไปแล้ว, เลิกแล้ว

throughout l)ta!-l)lawt ตลอด; (all the time)
l)ta!-l)lawt we·la ตลอดเวลา

throw v. yon, f)khwang โยน, ขว้าง

throw away h)thing! pai! ทิ้งไป

throw up (vomit) ah-jian อาเจียน

thru (See through.)

thumb (of hand) h)new f)pong นิ้วโป้ง

Thursday wan! h)phreu!-l)hat! วันพฤหัส

thus (in this way, in this manner) dang! nee,
l)yang h)nee ดั่งนี้, อย่างนี้; (therefore) dang!
h)nan!, h)phraw! l)cha!-h)nan! ดั่งนั้น เพราะฉะนั้น

tical, tcs., tics. [old-fashioned Eng. term for
"baht", not Thai words and not recommended
for use in place of official term "baht",
l)baht, บาท]

ticket n. (for admission, for a ride, etc.) r)tua,
l)bat! l)phan l)pra!-too ตั๋ว, บัตรผ่านประตู

tickle v. f)jee จี้

ticklish adj. h)jak!-l)ka!-f)jee จักจี้

tide (of sea) h)nam! น้ำ; (against tide) thuan
h)ham! ทวนน้ำ; (ebbtide, low tide) h)nam!
long! น้ำลง; (high tide) h)nam! f)kheun! น้ำขึ้น

tie n. (necktie) h)nek!-thai!, f)pha l)phook
khaw เน็คไท, ผ้าผูกคอ; (tie score) l)sa!-r)muh
kan! เสมอกัน

tie, tie up v. l)phook h)wai ผูกไว้

tie-clasp n. f)thee l)neep h)nek!-thai! ที่หนีบเน็คไท

tiger n. r)seua เสือ

tight adj. f)naen แน่น; (stingy) f)khee r)neeo
ขี้เหนียว; (too tight, as clothing) h)khap! คับ

tighten v. (make tight) h)rat! f)khao! f)hai!
f)naen รัดเข้าให้แน่น

tightly adv. f)naen f)naen แน่นๆ

till, until jon! l)kwa, jon! r)theung จนกว่า, จนถึง

time n. (clock time) we-la เวลา; (occasion,
event) khrao คราว; (occurrence) h)khrang!
ครั้ง; (What time is it?) we-la f)thao!-rai!
เวลาเท่าไร

timely (on time) than! we-la ทันเวลา; (good timing) l)thook jang!-l)wa! ถูกจังหวะ; (wrong timing) l)phit! jang!-l)wa! ผิดจังหวะ

time-table n. ta-rang we-la ตารางเวลา

timid adj. (bashful) ai, f)khee ai อาย, ขี้อาย

tin (the metal) dee-l)book! ดีบุก; (tin mine)
r)meuang f)rae dee-l)book! เหมืองแร่ดีบุก

tin, tincan l)kra!-r)pawng กระป๋อง

tin-opener, can-opener f)thee l)puht l)kra!-r)pawng ที่เปิดกระป๋อง

tip n. (advice) kham! h)nae!-nam! คำแนะนำ; (end of something) plai ปลาย; (money for waiter, etc.) nguhn tip! เงินทิป

tire, tyre (of vehicle) yang h)rot! ยางรถ; (inner-tube) yang nai! ยางใน

tire, tired (fatigued) l)neuay เหนื่อย; (make tired) tham! f)hai! l)neuay ทำให้เหนื่อย

tiresome (boring) f)na l)beua น่าเบื่อ

title (name of story etc.) f)cheu f)reuang ชื่อเรื่อง

title-deed (for land) l)cha!-l)not โฉนด

to (a certain extent) phiang, f)khae เพียง, แค่

to (a place) yang!, r)theung!, pai! f)thee ยัง, ถึง, ไปที่

to (someone) l)kae, f)hai! l)kae แก่, ให้แก่

toast (toasted bread) l)kha!-r)nom!-pang! f)ping! ขนมปังปิ้ง

toast v. (as bread) f)ping! ปิ้ง; (make a toast, at a party) l)deum f)hai! phawn ดื่มให้พร

tobacco n. ya l)soop ยาสูบ

today wan! h)nee วันนี้

toe (of foot) h)new h)thao! นิ้วเท้า

to each other, to one another kan!, f)seung! kan! h)lae! kan! กัน, ซึ่งกันและกัน

toenail n. h)lep! h)thao! เล็บเท้า

together (of people) f)ruam kan!, f)duay kan! ร่วมกัน, ด้วยกัน

toilet n. (bathroom) f)hawng h)nam!, f)hawng f)suam ห้องน้ำ, ห้องส้วม

toilet paper (tissue) l)kra!-l)dat cham!-h)ra! กระดาษชำระ

to let (for rent) f)hai! f)chao! ให้เช่า

tomato (veg.) h)ma!-r)kheua-f)thet มะเขือเทศ

tomato juice h)nam! h)ma!-r)kheua-f)thet น้ำมะเขือเทศ

tomorrow f)phroong! h)nee พรุ่งนี้

tongs (tool) kheem คีม

tongue (of body, animal, machine) h)lin! ลิ้น

tonight kheun h)nee คืนนี้

too (also) f)duay ด้วย; (too much) f)mak kuhn pai! มากเกินไป; (too bad) f)na r)sia dai น่าเสียดาย

tool n. f)khreuang-meu เครื่องมือ

tooth n. fan! ฟัน

toothache l)puat fan! ปวดฟัน

toothbrush n. praeng r)see fan! แปรงสีฟัน

toothpaste n. ya r)see fan ยาสีฟัน

toothpick n. h)mai! f)jim! fan! ไม้จิ้มฟัน

tooth powder ya r)see fan! h)chi!-h)nit! r)phong!
ยาสีฟันชนิดผง

top (lid of something) r)fa ฝา; (summit)
f)yawt ยอด

torn adj. (as of clothing) l)cheek l)khat ฉีกขาด

torture v. thaw-h)ra!-man ทรมาน

total n. (in figures) f)yawt ruam ยอดรวม

touch v. (with fingers) l)jap! จับ; (when things
touch each other) l)thook kan! ถูกกัน

tough adj. (as meat) r)neeo เหนียว; (strong)
r)khaeng! raeng แข็งแรง

tour v. (as a tourist) f)thawng f)theeo ท่องเที่ยว

tourist n. h)nak! f)thawng f)theeo นักท่องเที่ยว

tourist guide f)phoo nam! f)theeo ผู้นำเที่ยว

towel n. f)pha h)chet! tua ผ้าเช็ดตัว; (small
face towel) f)pha r)khon! r)noo ผ้าขนหนู

town n. meuang เมือง; (downtown, uptown)
klang meuang กลางเมือง

toy n. r)khawng f)lehn ของเล่น

trace n. f)rawng rawy รองรอย

trace v. (make a line) f)lak f)sehn ลากเส้น

tractor n. h)rot! h)thraek!-f)tuh รถแทรกเตอร์

trade v. (engage in trade) h)kha r)khai ค้าขาย;
(exchange for something else) f)laek l)plian
แลกเปลี่ยน

trademark (n., comr.) f)khreuang-r)mai kan
h)kha เครื่องหมายการค้า

trader n. f)phaw h)kha พ่อค้า

traditions n. l)pra!-pheh-nee ประเพณี

traffic n. (on streets) kan ja-ra-jawn การจราจร

traffic light n. fai! ja-ra-jawn ไฟจราจร; (green
light) fai! r)kheeo ไฟเขียว; (red light) fai!
daeng ไฟแดง; (yellow light) fai! r)leuang
ไฟเหลือง

traffic police tam!-l)ruat ja-ra-jawn ตำรวจจราจร

trail n. (path) thang duhn ทางเดิน

trailer (vehicle) h)rot! f)phuang รถพ่วง

train n. (railway) h)rot!-fai! รถไฟ

train v. l)feuk! l)hat! ฝึกหัด

training n. kan l)feuk! การฝึก

train schedule ta-rang n)rot!-fai! ตารางรถไฟ

train station l)sa!-r)tha-nee h)rot!-fai! สถานีรถไฟ

train ticket r)tua h)rot!-fai! ตั๋วรถไฟ; (round-trip ticket) r)tua h)rot!-fai pai! l)klap! ตั๋วรถไฟ ไปกลับ

tram n. (streetcar) h)rot! rang รถราง

transfer v. f)yok h)yai โยกย้าย; (transfer ownership) tham! kan ohn ทำการโอน

transformer (n., elect.) f)maw [f)khreuang] pla-eng fai! หม้อ(เครื่อง)แปลงไฟ

translate v. plae แปล; (interpret) pen! f)lam เป็น ล่าม

translation n. (in general) kan plae การแปล; (written translation) kham! plae คำแปล

translator n. h)nak! plae นักแปล; (interpreter) f)lam ล่าม

transport v. r)khon! l)song! ขนส่ง

transportation n. (in general) kan r)khon! l)song! การขนส่ง; (means of transportation, vehicle) pha-l)ha!-h)na! พาหนะ

transvestite n. (usually a male dressed as a female) l)ka!-thuhy กระเทย

trap n. l)kap! l)dak! กับดัก; (hole trap) r)loom! l)dak! หลุมดัก

trap v. (catch with traps) l)jap! f)duay l)kap! l)dak! จับด้วยกับดัก

trash n. l)kha!-l)ya! ขยะ

trash can n. r)thang! l)kha!-l)ya! ถังขยะ

travel v. duhn thang เดินทาง

tray n. l)that ถาด

tree n. f)ton! h)mai! ต้นไม้

trench (n., mil.) l)sa!-r)nam h)phlaw! สนามเพลาะ

tribe n. (of people) l)phao! เผ่า; (hill tribe) chao r)khao! ชาวเขา

trick n. f)look h)mai! ลูกไม้

trick v. (cheat) kong โกง; (deceive) l)lawk luang หลอกลวง

trigger (of a gun) kai! peun ไกปืน

trim v. (as the hair) lem! เล็ม; (trim something, as a bush) klao! เกลา

trip n. (journey) kan duhn thang การเดินทาง

troops (soldiers) kam!-lang! phon! กำลังพล

tropical country l)pra!-f)thet sohn h)rawn ประเทศ โซนร้อน

trouble n. khwam f)yoong!-f)yak ความยุ่งยาก

troublesome (hard, difficult) lam!-l)bak ลำบาก

trousers (male clothing) kang keng กางเกง

trowel (gardening) f)phlua meu หลัวมือ

truck n. (lorry) h)rot! ban!-h)thook! รถบรรทุก

true adj. jing! จริง; (genuine) r)khawng h)thae ของแท้; (loyal) f)seu l)sat! ซื่อสัตย์

truly (really) jing! jing! จริงๆ; (sincerely) l)yang jing! jang! อย่างจริงจัง

trunk (for storing things) l)heep หีบ; (of auto) l)kra!-prong h)thai h)rot! กระโปรงท้ายรถ (of tree) lam! f)ton! ลำต้น

trust v. (have confidence or faith in) h)wai! jai! ไว้ใจ

trustworthy adj. h)wai! jai! f)dai! ไว้ใจได้

truth (the truth) khwam jing! ความจริง

try (make effort) pha!-ya-yam พยายาม

try, try out (experiment) h)thot!-lawng ทดลอง

try on (as clothing) lawng l)sai! doo ลองใส่ดู

tube n. (container) l)lawt หลอด; (innertube of tire) yang nai! ยางใน; (pipe conduit) f)thaw ท่อ

tuberculosis (T.B.) wan!-h)na!-f)rok (thee. bee.) วัณโรค (ที.บี.)

Tuesday wan! ang!-khan วันอังคาร

tugboat reua f)lak joong เรือลากจูง

tumor (n., med.) h)neua f)ngawk เนื้องอก

tunnel n. oo!-mong อุโมงค์

turn (time to play or do something) ta, f)theeo ตา, เทียว; (take turns) l)phlat! kan! ผลัดกัน

turn (go to one side or the other) h)leeo เลี้ยว; (turn around) r)han! l)klap! หันกลับ; (turn back) l)klap! pai! กลับไป; (turn left) h)leeo h)sai เลี้ยวซ้าย; (turn right) h)leeo r)khwa เลี้ยวขวา; (turn car around) l)klap! h)rot! กลับรถ

turn off (as radio, light) l)pit! ปิด

turn on (as radio, light) l)puht เปิด

turn over (as car accident) f)khwam! คว่ำ; (as page of book) h)phlik! พลิก

turnip (veg.) r)hua l)phak! kat r)khao หัวผัก กาดขาว

turtle n. l)tao! เต่า

tusk (of elephant) nga h)chang งาช้าง

T.V. (television) thee. wee ที.วี.

tweezers n. l)naep, l)pak f)kheep แหนบ, ปากคีบ

twelve (12) l)sip!-r)sawng สิบสอง (๑๒)

twenty (20) f)yee-l)sip! ยี่สิบ (๒๐)

twice (two times) r)sawng h)khrang! สองครั้ง

twice as much r)sawng f)thao! l)kwa สองเท่ากว่า

twins (children) f)look l)faet ลูกแฝด

twist v. 1)bit! บิด; (be twisting, as a road) h)khot! h)kheeo คดเคี้ยว

two (2) r)sawng สอง (๒); (in telephone number, for clarity) tho โท

two or three (a few) r)sawng r)sam สองสาม

two times (twice) r)sawng h)khrang! สองครั้ง

type n. h)cha!-h)nit! ชนิด

type v. (typewrite) phim! l)deet พิมพ์ดีด

typewriter f)khrenang phim! l)deet เครื่องพิมพ์ดีด

typewiter ribbon f)pha phim! l)deet ผ้าพิมพ์ดีด

typhoid fever f)khai! f)rak l)sat h)nawy ไข้รากสาดน้อย

typhoon lom! f)tai!-l)foon! ลมไต้ฝุ่น

typist khon! phim!-l)deet คนพิมพ์ดีด; (clerk-typist) l)sa!-r)mian phim!-l)deet เสมียนพิมพ์ดีด

tyre (tire, for vehicles) yang h)rot! ยางรถ

ugly adj. f)na l)kliat น่าเกลียด; f)khee l)reh ขี้เหร่

ulcer n. pen! r)phlae เป็นแผล

umbrella n. f)rom! ร่ม

umpire (referee) f)phoo l)tat! r)sin! ผู้ตัดสิน

unbutton l)plot! l)kra!-doom! ปลดกระดุม

unchanging adj. f)mai! l)plian-plaeng ไม่เปลี่ยนแปลง

uncle (elder) loong! ลุง; (younger, maternal) h)na น้า; (younger, paternal) ah อา

unconscious f)mai! h)roo-l)seuk! tua ไม่รู้สึกตัว

uncover v. l)puht l)awk เปิดออก; (disclose) l)puht r)phuhy เปิดเผย

under f)khang f)tai! ข้างใต้; f)khang f)lang ข้างล่าง

undershirt f)seua h)chan! nai! เสื้อชั้นใน

understand v. f)khao! jai! เข้าใจ

undertaker n. (for funerals, cremations) l)sap!-l)pa!-l)ruh สัปเหร่อ

underwear f)seua f)pha h)chan! nai! เสื้อผ้าชั้นใน

undo v. f)kae l)awk แก้ออก

undress v. l)thawt f)seua ถอดเสื้อ

uneasy (worried) kang!-won! jai!, pen! l)huang กังวลใจ, เป็นห่วง

unemployed adj. f)wang ngan ว่างงาน

uneven (not smooth) f)mai! f)riap ไม่เรียบ

unexpectedly doy bang!-uhn โดยบังเอิญ

unfasten v. f)kae l)awk แก้ออก

unfortunate adj. (poor) f)yak jon! ยากจน; (pitiful) f)na r)song!-r)san น่าสงสาร; (unlucky) h)khraw! h)rai เคราะห์ร้าย

unfriendly adj. f)mai! pen! h)mit ไม่เป็นมิตร

ungrateful adj. neh-ra-koon! เนรคุณ

unhappy adj. f)mai! mee khwam l)sook! ไม่มี
ความสุข

uniform n. f)khreuang l)baep เครื่องแบบ

unintentional adj. f)mai! mee jet-ta-na ไม่มีเจตนา

unit n. l)nuay หน่วย; (mil. unit) l)nuay h)tha!-
r)han หน่วยทหาร

United Nations (U.N.) l)sa!-l)ha! l)pra!-cha-f)chat
(yoo. no.) สหประชาชาติ (ส. โน.)

United States (of America) l)sa!-l)ha!-h)rat! (ah-
meh-ri-ka) สหรัฐ (อเมริกา)

university h)ma!-r)ha h)wit!-h)tha!-ya-lai! มหา
วิทยาลัย

unless h)wehn l)tae เว้นแต่; f)nawk l)jak f)wa
นอกจากว่า

unload v. r)kon! long! ขนลง

unlock v. r)khai! koon!-jae ไขกุญแจ

unlucky f)chok f)mai! dee โชคไม่ดี; h)khraw!
h)rai! เคราะห์ร้าย

untie v. f)kae l)awk แก้ออก

until jon! l)kwa จนกว่า

untrue f)mai! jing! ไม่จริง

unusual l)pra!-l)lat ประหลาด; i)phit! l)pok!-l)ka!-
l)ti! ผิดปกติ

unwrap f)kae l)haw l)awk แก้ห่อออก

up f)kheun! ขึ้น

upcountry (in provinces) l)tang jang!-l)wat! ต่าง
จังหวัด

upon (on) bon! บน

upset stomach h)thawng r)sia ท้องเสีย

upside down f)khwam! คว่ำ

upstairs h)chan! bon! ชั้นบน

urge v. h)chak! chuan ชักชวน

urgent l)duan ด่วน

urinate v. (pass water) l)pat!-r)sa-h)wa! ปัสสาวะ;
(have urge to urinate) l)puat l)pat!-r)sa-h)wa!,
ปวดปัสสาวะ, (colloq.) l)puat f)yeeo ปวดเยี่ยว

urine n. h)nam! l)pat!-r)sa-h)wa! น้ำปัสสาวะ

urn n. l)kot โกฏ

us (See we.)

use v. h)chai! ใช้

used (second-hand) h)chai! h)laeo ใช้แล้ว

used to (do something) khuhy เคย

used to something (accustomed) khuhy chin!
เคยชิน

used up (all gone) l)mot! h)laeo หมดแล้ว

useful mee l)pra!-l)yot มีประโยชน์

useless f)mai! mee l)pra!-l)yot ไม่มีประโยชน์

usual (normal) l)pok!-l)ka!-l)ti! ปกติ; (as usual) tam khuhy ตามเคย

usually tam tham!-h)ma!-da ตามธรรมดา

uterus (womb) h)mot! f)look มดลูก

vacant f)wang ว่าง

vacate (move out) h)yai l)awk ย้ายออก

vacation kan la l)yoot! h)pak การลาหยุดพัก

vaccinate l)plook r)fee ปลูกฝี

valley l)hoop! r)khao! หุบเขา

valuable mee ra-kha f)mak มีราคามาก

value ra-kha ราคา

vase n. jae-kan! แจกัน

veal (meat of calf) h)neua f)look wua เนื้อลูกวัว

vegetable n. l)phak! ผัก

vehicle n. h)rot!, khan! รถ, คัน

vehicle registration (license plate) bai! h)tha!-bian h)rot! ใบทะเบียนรถ

vein (blood vessel) l)lawt [f)sehn] lo-l)hit! dam! หลอด (เส้น) โลหิตดำ

velocity (speed) khwam reh-o ความเร็ว

venereal disease (V.D.) kam-h)ma!-f)rok กามโรค

venetian blinds f)moo-f)lee มู่ลี่

ventilate v. l)thai theh ah-l)kaht ถ่ายเทอากาศ

very, very much f)mak มาก

veteran (mil.) h)tha!-r)han l)phan l)seuk! ทหาร
ผ่านศึก

veterinarian l)sat! f)phaet สัตว์แพทย์

via doy โดย

vibrate v. l)san! l)sa!-theuan สั่นสะเทือน

vice.... (deputy, assistant) rawng.... รอง....

vice-admiral phon! reua tho พลเรือโท

vice-president rawng l)pra!-tha-na-h)thi-baw-dee
รองประธานาธิบดี

vicinity n. baw-h)ri!-wehn บริเวณ

victim n. l)yeua, f)phoo h)rap! h)khraw! เหยื่อ,
ผู้รับเคราะห์

victor n. f)phoo h)cha!-h)na! ผู้ชนะ

Vietnam (country) l)pra!-f)thet wiat-nam ประเทศ
เวียดนาม; (North VN) wiat-nam r)neua เวียดนาม
เหนือ; (South VN) wiat-nam f)tai เวียดนามใต้

Vietnamese (language) pha-r)sa yuan ภาษาญวน;
(people) khon! yuan คนญวน

view n. (of scenery) wiew (view) วิว; (opinion)
khwam r)hen ความเห็น

village (subdiv. of Thai tambon) l)moo-f)ban
หมู่บ้าน

village chief f)phoo-l)yai f)ban ผู้ใหญ่บ้าน

villager chao f)ban ชาวบ้าน

vinegar n. h)nam! f)som! r)sai-choo น้ำส้มสายชู

violate v. h)la!-f)muht, tham! l)phit! ละเมิด,
ทำผิด

violet (color) r)see f)muang l)awn สีม่วงอ่อน

violin n. wai!-oh-lin! ไวโอลิน; (Thai-style) saw
f)duang, saw f)oo ซอด้วง, ซออู้

VIP l)book!-khon! r)sam!-khan! f)mak บุคคล
สำคัญมาก

visa v. wee-f)sa วีซ่า

visit v. f)yiam เยี่ยม

visiting hours we-la f)yiam เวลาเยี่ยม

visitor n. l)khaek แขก

vitamin wai-ta-min ไวตามิน

voice n. r)siang เสียง

volt (elect.) wohn โวลต์

voltage (elect.) jam!-nuan wohn จำนวนโวลต์

volume n. (books) f)lehm เล่ม; (quantity) paw-
h)ri!-man ปริมาณ

volunteer (person) f)phoo ah-r)sa l)sa!-l)mak!
ผู้อาสาสมัคร

volunteer v. ah-r)sa l)sa!-l)mak! อาสาสมัคร

vomit v. ah-jian อาเจียน

vote v. long! h)kha!-naen, l)awk r)siang
ลงคะแนน, ออกเสียง

vowel n. l)sa!-l)ra! สระ

vulgar adj. l)yap khai หยาบคาย

vulture (bird) h)nok! (ee) h)raeng นก(อี)แร้ง

wa n. (unit of linear measure in Thailand =
2 metres) wa วา; (square wa) ta-rang wah
ตารางวา

wade v. looy h)nam! ลุยน้ำ

wages n. f)kha f)jang! ค่าจ้าง

wagon (oxcart) kwian เกวียน

waist (of body) eh-o เอว

wait v. khawy, raw คอย, รอ

Wait a moment. raw l)pra!-r)deeo รอประเดี๋ยว

waiter n. khon! duhn h)to!, r)bawy คนเดินโต๊ะ,
บ๋อย

waitress n. r)ying l)suhf ah-r)han หญิงเสิร์ฟอาหาร

wake someone up l)plook! ปลุก

wake up (oneself) l)teun ตื่น

walk v. duhn เดิน; (for pleasure) duhn f)lehn เดินเล่น; (for exercise) duhn l)awk kam!-lang! เดินออกกำลัง

walking-stick h)mai! h)thao! ไม้เท้า

wall n. (interior) r)fa l)pha!-r)nang! ฝาผนัง; (outer) kam!-phaeng กำแพง

wallet n. l)kra!-r)pao กระเป๋า

want v. ao!, f)tawng-kan เอา, ต้องการ

war n. r)song!-khram สงคราม

wardrobe n. f)too f)seua f)pha ตู้เสื้อผ้า

warehouse n. khlang! l)kep! r)sin!-h)kha คลังเก็บ สินค้า

warm adj. l)ohp! l)oon! อบอุ่น

warm something up (food) l)oon! ah-r)han อุ่น อาหาร; (warm up an engine) l)oon! f)khreuang อุ่นเครื่อง

warn v. teuan เตือน

warrant officer (mil.) nai l)dap นายดาบ; (navy) phan! l)ja พันจ่า; (AF) phan! l)ja ah-l)kat พันจ่าอากาศ

warship n. reua h)rop! เรือรบ

wart n. l)hoot หูด

was (See be.)

wash v. (clothes) h)sak! f)pha ซักผ้า; (wash &
iron) h)sak! f)reet ซักรีด; (wash dishes) h)lang
cham ล้างชาม; (wash face) h)lang f)na ล้างหน้า;
(wash hair) l)sa! r)phom! สระผม; (wash hands)
h)lang meu ล้างมือ

washbasin n. l)ang h)lang meu อ่างล้างมือ

washing powder r)phong! h)sak! f)fawk ผงซักฟอก

washwoman khon! h)sak! f)pha คนซักผ้า; (who also
does ironing) khon! h)sak! f)reet คนซักรีด

waste v. r)sia, pleuang เสีย, เปลือง; (waste
money) pleuang nguhn เปลืองเงิน; (waste time)
r)sia we-la เสียเวลา

wastebasket n. r)thang! r)phong! ถังผง

wastes n. r)khawng l)set l)set ของเศษๆ

wat (Buddhist temple) h)wat! วัด

watch n. (for telling time) na-h)li!-ka นาฬิกา;
(wrist watch) na-h)li!-ka f)khaw meu นาฬิกา
ข้อมือ

watch v. (guard duty) f)fao! yam เฝ้ายาม; (look
at) mawng doo มองดู; (observe) r)sang!-l)ket
doo สังเกตดู

watchdog n. l)soo!-h)nak f)fao! f)ban สุนัขเฝ้าบ้าน

watchman khon!-yam คนยาม

watchmaker n. f)chang na-h)li!-ka ช่างนาฬิกา

water n. h)nam! น้ำ; (boiled water) h)nam! f)tom! h)laeo น้ำต้มแล้ว; (drinking water) h)nam! l)deum น้ำดื่ม; (pure water) h)nam! baw-h)ri!-l)soot! น้ำบริสุทธิ์

water v. (add water) tuhm! h)nam! เติมน้ำ; (water flowers) h)rot! h)nam! รดน้ำ

water bill (for water supply) f)kha h)nam! ค่าน้ำ

water buffalo khwai ควาย

waterfall n. h)nam! l)tok! น้ำตก

water faucet n. h)kawk h)nam! ก๊อกน้ำ

water-glass (drinking glass) f)thuay f)kaeo h)nam! ถ้วยแก้วน้ำ

water-jar n. (large jar for storing water in homes) l)ong h)nam! โอ่งน้ำ

water leech (insect) pling! ปลิง

watermelon n. taeng moh แตงโม

water pump n. f)khreuang l)soop h)nam! เครื่องสูบน้ำ

waterway (in general) thang h)nam! ทางน้ำ

waterworks n. kan l)pra!-pa การประปา

wave n. (of sea, air, radio) f)khleun คลื่น; (permanent wave, for hair) h)set! r)phom! เซ็ทผม

wave the hand 1)bok meu โบกมือ

wax (beeswax) f)khee f)pheung! ขี้ผึ้ง; (floo
wax) h)nam!-man! 1)khat! h)pheun น้ำมันขัดพื้น

wax v. (as a floor) long! h)nam!-man! ลงน้ำมัน

way n. (direction) h)thit! thang ทิศทาง; (whic'
way) thang r)nai! ทางไหน; (method) h)wi'
thee วิธี; (thoroughfare) r)hon! thang หนทาง
(one-way street) 1)tha!-r)non! wan!-we'
ถนนวันเวย

way in (entrance) thang f)khao! ทางเข้า

way out (exit) thang 1)awk ทางออก

we (or us) rao! เรา; (2 people) rao! h)thang
r)sawng เราทั้งสอง; (many people) f)phua'
rao!, rao! h)thang! r)lai พวกเรา, เราทั้งหลาย

weak adj. (colors, taste) 1)awn อ่อน; (physicall)
weak) 1)awn ae อ่อนแอ

wealthy adj. f)ram! ruay ร่ำรวย

weapon n. ah-h)woot! อาวุธ

wear v. (as clothing) 1)sai! ใส่

weather n. ah-l)kat อากาศ

weave v. thaw f)pha ทอผ้า

wedding (marriage ceremony) 1)taeng ngar
แต่งงาน

Wednesday wan! h)phoot! วันพุธ

weeds f)ya h)rok! หญ้ารก

week n. ah-h)thit!, l)sap!-l)pa!-da อาทิตย์, สัปดาห์

weekend n. wan! l)soot! l)sap!-l)pa!-da วันสุดสัปดาห์

weekly l)pra'-jam! l)sap'-l)pa!-da ประจำสัปดาห์

weigh (something) f)chang! h)nam!-h)nak! ชั่ง
น้ำหนัก

weight n. h)nam'-l)nak! น้ำหนัก; (how much
weight? how much do you weigh? how much
does it weigh? etc.) h)nam!-l)nak: h)hao!-rai!
น้ำหนักเท่าไร

welcome v. f)tawn h)rap! ต้อนรับ; (You're wel-
come--in reply to "Thank you.") f)mai! pen!-
rai! ไม่เป็นไร

weld v. f)cheuam, h)awk เชื่อม, อ๊อก

welder n. f) hang h)awk ช่างอ๊อก

well adj. (not s ck) l)sa!-bai dee สบายดี

well adv. dee, l)yang dee ดี, อย่างดี

well n. l)baw h)nam! บ่อน้ำ; (artesian) l)baw
h)nam! ba-dan บ่อน้ำบาดาล, (oil) l)baw h)nam!-
man! บ่อน้ำมัน

well-done (cooking) l)sook! l)sook! สุก ๆ

well-liked (popular) h)ni!-yom! นิยม

well water h)nam! l)baw น้ำบ่อ

were (See BE.)

west (direction) h)thit! l)ta!-wan! l)tok! ทิศ
ตะวันตก

West (region) f)phak ta!-wan! l)tok! ภาคตะวันตก;
(Europe and Americas) l)ta!-wan! l)tok!
ตะวันตก

wet adj. l)piak เปียก

wharf n. f)tha reua ท่าเรือ

what l)ah!-rai! อะไร; (meaning "which?")
....r)nai! ....ไหน

What a pity! f)na r)sia dai น่าเสียดาย

What did you say, please? (polite Thai way of
saying "Pardon.") l)ah!-rai! h)na! อะไรนะ

What do you call it? What's it called? f)riak f)wa
l)ah!-rai! เรียกว่าอะไร

What is your (his, her, its) name? f)cheu l)ah!-
rai! ชื่ออะไร

what place? (where?) f)thee r)nai! ที่ไหน

What time is it? l)kee mong h)laeo, we-la
f)thao!-rai! กี่โมงแล้ว, เวลาเท่าไร

wheat n. f)khao r)sa-lee ข้าวสาลี

wheel n. h)law ล้อ

when? f)meua-rai! เมื่อไร: (at what time) l)kee mong, we-la f)thao'-rai! กี่โมง, เวลาเท่าไร

when (not interrogative) f)meua เมื่อ

where? (at what place) f)thee r)nai! ที่ไหน

where (not interrogative) f)thee ที่

Where are you going? (polite Thai greeting) pai! r)nai! ไปไหน

Where have you been? (polite Thai greeting) pai! r)nai! ma ไปไหนมา

which? ....r)nai! ....ไหน

which (not interrogative) f)thee, f)seung! ที่, ซึ่ง

which one? an! r)nai! อันไหน

while (during a certain time) nai! we-la f)thee.... ในเวลาที่....

whip n. f)sae แส้

whip v. tee ตี

whirlpool n. h)nam! won! น้ำวน

whirlwind n. lom! won! ลมวน

whiskey, whisky f)lao! wit!-sa!-f)kee เหล้าวิสกี้

whisper v. l)kra!-h)sip! กระซิบ

whistle n. h)nok! l)weet นกหวีด

whistle v. r)phew l)pak ผิวปาก

white (color) r)see r)khao สีขาว

white ant (termite) l)pluak ปลวก

who? khrai! ใคร

who, whom (not interrogative) f)thee, f)seung! ที่, ซึ่ง

whore (prostitute) r)so-pheh-nee, (slang) l)ka!-l)ree โสเภณี, กะหรี่

whose? r)khawng khrai! ของใคร

why? tham!-mai! ทำไม

wicker (rattan, used for furniture) r)wai หวาย

wide adj. f)kwang กว้าง; (very wide) f)kwang r)khwang กว้างขวาง

widespread adj. f)phrae-r)lai แพร่หลาย

widow n. f)mae f)mai แม่หม้าย

widower n. f)phaw f)mai พ่อหม้าย

width n. khwam f)kwang ความกว้าง

wife n. mia, faen, phan!-h)ra!-ya เมีย, แฟน, ภรรยา; (minor wife, mistress) mia h)nawy เมียน้อย

wild adj. l)doo! h)rai ดุร้าย; (savage) l)pa l)theuan ป่าเถื่อน

will n. (determination) khwam! f)tang! jai! ความตั้งใจ; (legal document) h)phi!-nai!-kam! พินัยกรรม

will (helping verb, as in Eng.) l)ja! จะ

willing (to do something) yin! dee (tham!) ยินดี (ทำ)

win v. h)cha!-h)na! ชนะ

wind n. lom! ลม

wind v. (as a watch etc.) r)khai! lan ไขลาน

wind, wind up v. (in a roll) h)muan ม้วน

window f)na-l)tang หน้าต่าง

window-pane l)kra!-l)jok! f)na-l)tang กระจกหน้าต่าง

window-screens h)moong! f)luat มุ้งลวด

windshield (of a car) l)kra!-l)jok! f)na กระจกหน้า

windstorm lom! pha-h)yoo! ลมพายุ

windy adj. lom! raeng ลมแรง

wine (bev.) f)lao! wai!, f)lao! l)ah!-l)ngoon! เหล้าไวน์, เหล้าองุ่น

wing n. l)peek ปีก

wing commander (AF lt.-col.) na-wa ah-l)kat tho นาวาอากาศโท

wink v. (the eyes) l)ka!-h)phrip! ta กะพริบตา

winner n. f)phoo h)cha!-h)ɳa! ผู้ชนะ

winter (season) h)reu-doo r)nao ฤดูหนาว

wipe, wipe up h)chet! เช็ด; (wipe dry) h)chet! f)hai f)haeng เช็ดให้แห้ง

wire f)luat ลวด; (electric wire) r)sai fai!-h)fa สายไฟฟ้า

wire v. (run electric wiring) duhn r)sai fai!-h)fa เดินสายไฟฟ้า

wireman n. f)chang duhn r)sai ช่างเดินสาย

wish to...., would like to.... (do something) f)khrai! l)ja'...., l)pra!-r)song! l)ja!.... ใคร่จะ...., ประสงค์จะ

witch n. f)mae h)mot! แม่มด

with l)kap!, กับ, (by means of) f)duay ด้วย

withdraw v. r)thawn l)awk ถอนออก; (withdraw money) r)thawn nguhn ถอนเงิน

withdraw charges (leg.) r)thawn kha!-dee ถอนคดี

withered adj. l)heeo f)haeng เหี่ยวแห้ง

within phai-nai! ภายใน

without (on the outside) phai f)nawk ภายนอก; (lacking, not having something) l)prat l)sa!-l)jak ปราศจาก; (unless) h)wehn l)tae f)dai!.... เว้นแต่ได้....

witness (n., leg.) h)pha!-yan พยาน; (be a witness)
pen! h)pha!-yan เป็นพยาน; (have a witness)
mee h)pha!-yan มีพยาน

woman n. f)phoo r)ying!, l)sa!-tree ผู้หญิง, สตรี

wonder v. (not be sure) r)song!-r)sai! สงสัย

wonderful adj. (amazing) f)na l)at!-l)sa!-jan!
น่าอัศจรรย์; (strange) l)plaek l)pra!-l)lat แปลก
ประหลาด; (very good, excellent) h)wi!-l)set
วิเศษ

wood n. h)mai! ไม้

woods n. (forests) l)pa h)mai! ป่าไม้

word n kham!, l)sap! คำ, ศัพท์

work n. ngan งาน; (occupation) ah-f)cheep
อาชีพ; (profession) wi-cha-f)cheep วิชาชีพ

work v. (do work) tham! ngan ทำงาน

worker khon! ngan คนงาน

work-permit bai! ah-noo-yaht tham! ngan ใบ
อนุญาตทำงาน

workshop n. rong ngan โรงงาน

work together (cooperate) f)ruam meu ร่วมมือ

world n. f)lok โลก

worm n. tua r)nawn ตัวหนอน; (parasitic worm)
h)pha!-f)yat พยาธิ

worms n. (a children's disease well-known among most Thais) f)rok tan l)kha!-moy โรคตาลขะโมย

worn-out l)sia h)laeo, l)khat h)laeo เสียแล้ว, บาคแล้ว; (exhausted) f)mai! mee raeng r)leua luhy ไม่มีแรงเหลือเลย

worried adj. pen! l)huang เป็นห่วง; (depressed) f)kloom! jai! กลุ้มใจ

worse adj. h)rai l)kwa l)kao ร้ายกว่าเก่า

worship v. boo-cha บูชา

worst adj. leh-o f)thee l)soot! เลวที่สุด

worth n. (value) ra-kha ราคา

would, should (helping verb, same as "will") l)ja! จะ

would (should) like (to).... l)yak l)ja!.... อยากจะ....

wound n. (injury) l)bat r)phlae บาคแผล

wounded (injured) l)bat l)jep! บาคเจ็บ

wrap, wrap up l)haw ห่อ

wreck (auto accident) h)rot! chon! kan! รถชนกัน

wrench (tool) koon!-jae l)pak tai กุญแจปากตาย

wring, wring out v. l)biat เบียด

wrinkle n. (clothing) rawy f)yon! รอยย่น; (skin) r)nang! f)yon! หนังย่น

wrist (of body) f)khaw-meu ข้อมือ

wristwatch na-h)li!-ka f)khaw-meu นาฬิกาข้อมือ

write v. r)khian เขียน

writer n. h)nak! r)khian นักเขียน

wrong (not correct) l)phit! ผิด

wrong number (in telephoning) tho. l)phit! โทร. ผิด

X-ray l)eks-reh เอกซ์เรย์

yard (of house) l)sa!-r)nam f)ya สนามหญ้า

yard (3 feet) r)la หลา

yawn v. r)hao nawn หาวนอน

year pee ปี; (for ages of small children) l)khuap ขวบ

yearly l)pra!-jam! pee ประจำปี

yell v. l)ta!-kon ตะโกน

yellow (color) r)see r)leuang สีเหลือง

yes (yes, that's right) f)chai!, f)chai! h)laeo ใช่, ใช่แล้ว

yes, ma'am or yes, sir (spoken by females) h)kha!, f)chai! h)kha! คะ, ใช่คะ; (spoken by males) h)khrap!, f)chai! h)khrap! ครับ, ใช่ครับ

yesterday f)meua wan h)nee เมื่อวานนี้

yet (not yet) yang! ยัง; (still) yang!, yang!
   khong' ยัง, ยังคง; (still here, still there) yang!
   l)yoo ยังอยู่

yonder (over there) f)non, f)thee h)non โน่น,
   ที่โน้น

you (normal) khoon! คุณ; (respectful) f)than
   ท่าน

young (in age) ah-h)yoo! h)nawy อายุน้อย

your, yours (normal) r)khawng khoon! ของคุณ;
   (respectful) r)khawng f)than ของท่าน

You're welcome. (in response to "Thank you")
   f)mai! pen!-rai! ไม่เป็นไร

youthful adj. (for men) l)noom! หนุ่ม; (for
   women) r)sao สาว

zero r)soon ศูนย์

zinc n. r)sang!-l)ka!-r)see สังกะสี

zip, zipper n. sip! ซิบ

zone n. l)khet, sohn เขต, โซน

zoo n. r)suan l)sat! สวนสัตว์

APPENDIX
List of Phonetic Equivalents Used in This Dictionary
(Listed in English Alphabetical Order)

Notes.

1) **TONES.** Thai has 5 tones in speaking, but you can still be understood even if your tones are not correct. Even native Thai speakers do not carefully pronounce all the separate tones in Thai. Therefore, we show you the correct tone for a syllable only if we think it is important to try to use the correct tones in that particular word, as use of the wrong tone can of course cause someone to misunderstand your intended meaning. We indicate tones in the following manner (in front of the syllable with the indicated tone):-

    f) = **falling tone** (starting rather high and coming down)

    h) = **high tone** (said in a rather high, emphatic tone of voice)

l) = **low tone** (said in a rather low, even
tone of voice)

r) = **rising tone** (starting rather low and
going up)

(no indication = **normal tone**, said in a normal, even tone of voice)

2) **EXCLAMATION POINT.** Thai has 2 kinds of
vowel sounds: the **normal-duration sound** (like
a long vowel sound), and the **short-emphatic
sound** (spoken quickly and rather emphati-
cally). We indicate a short-emphatic vowel
sound by the use of an exclamation mark
(!) at the end of the syllable containing
the short-emphatic vowel sound. However,
even if you use the wrong kind of vowel
sound, you can still be understood, and
even native Thai speakers normally do not
carefully enunciate these vowel-sound dur-
ations in many cases.

3) **HYPHENS.** A hyphen (-) is used in our
phonetics to separate syllables of the same
word.

4) **OUR PHONETIC SYSTEM.** Our phonetic system
is based upon long practical experience

and has been used successfully already in other books. The following list does not include letters such as "B", "D", and others which are pronounced as in English.

Phonetic Equivalents

a, ah (as in father)

ae (as in man, tan)

aeo (ae + oh)

ah (See "a".)

ai (as in I, my)

ao (as in now, cow)

aw (as in law, saw)

awy (as in aw + ee)

ch (as in church)

e, eh (as in get, let)

ee (as in me, see)

eeo, ieo, io (ee + oh)

eh (See "E".)

eh-o, eo (eh + oh)

eu (similar to "oo" in "good")

eua (eu + uh)

ew, iu (as in few, new)

i, ih (as in hit, sit)

ia (ee + uh)

ieo, io (See "eeo".)

ih (see "i".)

io (See "eeo".)

iu (See "ew".)

j (as in joke, Joe)

k (at the beginning of a syllable, as in get, go--same as "hard G")

k (at the end of a syllable, normal "K", as in "back")

kh (normal "K", as kick, kiss)

ng (as in ring--a difficult sound only when coming at the first of a syllable)

o, oh (as in bone, home)

oe (See "uh".)

oh (See "o".)

oo (as in do, boot)

ooy (oo + ee)

oy (oh + ee)

p (at the beginning of a syllable, no English equivalent, mixture of "B" and "P", with explosive sound, often indicated in phonetics as "BP")

p (at the end of a syllable--normal "P" sound,
    as in lap, map)

ph (normal "P" sound, as in pan, put)

t (at the beginning of a syllable--no English
    equivalent, mixture of "D" and "T",
    with explosive sound, often indicated in
    phonetics as "DT")

t (at the end of a syllable, normal "T" sound,
    as in "hit")

th (normal "T" sound, as in tin, took)

ua (oo + uh)

uai, uay (oo + "ay" in "day")

uh, oe (as in but, hut)

uhy (uh + ee)

THAI–ENGLISH
DICTIONARY

พจนานุกรม

ไทย-อังกฤษ

a, ah aunt, uncle (younger, paternal) อา

a-cheep occupation อาชีพ

aekt act (put on "airs") แอ็กท์

aen-kaw-haw alcohol แอลกอฮอล

aep-puhn apple แอปเปิ้น

aer (air) air-conditioning แอร์

aes-pai-rin aspirin แอสไพริน

a-fri-ka Africa, African อาฟริกา

ah-r)han n. food อาหาร; ah-r)han h)chao! breakfast อาหารเช้า; ah-r)han f)kham! dinner อาหารค่ำ;
ah-r)han klang-wan! lunch อาหารกลางวัน; ah-r)han
pen! h)phit! food-poisoning อาหารเป็นพิษ

ah!-l)hi!-wa n. cholera อหิวาต์

ai! cough ไอ

ai adj. shy, timid อาย

ai!-h)nam! n. steam, vapour ไอน้ำ

ai!-h)ya!-kan n. public prosecutor อัยการ

a-jan n. teacher อาจารย์

a-jian v. vomit อาเจียน

a-kan (n., med.) condition, symptom อาการ; a-kan r)sa-l)hat! serious condition อาการอาหัส

a-kat [ah-l)kat] n. air, weather อากาศ; a-kat l)haeng tam!-bon! climate อากาศแห่งตำบล

a-kawn, a-kawn l)sa!-taem n. revenue stamp, duty stamp อากร, อากรแสตมป์

a-khan stone or brick building อาคาร

l)ak!-l)sep (adj., med.) infected, inflamed อักเสบ

a!-l)lai! adj. spare, extra, reserve อะไหล่; f)khreu-ang a!-l)lai! spare parts (cars, etc) เครื่องอะไหล่

a-me-ri-ka, a-me-ri-kan America, American อเมริกา, อเมริกัน

a-me-ri-ka f)tai! South America อเมริกาใต้

am-f)nat n. authority, power อำนาจ

am-nuay phawn bless, give blessings to อำนวยพร

am-phuh amphoe, district (subdiv. of changwat or province) อำเภอ

an! n. thing (in general) อัน; an! deeo kan! the same one, the same thing อันเดียวกัน

l)an v. read อ่าน

a!-na-h)khot! future, future time อนาคต

a-na-mai health, hygiene อนามัย

l)ang l)ap h)nam! n. bathtub อ่างอาบน้ำ

f)ang r)theung v. refer to อ้างถึง

f)ang f)wa v. claim, claim something is true
อ้างว่า

l)ang h)nam! n. wash bowl, washbasin อ่างน้ำ

ang-khan (wan! ang-khan) Tuesday อังคาร (วัน
อังคาร)

ang!-l)krit! English, English language, England
อังกฤษ

l)ang h)lang meu, l)ang h)lang f)na washbasin
อ่างล้างมือ, อ่างล้างหน้า

a!-l)ngoon! n grape องุ่น

an! r)nai! which one? อันไหน

a-noo-sa-wa-ree n. statue, memorial monument
อนุสาวรีย์

a-noo-yat v. approve, permit อนุญาต

an-ta-rai danger, dangerous อันตราย

ao! v. want, take or get something เอา

ao n. gulf, bay (body of water) อ่าว; ao thai
the Gulf of Thailand อ่าวไทย

ao! l)awk v. remove something เอาออก

ao! l)dek! ma h)liang adopt a child เอาเด็กมาเลี้ยง

ao! jai! l)sai! v. concentrate, pay attention
เอาใจใส่

ao! kan ao! ngan adj. conscientious, hard-working เอาการเอางาน

ao! ma v. bring เอามา

ao! pai! v. take away เอาไป

ao! l)priap take advantage of someone or some situation เอาเปรียบ

l)ap, l)ap h)nam! take a bath อาบ, อาบน้ำ

l)ap h)nam! l)fak! bua take a shower อาบน้ำฝักบัว

a!-phai! v. forgive, pardon อภัย

a!-phai!-h)ya!-f)thot n. pardon, amnesty อภัยโทษ

a!-rai! what, anything, something อะไร

a!-rai! f)kaw! f)dai! anything will be all right (anything will do, as you like) อะไรก็ได้

a!-rai! h)na! what did you say, please? (equivalent to Eng. "pardon me") อะไรนะ

al-l)rawy adj. delicious อร่อย

a-rom! n. mood (of a person) อารมณ์; a-rom! dee good mood อารมณ์ดี; a-rom! r)sia bad mood อารมณ์เสีย; f)jao! a-rom! moody person เจ้าอารมณ์

a-r)sa v. volunteer อาสา

a-r)sai! depend upon (for support) อาศัย

a-r)sai! l)yoo, live in a place อาศัยอยู่

a-r)sa l)sa!-l)mak! v. volunteer; n. volunteer, U.S. Peace Corps member อาสาสมัคร

a-sia Asia อาเซีย

l)at, l)at l)ja! v. may (possibility) อาจ, อาจจะ

l)at! l)cheet v. grease (lubricate) a car อัดฉีด

a!-h)thi!-bai v. explain อธิบาย

a!-h)thi!-baw-dee director-general (of a Thai- govt. dept.) อธิบดี

a!-h)thi!-kan-baw-dee, rector (of a univ.) อธิการบดี

a-h)thit! n. week อาทิตย์; **a-h)thit! f)na** next week อาทิตย์หน้า; **a-h)thit! f)thee h)laeo** last week อาทิตย์ที่แล้ว

a-h)thit! [wan! a!-h)thit!] Sunday อาทิตย์ (วันอาทิตย์)

l)at! r)sam!-nao! make copies by machine, dupli- ate อัดสำเนา

l)at!-l)ta!-no-h)mat! automatic, automatically อัตโนมัติ

l)at!-tra n. rate อัตรา; **l)at!-tra kan l)kuht** birth rate อัตราการเกิด; **l)at!-tra kan f)laek-l)plian** exchange rate อัตราการแลกเปลี่ยน

a-wa-l)kat n. space, outer space อวกาศ

l)awk v. come out, go out, start out, leave ออก

l)awk l)baep v. design ออกแบบ

l)awk bin! v. take off (airplanes) ออกบิน

l)awk duhn thang, depart, leave on trip ออกเดินทาง

l)awk f)hai! issue, issued (officially, as a permit) ออกให้

l)awk kam!-lang! exercise, take exercise ออกกำลัง

l)awk ma come out ออกมา

l)awk pai! go out, leave ออกไป

l)awk r)siang pronounce (a word), vote (orally) ออกเสียง

f)awm roundabout, indirect, make a detour อ้อม

awn n. ounce ออนซ์

l)awn adj. (colors) weak, light; young, soft, tender, flexible อ่อน

l)awn ae adj. weak, frail, feeble อ่อนแอ

l)awn f)noom adj. soft, yielding (as pillow) อ่อนนุ่ม

l)awn phlia adj. weary, weak อ่อนเพลีย

l)awn r)wan adj. sweet in manner, gentle อ่อนหวาน

a-h)woot! n. weapon อาวุธ

aws-treh-lia Australia(n) ออสเตรเลีย

aws-tria Austria(n) ออสเตรีย

f)awy sugarcane อ้อย

a-h)yat! h'sap! (leg.) attach property assets อายัดทรัพย์

a-h)yoo! age, be a certain age อายุ

a-h)yoo! h)nawy young, not old อายุน้อย

a-h)yoo! f)thao!-rai! How old (are you, is he, is she, is it)? อายุเท่าไร

ba bar (of drinking) บาร์

f)ba crazy, insane บ้า; f)ba f)ba baw baw (colloq.) odd, crazy, dotty บ้าๆบอๆ

baed-min-tan badminton แบดมินตัน

l)baek carry something very heavy แบก

baen adj. flat แบน

baeng banknote (currency) แบงค์

l)baeng kan! v. share, divide แบ่งกัน

l)baep n. model, type, style, form แบบ; l)baep fawm printed form แบบฟอร์ม

baht baht (official Thai currency) บาท

bai! (classifier noun for round & hollow objects, such as fruit, eggs, containers, or sheets of paper such as certificates, tickets, permits etc.) ใบ

f)bai! adj. dumb (cannot speak) ใบ้

l)bai afternoon (time) บ่าย; **l)bai...., ...o'clock** (in afternoon) บ่าย....

bai! a-noo-f)yat n. permit, licence ใบอนุญาต

bai! a-noo-f)yat l)khap! l)khee driver's license ใบอนุญาตขับขี่

bai! a-noo-f)yat tham! ngan work permit ใบอนุญาตทำงาน

bai! cha tea leaves ใบชา

bai! f)hoon! (fin.) share certificate ใบหุ้น

bai! l)kep! nguhn n. bill (for collection) ใบเก็บเงิน

bai! l)khap! l)khee driver's license ใบขับขี่

bai! l)kuht (soo-ti-bat) birth certificate ใบเกิด (สูติบัตร)

bai! h)mai! leaves (of trees) ใบไม้

bai! f)meed kon razor blade ใบมีดโกน

bai! f)naep attachment (to a document) ใบแนบ

bai! plew! n. leaflet ใบปลิว

bai! h)rap! nguhn n. receipt ใบรับเงิน

bai! h)rap!-rawng n. testimonial, certificate ใบรับรอง

bai! l)sa!-l)mak! n. application form ใบสมัคร

bai! l)sang! ya, bai! l)sang! f)phaet n. prescription
(for drugs, medicine) ใบสั่งยา, ใบสั่งแพทย์

bai! l)set!, bai! l)set! h)rap nguhn n. receipt ใบ
เสร็จ, ใบเสร็จรับเงิน

bai! l)tang h)dao [r)thai-bian l)tang h)dao] alien
registration card/papers ใบต่างด้าว(ทะเบียนต่างด้าว)

bai! h)thai-bian h)rot! license plate (for a vehicle) ใบทะเบียนรถ

ba-lee, pha-r)sa ba-lee Pali (sacred religious
language of Thai Buddhism) บาลี, ภาษาบาลี

l)bai-l)mee Chinese egg noodles บะหมี่

bam!-roong! v. improve, maintain บำรุง

ban (classifier noun) doors, windows บาน; v.
bloom, blossom

f)ban n. house, home บ้าน; [l)moo-f)ban] village
(subdiv. of tambon) หมู่บ้าน

ban!-cha v. command, order บัญชา

ban!-chee n, account บัญชี; ban!-chee h)thai-na-khan
bank account บัญชีธนาคาร

ban-da all, all of (used in front of nouns) บรรดา

ban!-dai n. stairway, ladder บันได

f)ban!-eh-o waist (of body) ชั้นเอว

bang! v. obstruct view, shield, veil บัง

bang adj. thin (for things) บาง

bang adj. some บาง

f)bang (pron., adv.) any, some, somewhat บ้าง

bang!-ka-lo n. bungalow, motel บังกาโล

bang!-h)khap! v. force บังคับ

bang!-l)kuht f)kheun! v. happen บังเกิดขึ้น

bang r)ssen Bang Saen beach resort (near Pattaya) บางแสน

bang thee perhaps, sometimes บางที

bang!-uhn accidentally, by chance บังเอิญ

f)ban f)hai! f)chao! house for rent บ้านให้เช่า

ban!-l)joo! v. pack บรรจุ

f)ban f)lek f)thee house number บ้านเลขที่

f)ban h)mai wooden house บ้านไม้

ban-na-thi-kan n. editor บรรณาธิการ

f)ban f)nawk rural areas, countryside บ้านนอก

ban-pha-boo-root ancestors บรรพบุรุษ

f)ban h)phak! residence (house) บ้านพัก

ban-h)phap! n. hinge บานพับ

f)ban r)so-pheh-nee house of prostitution บ้านโสเภณี

f)ban l)teuk! stone or brick house บ้านตึก

ban!-h)theuk! v. record บันทึก; b)an!-h)theuk! r)siang
  record sound บันทึกเสียง

ban!-h)thook! v. load (as a truck) บรรทุก

ban-ya-l)kat n. atmosphere บรรยากาศ

ban!-h)yat! v. legislate บัญญัติ

bao! adj. light (in weight) เบา

bao! bao! adv. softly, gently เบาๆ

bao!-r)wan n. diabetes เบาหวาน

l)bap-kam! sin, sinful บาปกรรม

bas-ket-bawn basketball บาสเกตบอลล์

l)bat! chuhn invitation card บัตรเชิญ

l)bat l)jep! adj. injured, wounded บาดเจ็บ

l)bat!-kree v. solder บัดกรี

l)bat r)luang Catholic priest บาดหลวง

l)bat! h)nee now, at this time บัดนี้

l)bat! l)phan l)pra!-too admission ticket บัตรผ่าน
  ประตู

l)bat r)phlae n. wound (injury) บาดแผล

l)bat! l)pra!-cha-chon! Thai I.D. card (required
  for all adults) บัตรประชาชน

l)bat! l)pra!-jam! tua (old name for Thai I.D.
  card) บัตรประจำตัว

l)baw h)nam! n. well, water-hole บ่อน้ำ

l)bawk, l)bawk f)wa say, tell (that) บอก, บอกว่า

l)bawk f)hai! f)sap v. inform บอกให้หราบ

l)baw khlon mud puddle บ่อโคลน

l)bawk f)wa v. state, say that.... บอกว่า

l)baw h)nam!-man! n. oil-well บ่อน้ำมัน

baw-ri-boon adj. complete, in full บริบูรณ์

baw-ri-r)han v. administer, execute บริหาร

baw-ri-l)jak v. contribute, donate บริจาค

baw-ri-kan (v., n.) service บริการ

baw-ri-kan nam! f)theeo tour services บริการนำเที่ยว

baw-ri-kan r)theung! f)hawng room service บริการ
ถึงห้อง

baw-ri-l)sat! n. company (comr.) บริษัท

baw-ri-l)sat! jam!-l)kat! (n., comr.) limited
company บริษัทจำกัด

baw-ri-l)soot adj. pure, innocent บริสุทธิ์

baw-ri-wen n. vicinity บริเวณ

l)bawy, l)bawy l)bawy often บ่อย, บ่อย ๆ

r)bawy (from "boy") waiter, houseboy บ๋อย

r)bawy f)hawng bellboy (hotel) บ๋อยห้อง

l)beep, l)beep h)khan! v. squeeze, compress บีบ,
บีบคั้น

ben-seen! (benzine) gasoline, petrol เบนซิน

ben-yiam Belgium, Belgian เบลเยี่ยม

l)bet! fish hook เบ็ด

l)beua, l)beua-l)nai! adj. bored, sick of something
เบื่อ, เบื่อหน่าย

f)beuang n. side, part (of something) เบื้อง

beung! n. swamp, marshland, lake บึง

bia (bev.) beer เบียร์

f)bia l)pra!-choom! allowances for attending meet-
ings เบี้ยประชุม

bi-da n. father บิดา

bin!, bin! l)kep! nguhn bill (for collection) (Note.
"bin!" is also colloq. for "receipt".) บิล, บิลเก็บ
เงิน

bin!, bin! pai! v. fly, go by plane บิน, บินไป

bin!-liat billiards (the game) บิลเลียด

l)bit! v. twist บิด

l)bit! (med.) dysentery บิด

bo bow (of ribbon, etc.) โบว์

l)bok! land, on the land บก

l)bok meu, wave the hand โบกมือ

bon! on (on top of something), upon บน

l)bon! v. complain, grumble บ่น

bon! reua aboard ship บนเรือ

boo-cha v. worship, show reverence to บูชา

h)book! (from "book") reserve, book a ticket บุ๊ค

l)book! v. attack บุก

book-kha-la-kawn personnel (in general) บุคลากร

book-kha-lik-ka-lak-sa-na n. personality บุคลิกลักษณะ

book-khon individual, individual person บุคคล

book-rook (book-ka-rook) v. trespass บุกรุก

boon n. merit, virtue, good deeds บุญ

boo!-l)ree n. cigarette บุหรี่

boo!-l)root! n. man บุรุษ

boo!-l)root! prai-sa-nee n. postman บุรุษไปรษณีย์

l)boot! son daughter บุตร

bo-ran ancient, old-fashioned โบราณ

l)bot! v. grind, pulverize, crush บด

l)bot! n. lesson, chapter บท

l)bot n. church, chapel of Buddhist temple โบสถ์

l)bot!-khwam newspaper editorial บทความ; l)bot!-khwam f)reuang articles in newspaper etc. บทความเรื่อง

l)bot!-rian n. lesson, lesson learned บทเรียน

bra-sin! Brazil, Brazilian บราซิล

l)brek brakes (of motor vehicle), (v.) put on
  brakes เบรค

l)buak v. add (numbers); adj. plus, positive บวก

buam v. swell, become swollen บวม

f)buan v. spit out บ้วน

l)buat v. enter Buddhist priesthood บวช

l)buhk nguhn receive mooey due (wages, sala-
  ries, allowances, or for some stipulated use)
  เบิกเงิน; buhk nguhn f)luang f)na ask for and get
  an advance on salary etc. เบิกเงินล่วงหน้า

buh tho-ra-l)sap! telephone number เบอร์โทรศัพท์

cha adj. numb, no circulation ชา

cha n. tea ชา

h)cha, h)cha h)cha slow, slowly ช้า, ช้าๆ

l)cha!-l)bap! (classifying noun for papers, documents) ฉบับ

f)chae v. soak, immerse in liquid แช่

f)chaeng v. curse, put a curse on someone แช่ง

chai male, man (also shows male form of word,
  for persons) ชาย

f)chai!, f)chai! h)laeo that's right ใช่, ใช่แล้ว

h)chai! v. use, spend, expend ใช้

h)chai! ŋguhn pay back money, reimburse ใช้เงิน

r)chai v. project, give off light (as a flashlight,
   projector) ฉาย; r)chai r)naŋ! project (show)
   a film ฉายหนัง

chai cha-kan able-bodied young man ชายฉกรรจ์

chai daen n. border, frontier, boundary ชายแดน

chai-l)hat n. beach, sandy seaside ชายหาด

f)chai! r)mai!? Is that right? Isn't that right?
   ใช่ไหม

f)chai! l)mot! used up, all used up, all gone
   ใช้หมด

chai l)sot n. bachelor (male) ชายโสด

chai tha-leh n. seaside ชายทะเล

chai!-yo Hooray! ไชโย

h)chak! v. pull, draw out, pull at, have spasms
   or convulsions ชัก

l)chak n. screen, partition (for dividing rooms),
   act of a play or show ฉาก

h)chak!-chuan v. urge, try to persuade ชักชวน

h)cha l)kwa h)nee slower, more slowly, slower
   than this ช้ากว่านี้

h)chak! f)wao fly a kite (slang for "masturbate") ชักว่าว

l)cha!-r)lam n. shark ฉลาม

l)cha!-l)lat adj. bright, clever ฉลาด

l)cha!-r)lawng v. celebrate ฉลอง

l)cha!-r)liang n. porch, veranda เฉลียง

l)cha!-r)luhy v. give answers (to exam questions, to problems) เฉลย

cha-luhy l)seuk! prisoner-of-war เชลยศึก

cham n. bowl, dishes in general ชาม

h)cham! adj. bruised, painful ช้ำ

cham! nan adj. skilled, expert ชำนาญ

cham!-nan kan h)tha!-r)han military occupational specialty (MOS) ชำนาญการทหาร

cham!-h)ra! v. pay (a debt or a bill), clean, get rid of dirt etc. ชำระ

cham!-h)root! adj. out of order, broken ชำรุด

h)chan! n. class (school), storey (floor), rank (1st, 2nd, etc.), shelf ชั้น

r)chan! I, me (mostly female speakers) ฉัน

cha!-na! v. win, defeat ชนะ

l)cha!-h)nan! therefore, consequently ฉะนั้น

h)chan! bon! upstairs ชั้นบน

h)cha!-nee gibbon (animal) ชะนี

f)chang n. artisan, tradesman ช่าง

h)chang n. elephant ช้าง

f)chang fai!-h)fa n. electrician ช่างไฟฟ้า

f)chang h)fit! n. mechanic ช่างฟิต

f)chang l)kaw l)it! n. bricklayer ช่างก่ออิฐ

f)chang r)khian n. artist, painter ช่างเขียน

f)chang! h)nam!-l)nak! weigh something ชั่งน้ำหนัก

f)chang f)phap n. photographer ช่างภาพ

f)chang phim! n. printer ช่างพิมพ์

f)chang l)pok! n. bookbinder ช่างปก

f)chang rawng-h)thao! n. shoemaker ช่างรองเท้า

f)chang riang n. typesetter ช่างเรียง

f)chang l)tat! r)phom! n. barber ช่างตัดผม

f)chang l)tat! f)seua n. tailor ช่างตัดเสื้อ

f)chang l)tat! f)seua l)sa!-tree n. dressmaker ช่าง
    ตัดเสื้อสตรี

chang-wat See jang-l)wat!

f)chang f)wat f)roop artist, painter ช่างวาดรูป

h)cha!-h)nit! n. type, kind ชนิด

h)chan! f)lang downstairs ชั้นล่าง

')chan! l)neung!, h)chan! f)thee l)neung! 1st-class 1st-grade, 1st floor (1st storey) ชั้นหนึ่ง, ชั้นที่หนึ่ง

h)cha!-nuan n. fuse, primer ชนวน

chao n. native of, citizen of, inhabitant of, follower of ชาว

f)chao! v. rent, lease เช่า

h)chao!, h)chao! h)chao! (time) early in the morning (a.m.) เช้า, เช้าๆ

chao! a-me-ri-kan American (person) ชาวอเมริกัน

chao ang-krit English (person) ชาวอังกฤษ

chao a-rab Arab (person) ชาวอาหรับ

chao a-sia, chao eh-sia Asian (person) ชาวอาเชีย, ชาวเอเชีย

chao f)ban n. villager, average citizen ชาวบ้าน

chao na rice-farmer ชาวนา

chao h)phoot! Buddhist (person) ชาวพุทธ

chao r)suan fruit-grower ชาวสวน

h)chao! l)troo (time) early morning เช้าครู่

l)cha!-h)phaw! adj. private, personal เฉพาะ

l)cha!-h)phaw!., doy l)cha!-h)phaw! especially, in particular เฉพาะ, โดยเฉพาะ

h)cha!-ra adj., aged, elderly ชรา

f)chat n. nationality, life ชาติ

h)chat!, h)chat! jen adj. clear, easy to understand ชัด, ชัดเจน

cha-wa-f)lek n. shorthand ชวเลข

chawk n. chalk ชอล์ก

h)chawn n. spoon (for eating) ช้อน

h)chawn cha teaspoon ช้อนชา

f)chawng n. opening, mountain pass, channel ช่อง

f)chawng f)khlawt n. vagina, vaginal canal ช่องคลอด

h)chawn khao tablespoon ช้อนคาว

h)chawn f)sawm n. tableware, spoon and forks ช้อนส้อม

h)chawn h)to! n. tablespoon ช้อนโต๊ะ

f)chawp v. like, fond of ชอบ

chee n. nun, sister ชี

h)chee v. point out, point at ชี้

l)cheek v. tear, rip ฉีก

f)cheep (pertaining to life, concerning life) ชีพ

f)cheep-pha-jawn n pulse ชีพจร

l)cheet v. spray, inject ฉีด

h)chee h)thit!-thang give directions, show the way ชี้ทิศทาง

l)cheet ya inject medicine ฉีดยา

chee-wa-wit-tha-ya n. biology ชีววิทยา

chee-h)wit! n. life ชีวิต

f)chen like, as, for example, such as เช่น

f)chen deeo l)kap! the same as เช่นเดียวกับ

f)chen khuhy as usual เช่นเคย

f)chen-h)nan! like that, that way เช่นนั้น

f)chen-h)nee like this, this way เช่นนี้

h)chet! v. dry, wipe dry, wipe up เช็ด

f)cheu first name (of a person), name of a place ชื่อ

f)cheua v. believe เชื่อ

h)cheua n. family line เชื้อ

h)cheua-f)chat n descent, race เชื้อชาติ

h)cheua chuhn v. invite เชื้อเชิญ

f)cheua fang! v. obey เชื่อฟัง

f)cheua jai! v. believe, have faith in เชื่อใจ

f)cheuak n. string, cord, rope เชือก

f)cheuak l)phook rawng-h)thao! n. shoelaces เชือกผูกรองเท้า

f)cheuam v. weld, join together เชื่อม

f)cheuang adj. tame, domesticated เชื่อง

h)cheua phluhng n. fuel, combustibles เชื้อเพลิง

f)cheu a-rai? What is (your, his, her, its) name? ชื่ออะไร

f)cheua f)rok n. germs, bacteria เชื้อโรค

f)cheua r)theu v trust, believe in. respect เชื่อถือ

f)cheu h)lae! nam l)sa!-koon! full name (first and last name of a person) ชื่อแลนามสกุล

f)cheu f)len n. nickname ชื่อเล่น

h)cheun aɔj. damp, moist, humid ชื้น

h)cheun l)chae! adj. wet and damp ชื้นแฉะ

f)cheun jai! adj. refreshing, pleasant ชื่นใจ

f)cheu plawm n. alias (false name) ชื่อปลอม

f)cheu r)siang n. reputation ชื่อเสียง

chim! taste ชิม

h)chin! n. piece (of something) ชิ้น

ching! v. fight over, compete for ชิง

ching!-h)cha n., v. swing ชิงช้า

cho-fuh n. chauffeur โชเฟอร์

f)chok n. luck, fortune โชค

h)chok! kan! v. fight, fight with fists ชกกัน

f)chok f)mai! dee, f)chok h)rai bad luck โชคไม่ดี, โชคร้าย

h)chok! muay box (the sport), boxing ชกมวย

h)chok! l)tawy hit with the fist ชกต่อย

chom! v. compliment, admire, look at (with pleasure) ชม

chom! chuhy v. compliment, praise ชมเชย

chom! phoo [r)see chom!-phoo] pink (color) ชมพู

chon, chon! kan! v. collide ชน, ชนกัน

chon-na-l)bot! rural areas ชนบท

chon! l)pra!-than irrigation ชลประทาน

l)chook!-r)chuhn emergency ฉุกเฉิน

choom!-r)sai tho!-h)ra!-l)sap! telephone exchange ชุมสายโทรศัพท์

h)choot! n. set, a suit or team (of something or people) ชุด

h)choot l)ap-h)nam! bathing-suit ชุดอาบน้ำ

h)choot! nawn n. pajamas ชุดนอน

h)choot! r)sa-kon! suit of clothes (for men, Western style) ชุดสากล

f)chua! adj. bad, evil (for persons, usually) ชั่ว

f)chua! for a certain period of time ชั่ว

f)chua! l)kha!-l)na! just for a moment ชั่วขณะ

f)chua! khrao temporarily ชั่วคราว

f)chua! f)khroo for a short time ชั่วครู่

f)chua!-mong hour (one hour) ชั่วโมง

chuan v. ask someone to do something, invite someone ชวน

f)chuay, f)chuay-r)leua v. assist, help ช่วย, ช่วยเหลือ

f)chuay chee-h)wit! v. save, rescue ช่วยชีวิต

f)chuay f)duay Help! (emergency) ช่วยด้วย

chuhn v. invite someone (to do something) เชิญ

chuhn f)nang! Please sit down. เชิญนั่ง

r)chuhy r)chuhy adj. indifferent, impassive, without any opinion one way or the other เฉยๆ

l)da v. curse, scold roughly ด่า

daen n. land (in general) แดน

daeng [r)see daeng] red (color) แดง (สีแดง)

l)daet n. sunlight แดด

dai!, dai! dai! adj. any ใด, ใดๆ

f)dai! v. can, get, may (permission), (also shows past tense, when used in front of other verbs); all right (showing agreement or willingness) ได้

f)dai n. thread (for sewing) ด้าย

f)dai! kam!-rai! v. profit, make a profit ได้กำไร

f)dai! l)klin! v. smell, perceive an odor ได้กลิ่น

f)dai l)lawt spool of thread ด้ายหลอด

f)dai! ma v. acquire, get ได้มา

f)dai! r)mai? Is that all right? Can you (can I,) can he, etc.)? ได้ไหม

f)dai! l)pra!-l)yot adj. advantageous ได้ประโยชน์

f)dai! l)priap get or have an advantage over someone, get the best end of a bargain ได้เปรียบ

f)dai! yin! v. hear ได้ยิน

l)dak! n., v. trap ดัก

dam! [r)see dam!] black (color) ดำ (สีดำ)

dam! dam! dark-skinned, dark or black all over ดำ ๆ

dam!-nuhn v. proceed, carry on ดำเนิน

dan! v. push ดัน

f)dan n. side, part, aspect or sector ด้าน

l)dan immigration border checkpoint ด่าน

dang! adj. loud, (colloq.) famous ดัง

dang! l)klao (used mostly in legal documents) said...., the said.... ....ดังกล่าว

dang! h)nan! accordingly, consequently ดังนั้น

f)dan r)lang behind, in back of ด้านหลัง

f)dang f)na in front of, ahead ด้านหน้า

dao! v. guess เดา

dao n. star, planet ดาว

l)dap! v. extinguish, put out ดับ

l)dap n. sword, sabre ดาบ

l)dap plai peun n. bayonet ดาบปลายปืน

da-ra r)nang! film star ดาราหนัง

l)dawk-f)bia n. interest (on loans) ดอกเบี้ย

l)dawk l)ka!-l)lam! n. cauliflower ดอกกะหล่ำ

l)dawk f)kluay-h)mai! n. orchid ดอกกล้วยไม้

l)dawk koon!-jae n. lock ดอกกุญแจ

l)dawk-h)mai! n. flower ดอกไม้

dawng pickle, pickled (of food) ดอง

dee good, well ดี

dee-l)book! tin (mineral) ดีบุก

dee. dee thee. DDT (for spraying) ด.ด.ท.

dee jai! adj. happy, glad ดีใจ

dee f)kheun! better (than before) ดีขึ้น

dee l)kwa better, better than (something else) ดีกว่า

deco only one...., ...เดียว

r)deeo, r)deeo l)kawn Just a minute! เดียว, เดียวก่อน

r)deeo deeo just a minute เดียวเดียว

deeo kan! the same.... ....เดียวกัน

r)deeo h)nee now, right now เดียวนี้

dee f)san jaundice (disease) ดีซ่าน

dee f)thee l)soot! best, the best ดีที่สุด

l)dek! n. child, young person เด็ก

l)dek! l)awn new baby, young baby เด็กอ่อน

l)dek!-chai n. boy เด็กชาย

l)dek! daeng daeng very young baby เด็กแดงๆ

l)dek! tha-h)rok! n. baby, infant เด็กทารก

l)dek!-r)ying! n. girl (under 15) เด็กหญิง

deuan n. month เดือน

l)deuat v. boil, be boiling เดือด

l)deuat h)rawn in trouble, having trouble เดือดร้อน

l)deuk! late (at night) ดึก

l)deum v. drink ดื่ม

l)deum f)lao! drink alcoholic beverages ดื่มเหล้า

deung! v. pull, tug at ดึง

l)dih!-r)chan! I, me (mostly female speakers) ดิฉัน

dik!, dik!-chan-nuh-ree n. dictionary ดิก, ดิกชันเนอรี่

din! n. earth, ground ดิน

din!-r)saw n. pencil ดินสอ

l)dip! adj. raw, unripe ดิบ

dom!, dom! doo v. smell, smell of ดม, ดมดู

dong! n. forest, jungle ดง

don!-tree n. music ดนตรี

doo v. look; look at, watch ดู

l)doo! adj. fierce, wild; v. scold, bawl out ดุ

doo-lae v. look after, take care of ดูแล

doo r)meuan v. appear, seem ดูเหมือน

doo r)nang! see a movie (film) ดูหนัง

doo r)nang!-r)seu v. study (books) ดูหนังสือ

l)doot v. suck ดูด

doo l)thook v. insult, look down on ดูถูก

l)dot v. jump, leap โดด

l)dot f)rom v. parachute (from a plane), (slang) slip away from school without permission โดดร่ม

doy by, via โดย

doy at-ta-no-mat automatic, automatically โดย อัตโนมัติ

doy bang-uhn accidentally, by chance โดยบังเอิญ

doy cha-lia average (mathematical), on the average โดยเฉลี่ย

doy l)cha!-h)phaw! especially, particularly โดย เฉพาะ

doy lam!-phang! alone, by oneself โดยลำพัง

doy l)phan via, passing through, by way of โดย ผ่าน

doy thang by means of, via, by way of โดยทาง

doy f)yaw briefly, in brief โดยย่อ

l)duan adj. urgent, express ด่วน

duang n. round object, star, moon, etc. ดวง

duang a-thit the sun ดวงอาทิตย์

duang jan! the moon ดวงจันทร์

duang-tra prai-sa-nee n. postage stamp ดวงตราไปรษณีย์

f)duay also, by means of ด้วย

f)duay kan! together ด้วยกัน

duhm at first, originally เดิม

duhn v. walk, move, circulate (as blood), run (as a motor or clock), operate (as an airline etc.) เดิน

duhn ah-l)kat operate airplanes, navigate (aerially) เดินอากาศ

duhn l)kha!-buan v. parade, demonstrate (in protest) เดินขบวน

duhn f)na v. advance, move forward เดินหน้า

duhn reua v. operate ships, navigate เดินเรือ

duhn thang v. travel, take a trip เดินทาง

duhn h)to! v. serve food, wait on tables เดินโต๊ะ

l)eek again, once again, more (of something), some more, till (for telling time), other, another อีก

l)eek f)chua f)khroo in a while อีกชั่วครู่

l)eek khon! l)neung! another person, someone else อีกคนหนึ่ง

l)eek h)khrang!, l)eek h)khrang! l)neung one more time, once again, once more อีกครั้ง, อีกครั้งหนึ่ง

l)eek f)mai! h)cha a short time from now, in a short time from now อีกไม่ช้า

l)eek nan a long time from now อีกนาน

l)eek l)nawy soon, before long อีกหน่อย

l)eek thee one more time อีกที

l)eek l)yang l)neung! another thing อีกอย่างหนึ่ง

ee-r)san northeast(ern), Northeast Thailand อีสาน

ee-sook ee-sai n. chickenpox อีสุกอีใส

eh! huh? what's that? (showing doubt, surprise, or lack of clear understanding) เอะ, เอ๊ะ

eh-sia (a-sia) Asia, Asian เอเชีย (อาเซีย)

l)ek ,number one, 1st-class เอก

ek-ak-kha-rat-cha-thoot n. ambassador เอกอัครราชทูต

eng self [as in "r)khao! eng" = he himself] เอง

e-o (eh-o) n. waist (of the body) เอว

l)et! one [for ending of number 11, "l)sip'-l)et!" and for numbers from 21 on up ending in "one"] เอ็ด

euam meu v. reach out with one's hand เอื้อมมือ

euk-ka-theuk adj. noisy. boisterous อึกทึก

l)eun, l)eun l)eun another, others อื่น, อื่นๆ

h)fa n. sky ฟ้า; r)see h)fa = light-blue color, sky blue สีฟ้า

r)fa n. cover, lid ฝา

faen (colloq., from Eng, "fan") boyfriend, girlfriend, lover, wife, husband แฟน

fai! n. electricity, fire, flame, light ไฟ

f)fai n. cotton ฝ้าย

1)fai n. bureau, branch (of a govt.); (used for
people or groups of people) party, group ฝ่าย

fai! h)chaek n. cigarette-lighter ไฟแช็ค

fai!-r)chai n. flashlight ไฟฉาย

fai! daeng n. red light (traffic light) ไฟแดง

fai! h)fa electric, electricity ไฟฟ้า

fai! r)kheeo n. green light (traffic light) ไฟเขียว

fai! f)mai! be on fire, be burning, Fire! ไฟไหม้

fai! f)na h)rot! n. headlights (of a vehicle)
ไฟหน้ารถ

fai! r)san!-yan n. traffic lights ไฟสัญญาณ

h)fak! 1)khai hatch eggs ฟักไข่

h)fak!-thawng n. pumpkin, squash ฟักทอง

1)fak h)wai! v. deposit, entrust something or
someone to someone else's care ฝากไว้

h)fa f)laep n. lightning ฟ้าแลบ

fan! n. tooth; v. chop, slash ฟัน

r)fan! v. dream ฝัน

fang! v. listen, listen to ฟัง

fang n. straw, rice straw ฟาง

1)fang!, 1)fang! h)nam! bank (of a river or other
waterway), shore ฝั่ง, ฝั่งน้ำ

r)fang! v. bury ฝัง

c)fang! l)sop! bury a body ฝังศพ

i)fang! h)thal-leh n. seashore, seacoast ฝั่งทะเล

r)fan! h)lal-muh v. talk in one's sleep ฝันละเมอ

r)fan! h)rai nightmare, have a nightmare ฝันร้าย

f)fao! v. guard, watch เฝ้า

f)fao!, f)khao! f)fao! have an audience with royalty เฝ้า, เข้าเฝ้า

f)fao! khawy watch or wait for (in attentive observation) เฝ้าคอย

r)fa l)pha!-r)nang! n. wall (interior wall) ฝาผนัง

r)fa l)pit! n. cover, lid ฝาปิด

l)fa!-l)rang! (colloq.) foreigner (usually western) ฝรั่ง

fa-rang-set France, French ฝรั่งเศส

h)fa h)rawng thunder (in the sky) ฟ้าร้อง

h)fawng v. sue (in court), denounce someone ฟ้อง

fawng h)nam! n. sponge ฟองน้ำ

r)fee n. boil ฝี

r)fee l)dat n. smallpox ฝีดาษ

r)fee meu n. manual skill ฝีมือ

l)feuk!-l)hat! v. drill, practice, train ฝึกหัด

few! l)khat (elect.) blown-out fuse ฟิวส์ขาด

l)fin! n. opium ฝิ่น

flaet (flat) n. flat, apartment แฟลต

r)fon! n. rainfall ฝน

r)fon! prawy n. shower (of rain) ฝนปรอย

r)fon! l)tok! it's raining ฝนตก

f)fook n. mattress ฟูก

l)foon! n. dust ฝุ่น

f)ha five (5) ห้า (๕)

r)ha v. look for หา

r)hae n. fish-net (small) แห

f)haeng adj. dry แห้ง

l)haeng place, of, in (a place) แห่ง

f)hai! v. give, let, order to do something ให้

r)hai! n. earthen jug or jar ไห

r)hai v. get well (after sicknesss), disappear,
be missing or lost หาย

f)hai! l)awk v. discharge (from employment)
ให้ออก

f)hai! f)chao! for rent, to let; v. lease or rent
to someone ให้เช่า

f)hai! f)dai! do something (without fail) ให้ได้

r)hai jai! v. breathe หายใจ

r)hai jai! i)mai! l)awk v. cannot breathe, suffocate หายใจไม่ออก

f)hai! kan v. testify (give testimony), make an
official legal statement ให้การ

r)bai kan! be even, get even หายกัน

r)hai pai! adj., v. disappeared, disappear หายไป

f)hai! r)sin!-bon! v. bribe (someone) ให้สินบน

f)hai! yeum v. lend, let someone borrow something ให้ยืม

l)hak! v. break, break apart หัก

l)hak, l)hak f)wa if หาก, หากว่า

hal-lo hello (when answering phone) ฮัลโล

f)ham v. forbid ห้าม

f)ham h)law n., v., brake, brakes (of a vehicle)
ห้ามล้อ

l)han! v. slice, cut into pieces หั่น

f)han n. goose ห่าน

r)han! v. turn around หัน

r)han v. divide (arithmetically) หาร

f)hang n. firm, store, company (in general)
ห้าง

l)hang, l)hang l)jak far away, distant ห่าง, ห่างจาก

r)hang n. tail หาง

r)han! tua v. turn oneself around หันตัว

l)hao! v. bark, howl เห่า

r)hao nawn v. yawn หาวนอน

l)hap h)nam! carry water (in buckets etc., balanced on shoulder) หาบน้ำ

f)ha-l)sip fifty (50) ห้าสิบ (๕๐)

l)hat! v. practice, train หัด

l)hat sai sandy beach หาดทราย

l)haw n package, parcel; v. wrap into packages ห่อ

r)haw n. tower, hall หอ

r)ha f)wa v. accuse, charge with หาว่า

l)haw f)hoom! v. wrap all around (for protection) ห่อหุ้ม

r)haw kan h)kha n. chamber of commerce หอการค้า

l)haw r)khawng parcel, package; v. wrap up something ห่อของ

r)hawm v. be fragrant, have nice smell หอม

r)hawn v. bark, howl (dogs) หอน

f)hawng n. room ห้อง

f)hawng ah-r)han n. dining room ห้องอาหาร

f)hawng f)chao! rented room or apartment ห้องเช่า

f)hawng l)deeo single room (in hotel) ห้องเดี่ยว

f)hawng l)kep! r)khawng n. storeroom ห้องเก็บของ

f)hawng f)khoo n. double room (in hotel) ห้องคู่

f)hawng khrua n. kitchen ห้องครัว

f)hawng h)nam! n. bathroom, restroom, lavatory
ห้องน้ำ

f)hawng nawn n. bedroom ห้องนอน

f)hawng nawn tiang l)deeo single room (in hotel)
ห้องนอนเตียงเดี่ยว

f)hawng nawn tiang f)khoo double room (in hotel)
ห้องนอนเตียงคู่

f)hawng h)phak! ah-r)han n. pantry ห้องพักอาหาร

f)hawng l)pra!-choom! n. conference or meeting
room ห้องประชุม

f)hawng h)rap! l)khaek   n. living room, parlor
ห้องรับแขก

f)hawng rian n. classroom ห้องเรียน

f)hawng l)sa!-l)moot! n. library (normal size)
ห้องสมุด

f)hawng l)soo!-r)kha, f)hawng f)suam n. toilet, rest
room ห้องสุขา, ห้องส้วม

r)haw l)sa!-l)moot! n. library (large) หอสมุด

r)haw l)sa!-l)moot! l)haeng f)chat the National
Library of Thailand หอสมุดแห่งชาติ

r)hawy n. shell, oyster, shellfish, seashell หอย

r)hawy nang-rom! n. oyster หอยนางรม

r)ha f)yak difficult to find, rare หายาก

l)heep n. large box, case หีบ

l)heep phleng, l)heep phleng h)chak! n. accordion
หีบเพลง, หีบเพลงชัก

l)heep r)siang n. phonograph หีบเสียง

l)heep l)sop! n. casket, coffin หีบศพ

r)hen! v. see เห็น

r)hen! f)chawp v. approve, be in favor of เห็นชอบ

r)hen! f)duay v. agree with, approve of เห็นด้วย

r)hen! jai! v. sympathize with เห็นใจ

r)hen! l)ja! f)tawng had better, probably should
เห็นจะต้อง

r)hen! l)kae tua adj. selfish เห็นแก่ตัว

r)hen! khoon!-f)kha v. appreciate เห็นคุณค่า

l)hep! n. woodtick เห็บ

he-ran-yik n. treasurer (of company, association,
etc.) เหรัญญิก

l)het! khon n. mushrooms เห็ดโคน

l)het r)phon! n. cause, reason เหตุผล

r)heung! adj. jealous (romantically) หึง

l)heut n. asthma หืด

f)hew! v. carry something (rather heavy) หิ้ว

r)hew, r)hew f)khao hungry, be hungry หิว, หิวข้าว

r)hew h)nam [l)kra!·r)hai h)nam!] thirsty, be
   thirsty หิวน้ำ, กระหายน้ำ

l)hi!·h)ma! n. snow หิมะ

l)hi!·h)ma! l)tok! v. snow, it's snowing หิมะตก

r)hin! n. rock, stone หิน

f)hing! n. shelf หิ้ง

l)hok! six (6) หก (๖)

l)hok! v. spill หก

l)hok! h)lom! v. fall down หกล้ม

l)hok!·l)sip! sixty (60) หกสิบ (๖๐)

l)hom! v. cover up body with clothes, blankets,
   etc. ห่ม

r)hon! time, times (as one time, two times etc.)
   หน

r)hong! n. swan หงส์

r)hoo n. ear, handle (of glass, cup etc.) หู

f)hoon!, f)hoon! l)suan (n., fin.) share, stock หุ้น, หุ้นส่วน

r)hoo l)nuak adj. deaf หูหนวก

l)hoop! r)khao! n. valley หุบเขา

l)hot! v. shrink หด

r)hua n. head, top part of something หัว

r)hua r)hawm n. onions หัวหอม

r)hua jai! n. heart หัวใจ

r)hua f)kham! early part of the evening หัวค่ำ

r)hua l)khao! n. knee หัวเข่า

r)hua l)kra!-thiam n. garlic หัวกระเทียม

r hua l)lai! n. shoulder หัวไหล่

r)hua h)lan bald-headed หัวล้าน

r)hua f)na n. chief (boss) หัวหน้า

l)huang adj. worried ห่วง

r)hua nom! n. nipple หัวนม

r)hua l)phak!-l)kat n. turnip หัวผักกาด

r)hua l)phak!-l)kat daeng n. carrot หัวผักกาดแดง

r)hua h)raeng n. soldering iron หัวแร้ง

r)hua-h)raw! v. laugh หัวเราะ

r)hua thian n. spark plug หัวเทียน

f)huay n. creek, stream ห้วย

l)im, l)im h)laeo adj. full (after eating) อิ่ม, อิ่มแล้ว

in-dian daeng "red" Indian (American Indian) อินเดียนแดง

l)it! n. brick (for construction) อิฐ

l)it!·r)cha adj. jealous, envious อิจฉา

l)ja! v. shall, will, going to จะ

l)jaek v. distribute, hand out แจก

l)ja l)ek (RTN) petty·officer, 3rd class จ่าเอก

jae·kan! n. vase แจกัน

l)jaek f)khreuang l)deum serve drinks (at a party) แจกเครื่องดื่ม

l)jaem-r)sai! adj. clear, alert, fresh แจ่มใส

f)jaeng, t)jaeng f)hai! f)sap notify แจ้ง, แจ้งให้ทราบ

f)jaeng khwam advertise, file a complaint (as with police) แจ้งความ

jaeo reua row a boat แจวเรือ

jai! n. soul, inner being, mind ใจ

l)jai, l)jai nguhn pay out (money) จ่าย, จ่ายเงิน

jai! dam! adj. mean, black-hearted ใจดำ

jai! dee adj. good-hearted, generous ใจดี

jai! f)khaep adj. narrow-minded ใจแคบ

jai! f)kwang-r)khwang adj. broad-minded ใจกว้าง
ขวาง

l)jai l)ta!-l)lat do shopping (for food needs, usually daily) จ่ายตลาด

l)ja! r)khai for sale, will sell จะขาย

h)jak!-l)ka!-f)jee adj. ticklish จักจี้

jak-kra-yan n. bicycle จักรยาน

jak-kra-yan-yon n. bicycle with motor, motorcycle จักรยานยนต์

l)jak pai! v. depart from someone or a place จากไป

l)jak! h)yep! f)pha n. sewing maching จักรเย็บผ้า

jam!, jam! f)dai! v. remember, can remember จำ, จำได้

jam v. sneeze จาม

jam!-nam! v. pawn จำนำ

jam!-nawng v. mortgage จำนอง

jam-nuan n. amount จำนวน

l)ja!-l)mook n. nose จมูก

jam!-pen! must, necessary จำเป็น

jam!-f)phuak n. group, type จำพวก

jam!-f)tawng must, required จำต้อง

jan! (wan! jan!) Monday จันทร์ (วันจันทร์)

jan! [h)phra!-jan!] n. the moon จันทร์ (พระจันทร์)

jan n. plate (for eating) จาน

l)ja nai l)sip! tam!-l)ruat police sgt.-major, police
  1st-sgt. จ่านายสิบตำรวจ

l)ja f)na sawng address an envelope จ่าหน้าซอง

jang! very much จัง

f)jang v. employ, hire จ้าง

jang!-l)wa! n. rhythm, timing จังหวะ

jang!-l)wat! n. province, changwat จังหวัด

jan rawng f)thuay n. saucer จานรองถ้วย

f)jao! n. prince, ruler, holy being เจ้า

f)jao! ah-f)wat n. abbot (of Buddhist temple)
  เจ้าอาวาส

f)jao! l)bao n. bridegroom เจ้าบ่าว

f)jao! chai, f)jao!-h)fa chai n. prince เจ้าชาย,
  เจ้าฟ้าชาย

f)jao! h)fa n. prince, princess เจ้าฟ้า

f)jao!-h)fa r)ying!, f)jao! r)ying n. princess
  เจ้าฟ้าหญิง, เจ้าหญิง

f)jao!-r)khawng n. owner เจ้าของ

f)jao!·r)khawng f)ban n. landlord (house) เจ้าของ
  บ้าน

f)jao!-r)khawng f)thee n. landlord (land) เจ้าของที่

f)jao! krom n. director-general of a Thai-govt. dept. เจ้ากรม

f)jao! meu n. dealer, banker (card games etc.) เจ้ามือ

f)jao!-f)na-f)thee n. official, officer เจ้าหน้าที่

f)jao!-f)nee n. creditor เจ้าหนี้

f)jao!-f)phap n. host เจ้าภาพ

f)jao! r)sao n. bride เจ้าสาว

f)jao! r)ying! n. princess เจ้าหญิง

l)jap! v. catch, take hold of, touch จับ

l)jap! koom! v. arrest จับกุม

l)jap! meu shake hands จับมือ

ja-ra-jawn n. traffic จราจร

ja-ruhn adj. prosperous, advanced เจริญ

l)ja r)san n. court clerk จ่าศาล

l)ja l)sip! l)ek sgt.-major, master-sgt. จ่าสิบเอก

l)ja l)sip tho sgt. 1st-class จ่าสิบโท

l)ja l)sip! tree staff-sgt. จ่าสิบตรี

l)jat! very much จัด

l)jat! v. arrange, manage จัด

l)jat! r)ha v. provide supplies จัดหา

l)ja tho seaman, 1st-class จ่าโท

l)jat! kan v. manage จัดการ

l)ja tree seaman, 2nd-class อ่าครี

l)jat! h)seu v. procure จัดซื้อ

l)jat! f)tang! v. establish จัดตั้ง

l)jat! h)to! ah-r)han set the table (for a meal)
จัดโต๊ะอาหาร

jaw, jaw r)nang n. film screen จอ, จอหนัง

l)jaw! v. puncture, perforate เจาะ

jawm phon! field marshal จอมพล

jawm phon! ah-l)kat general of the air force
(5-star) จอมพลอากาศ

jawm phon! reua admiral of the fleet (5-star)
จอมพลเรือ

jawng, jawng h)wai! v. reserve, make a reser
vation จอง, จองไว้

f)jawng, f)jawng doo v. stare, stare at จ้อง, จ้องดู

jawng f)thee f)nang!, jawng r)tua reserve a ticket
(seat) จองที่นั่ง, จองตัว

l)jawp n. hoe จอบ

jaw-ra-kheh n. alligator จระเข้

l)jawt, l)jawt h)rot park a vehicle จอด, จอดรถ

jawt f)pai Next stop! (when riding a bus)
จอดข้าง

f)jee v. tickle, (slang) rob with a gun จี้

jeen China, Chinese จีน

l)jeep v. flirt จีบ

l)jep! feel pain, hurt, be sore เจ็บ

l)jep l)puat pain and soreness (in general) เจ็บปวด

l)jep! f)khai! sickness and illness (in general) เจ็บไข้

je-ra-ja v. negotiate, discuss เจรจา

l)jet! seven (7) เจ็ด (๗)

l)jet!-l)sip! seventy (70) เจ็ดสิบ (๗๐)

jeung! so, then, therefore จึง

l)jeut adj. tasteless, not spicy, not hot in taste จืด

f)jim! f)an! pick the teeth (with toothpicks) จิ้มฟัน

jing! true, real จริง

jing! jing! really, truly จริงๆ

f)jing!-l)jok! n. small household lizard จิ้งจก

l)jit!, l)jit!-jai! n. soul, inner being, mind, spirit จิต, จิตใจ

jom!, jom! h)nam! sink, go under the water จม, จมน้ำ

jom! h)nam! tai v. drown จมน้ำตาย

jom-tee v. attack โจมตี

jon! adj., adv. poor, in poverty จน

jon!, jon! r)theung! till, until จน, จนถึง

jon n. bandit โจร

jong! v. (command, order) be, must จง

jon! l)kra!-f)thang! to the point (extent) that
จนกระทั่ง

jon! l)kwa till (until) a certain time (extent)
จนกว่า

l)jook!, l)jook! l)khuet n. stopper, cork จุก, จุกขวด

l)joop n , v. kiss จูบ

l)joot! v. point, dot, period (full stop), decimal
point จุด

l)joot!, l)joot! fai! v. light, set fire to จุด, จุดไฟ

l)jop!, l)jop! h)laeo finished, ended จบ, จบแล้ว

l)jot!, l)jot! h)wai! v. jot down, make a note of
จด, จดไว้

l)jot!-r)mai n. letter (correspondence) จดหมาย

l)jot! tha-bian v. register จดทะเบียน

juan, juan, h)' o about to, almost, nearly จวน,
จวนแล้ว

ka n. crow; v. make an X-mark or a check-
mark กา

ka- ka h)nam! n. teakettle กา, กาน้ำ

l)ka! v. estimate กะ

kae (very informal, sometimes offensive) he, she, him, her, you แก

f)kae, f)kae l)awk v. undo, unwrap, unfasten, untie แก้, แก้ออก

f)kae, f)kae l)puat relieve pain แก้, แก้ปวด

f)kae, f)kae·r)khai! v. correct, improve, repair, revise แก้, แก้ไข

l)kae! n. sheep; v. carve, etch, pick out with fingers แกะ

l)kae old (for people), dark (for colors) strong (for drinks) แก่

l)kae to or for (a person) แก่

f)kaem n. cheek (of face) แก้ม

kaeng n. curry (food, of many kinds, eaten with rice) แกง

kaeng l)jeut mildly-seasoned Thai-style soup or curry แกงจืด

kaeng l)ka!-l)ree curry (Indian-style) แกงกะหรี่

kaeng l)phet! hot (spicy) curry (of many kinds) แกงเผ็ด

f)kaeo n. glass (material) แก้ว

f)kaeo, f)kaeo h)nam! water-glass, drinking glass
แก้ว, แก้วน้ำ

f)kae pan!-r)ha   v. solve, resolve a problem
แก้ปัญหา

f)kae f)pha v. disrobe, undress แก้ผ้า

f)kae tua   v. make an alibi or excuse, make
amends แก้ตัว

ka-fae n. coffee กาแฟ

l)kai! n. chicken, hen, (slang) prostitute ไก่

kai! peun n. trigger ไกปืน

l)ka!-l)lam!-plee n. cabbage กะหล่ำปลี

ka-la-see n. sailor กะลาสี

kam! l)jat! v. exterminate, get rid of กำจัด

kam!-lai! [f)khaw-meu] n. bracelet กำไล (ข้อมือ)

kam!-lang!   n. power, energy, mathematical or
exponential power กำลัง

kam!-lang! h)ma n. horsepower กำลังม้า

kam!-lang phon (n., mil.) personnel กำลังพล

kam-ma-kan n, member of committee or of
board of directors, company director กรรมการ

kam-ma-kawn n. laborer กรรมกร

kam-ma-rok n. venereal disease กามโรค

kam!-ŋan! n. tambon (commune, precinct) headman (chief) กำนัน

kam!-l)not! v., adj. schedule, specify, stipulate กำหนด

kam!-phoo·cha Cambodia, Khmer กัมพูชา

kam!-rai! n. profit กำไร

kan! (to) each other, (to) one another กัน

f)kan! v. block, obstruct กัน

kan (prefix used to make nouns from verbs, like gerunds in Eng, as in KAN KIN! = eating, or to form other kinds of nouns in general) การ

ka h)nam!-cha n. teapot กาน้ำชา

kan!-cha n. marijuana กัญชา

kang-keng n. trousers กางเกง

kang·keng nai! n. undershorts กางเกงใน

kang h)moong! put up a mosquito-net กางมุ้ง

kang!-won! jai! adj. anxious, uneasy, worried กังวลใจ

kan h)kha, kan h)kha·r)khai n. trade, commerce การค้า, การค้าขาย

kan f)khleuan-r)wai! n. activities, movements การเคลื่อนไหว

kan r)khon!-l)song! n. transportation work การ
ขนส่ง

kan kho-sa-na n. advertising work การโฆษณา

kan kho-sa-na chuan f)cheua n. propaganda การ
โฆษณาชวนเชื่อ

kan!-krai! n. scissors กรรไกร

kan-la-rok n. bubonic plague กาฬโรค

kan f)leuak f)tang! n. election การเลือกตั้ง

kan long! thoon! n. investment work การลงทุน

kan meuang n. politics การเมือง

kan ngan n. work (in general) การงาน

kan h)phal-nan! n. gambling การพนัน

kan l)pha l)tat! n. surgery การผ่าตัด

kan phat-tha-na n. development work การพัฒนา

kan l)pra!-choom! n. meeting, conference การประชุม

kan l)pra!-kan! phai! n. insurance work การประกันภัย

kan h)rop! (n., mil.) combat, battle การรบ

kan l)sa!-daeng n. show, performance, demonstration การแสดง

kan l)sep l)tit! n. addiction (to drugs etc.) การ
เสพติด

kan l)seuk!-r)sa n. education การศึกษา

kan r)som!-h)rot!, kan l)taeng-ngan n. wedding
การสมรส, การแต่งงาน

kan tham! na n. rice-farming การทำนา

f)kan! thang v. block (shut off) the way กั้นทาง

kaa f)thawng-theeo n. tourism การท่องเที่ยว

kan!-ya, kan!-ya yon! Septem'ber กันยา, กันยายน

kao! v. scratch oneself (with fingers) เกา

kao n. glue, paste, gum กาว

f)kao! nine (9) เก้า

f)kao v. step, take a step; n. step, pace ก้าว

l)kao!, l)kao!-l)kae old (for things) or long-stand-
ing (as for friends) เก่า, เก่าแก่

f)kao!-f)ee n. chair เก้าอี้

kao!-r)lee Korea(n) เกาหลี

f)kao-f)na v. progress, advance ก้าวหน้า

f)kao!-l)sip! ninety (90) เก้าสิบ (๙๐)

l)kap! with, and กับ

l)kap!-l)dak!   n. trap, snare กับดัก; l)kap!-l)dak!
r)noo mousetrap กับดักหนู

l)kap! f)khao n. food (in general, eaten with
rice) กับข้าว

ka-ra-ka-da, ka-ra-ka-da-khom July กรกฎา,กรกฎาคม

l)ka!-l)ree (slang) prostitute กะหรี่

ka·roo·na kindly, please กรุณา

ka·set, ka·set·ta·kam, ka·si·kam agriculture เกษตร, เกษตรกรรม, กสิกรรม

l)**kat!** v. bite กัด

l)**kal·thuhy** n. transvestite (usually male dressed as female) กะเทย

ka f)tom h)nam! teakettle (for boiling water) กาต้มน้ำ

f)**kaw!** (general connecting word, usually not translated but sometimes similar in meaning to "also") ก็

l)**kaw!** n. island เกาะ

f)**kaw! f)dai!, f)kaw! dee** all right, that's all right okay, that's good ก็ได้, ดี

h)**kawk, h)kawk h)nam!** n. water faucet ก๊อก, ก๊อกน้ำ

f)**kawn** n. block or lump of something (as sugar etc.) ก้อน

l)**kawn** before, first (before something else) ก่อน

kawng n. pile, heap (of something) กอง

kawng n. division (part of a dept., of a Thai-govt. ministry) กอง

kawng ah-f)cheep khon! l)tang f)dao Div. of Alien Occupations (Dept. of Labour) กองอาชีพคนต่างด้าว

kawng ban-cha-kan (n., mil.) headquarters กองบัญชาการ

kawng ban-cha-kan h)tha!-r)han r)soong l)soot! (n., mil.) Supreme Headquarters กองบัญชาการทหารสูงสุด

kawng jon band of guerrillas, outlaws, or terrorists กองโจร

kawng phan! (n., mil.) battalion กองพัน

kawng phon!, kawng phon! l)yai! (n., mil.) division กองพล, กองพลใหญ่

kawng phon! h)nawy [phon! h)nawy] (n., mil.) brigade กองพลน้อย (พลน้อย)

kawng h)rawy (mil.) company กองร้อย

kawng h)thap! ah-l)kat Royal Thai Air Force (RTAF) กองทัพอากาศ

kawng h)thap! l)bok Royal Thai Army (RTA) กองทัพบก

kawng h)thap! reua Royal Thai Navy (RTN) กองทัพเรือ

kawng l)truat khon! f)khao! meuang Immigration Div. กองตรวจคนเข้าเมือง

f)kawn r)hin n. rock, stone ก้อนหิน

f)kawn l)it! n. brick (usually for building) ก้อนอิฐ

l)kaw-f)sang v. build, construct ก่อสร้าง

l)kawt, l)kawt h)rat! v. embrace, hug กอด, แอกรัด

l)kee.... how many...? กี่....

kee-la n. athletics, sports กีฬา

kee-lo n. kilo (1 kilo = 2.2 pounds) กิโล

kee-lo-met n. kilometre (1 km. = 0.62 miles) กิโลเมตร

l)kee mong? At what time? What time is it? กี่โมง

l)keeo conc rning, about (a certain subject); v. hook, fasten เกี่ยว

l)keeo, l)kep! l)keeo v. harvest crops เกี่ยว, เก็บเกี่ยว

l)ke-o l)kap! concerning, pertaining to, regarding, about เกี่ยวกับ

l)keeo f)khawng involved, be involved in, concerned with เกี่ยวข้อง

l)keng adj. skillful, clever (at doing things) เก่ง

ken h)tha!-r)han v. (mil.) draft, conscript เกณฑ์ ทหาร

l)kep! v. collect, put away, keep เก็บ

l)kep!, l)kep! h)rak!-r)sa v. store, keep in storage เก็บ, เก็บรักษา

l)kep!, l)kep! h)wai! v. pick up, put away เก็บ, เก็บไว้

l)kep! l)keeo, l)kep! l)keeo f)khao harvest crops (especially rice) เก็บเกี่ยว, เก็บเกี่ยวข้าว

l)kep! r)khawng v. pack up, get ready to leave, put things away เก็บของ

l)kep! l)kra!-r)pao! pack one's bags เก็บกระเป๋า

l)kep! nguhn, l)kep! l)sai-tang collect money, collect a bill เก็บเงิน, เก็บสตางค์

l)kep! nguhn h)wai! save money, keep money aside เก็บเงินไว้

l)kep! h)wai! store, keep, set aside, save เก็บไว้

l)keuap almost, about, nearly เกือบ

f)kha cost of something, price ค่า

f)kha v. kill ฆ่า

h)kha! or f)kha! (spoken by females only) sir, ma'am, yes, yes sir, yes ma'am คะ, ค่ะ

h)kha, h)kha r)khai v. trade, do business ค้า, ค้าขาย

r)kha n. leg (of body) ขา

f)kha l)awk [l)kheet l)awk] mark out, rub out, cross out ฆ่าออก, ขีดออก

l)kha!-buan n. procession, in a line, in a row ขบวน

f)kha h)chai l)jai n. expenses, costs ค่าใช้จ่าย

f)kha f)chao! n. rent ค่าเช่า

f)kha h)cheua-f)rok v. sterilize ฆ่าเชื้อโรค

kha-dee n. lawsuit, case in court คดี

l)khaek n. visitor, guest (also general term for Asian nationals from Moslem or Hindu areas) แขก

r)khaen n arm (of body) แขน

l)khaeng, l)khaeng kan! v race, compete แข่ง, แข่งกัน

r)khaeng! adj. hard, stiff แข็ง

l)khaeng-r)khan! v. compete (as in sports) แข่งขัน

r)khaeng!-raeng adj. strong, powerful แข็งแรง

r)khaen f)seua n. shirtsleeve แขนเสื้อ

f)khaep adj. narrow แคบ

f)kha fai, f)kha fai-h)fa electric bill (charges) ค่าไฟ, ค่าไฟฟ้า

f)khai! n. fever ไข้

f)khai, f)khai h)tha!·r)han n. military camp ค่าย, ค่ายทหาร

l)khai! n. egg ไข่; l)khai! dao fried eggs ไข่ดาว; l)khai! jeeo egg omelette ไข่เจียว; l)khai! f)luak softboiled eggs ไข่ลวก; l)khai! f)tom! boiled eggs ไข่ต้ม

r)khai!, r)khai! koon!·jae v. unlock ไข, ไขกุญแจ

r)khai v. sell ขาย

f)khai! l)jap! l)san!, f)khai! ma·lah·ria n. malaria ไข้จับสั่น, ไข้มาลาเรีย

r)khai!·khuang n. screwdriver ไขควง

r)khai! lau v. wind (a watch, toy etc.) ไขลาน

r)khai! leh·r)lang! v auction ขายเลหลัง

l)khai! h)mook! n. pearl ไข่มุก

f)khai! thaw·ra·phit n. smallpox ไข้ทรพิษ

f)khai!·l)wat! (med.) a bad cold, with fever ไข้หวัด

f)khai!·l)wat! l)yai! n. the flu, influenza ไข้หวัดใหญ่

r)kha kan!·krai! n. jaws (of the face) ขากรรไกร

h)kha·r)khai v. trade, do business (in general) ค้าขาย

f)kha khrawng f)cheep   (fin.) cost of living
ค่าครองชีพ

kham! n. word (also used as prefix for spoken
or written things, such as kham! h)nae! nam!
= advice, kham! chuhn = invitation etc.)   คำ

f)kham! n. dusk, early evening   ค่ำ

f)kham v. cross, go across; prep. across   ข้าม

l)kha!-r)men (kam!-phoo-cha) Khmer, Cambodia
เขมร (กัมพูชา)

kham!-nuan v. compute, calculate   คำนวณ

kha-moy v. steal, rob; n. thief   ขโมย

kham! l)tawp n. answer   คำตอบ

kham! r)tham n. question   คำถาม

khan! v. itch   คัน

khan! n. (classifying noun for vehicles & some
other nouns, as in "(h)rot! r)sawng khan!" = 2
cars)   คัน

h)khan! l)beep h)khan!   v. squeeze out (as
juices), press   คั้น (บีบคั้น)

r)khan! l)khop!.r)khan!] adj. amusing, humorous
ขัน(ขบขัน)

h)kha!-h)na! n. college or faculty of univ., group
of people   คณะ

l)kha!-l)na! at a certain moment or time (as in "l)kha!-l)na! h)nee" = at this time) ขณะ

kha-naen n. grade, point, score, mark (exams), ballot (voting) คะแนน

kha-naen r)siang n. vote คะแนนเสียง

h)khal-h)na! kam-ma-kan n. committee, board of directors คณะกรรมการ

f)kha h)nam!. f)kha h)nam! l)pral·pa water bill (charges) ค่าน้ำ, ค่าน้ำประปา

l)khal-l)nat n. size ขนาด

khang n. chin (of face) คาง

f)khang n. side, part (of something) ข้าง

r)khang!, r)khang! h)wai! v. lock up, shut in a place, jail ขัง, ขังไว้

f)khang bon! above, upstairs, on top ข้างบน

f)khang f)khang alongside, beside ข้างๆ

f)khang khiang adjacent, nearby, beside ข้างเคียง

f)khang r)khwa on the right, right-hand side ข้างขวา

f)khang f)lang downstairs, below ข้างล่าง

f)khang r)lang! behind, in back of ข้างหลัง

f)khang f)na in front, in front of, ahead, forward ข้างหน้า

f)khang f)na [phai f)na, nai! a-na-khot!] ~~in the~~
future บ้างหน้า (ภายหน้า, ในอนาคต)

f)khang nai! inside บ้างใน

f)khang f)nawk outside บ้างนอก

f)khang h)sai on the ~~left~~, left-hand side บ้างซ้าย

f)khang f)tai below, underneath บ้างใต้

l)kha!-r)nom! n. candy, sweets ขนม

l)kha!-r)nom!-pang! n. bread ขนมปัง

l)kha!-r)nom!-pang! f)ping! n. toast (bread) ขนมปังปิ้ง

khan! f)reng h)nam!-man! n accelerator, gas
pedal (of a car) คันเร่งน้ำมัน

f)khao! f)khao! ma (pai!) v. enter, come (go) in,
attend (a meeting etc.) เข้า, เข้ามา (ไป)

f)khao n. rice ข้าว

l)khao n. news, information, intelligence ข่าว

r)khao! he, she, him, her, they, them เขา

r)khao! [phoo r)khao!] n. hill, mountain เขา

r)khao [r)see r)khao!] white (color) ขาว (สีขาว)

f)khao!-jai! v. understand เข้าใจ; f)khao!-jai! l)phit!
misunderstand เข้าใจผิด

l)khao leu n. rumors ข่าวลือ

f)khao! meuang v. immigrate เข้าเมือง

f)khao! nawn (pai! nawn) v. go to bed เข้านอน
(ไปนอน)

f)khao r)neeo n. glutinous rice ข้าวเหนียว

f)khao l)phat! n. fried rice (with vegetables,
meat etc.) ข้าวผัด

f)khao f)phot n. corn ข้าวโพด

khao!-h)rop! v. respect เคารพ

f)khao! f)ruam v. participate เข้าร่วม

f)khao r)sa-lee n. wheat ข้าวสาลี

h)khap! adj. tight, too tight (as clothing) คับ

l)khap!, l)khap! h)rot! drive a car ขับ, ขับรถ

l)khap!-f)lai! v. drive off, chase away ขับไล่

f)kha-l)seuk! n. enemy (in war) ข้าศึก

f)kha l)song! n. postage, freight (charges) ค่าส่ง

f)khat!, f)khat f)wa v. expect (that something
will happen) คาด, คาดว่า

l)khat! v. polish, shine, wax ขัด

l)khat v. miss (be absent), be lacking, torn,
wornout ขาด

f)kha tho-ra-sap! n. telephone bill ค่าโทรศัพท์

h)khat!-h)khan v. oppose, protest คัดค้าน

l)khat!-f)khawng v. disagree, have some difficulty, object ขัดข้อง

l)khat!-r)khwang v. block, obstruct ขัดขวาง

l)khat! rawng-h)thao! shine shoes ขัดรองเท้า

l)khat thoon! (fin.) lose money (in business),
take a loss ขาดทุน

f)kha tua tai commit suicide ฆ่าตัวตาย

khaw n. neck, throat (of body) คอ

h)khaw! v. knock, tap (usually with knuckles)
เคาะ

f)khaw [classifying noun & general prefix for
nouns pertaining to written things, as "f)khaw
l)sawp" = exam questions] ข้อ

r)khaw v. request, ask for ขอ

r)khaw n. small hook, hanger ขอ

r)khaw doo Let me see. Show me. ขอดู

f)khaw-meu n. wrist (of body) ข้อมือ

h)khawn n. hammer ค้อน

r)khaw l)nawy Please give me a little. ขอหน่อย

r)khawng n. things, belongings; (prep., v.) of,
belong to [used after something to show
possession by following noun or pronoun, as
in "f)ban r)khawng r)chan! = my house] ของ

r)khawng khoon! your, yours ของคุณ

r)khawng khrai! whose? ของใคร

r)khawng r)khwan! n. gift, present ของขวัญ

l)khawp n. edge ขอบ

l)khawp khoon! (normal) Thank you. ขอบคุณ;
(more respectful) l)khawp h)phraʔ-khoon! ขอบ
พระคุณ

h)khaw! l)praʔ-too knock at a door เคาะประตู

f)khaw-h)thaoʔ n. ankle (of body) ข้อเท้า

r)khaw f)thot [r)khaw ahʔ-phai!] Excuse me.
Pardon me. ขอโทษ (ขออภัย)

khawy v. wait คอย

f)khawy, f)khawy f)khawy gradually, little by
little, softly ค่อย, ค่อยๆ

r)khaw yeum Please let me borrow.... ขอยืม....

f)khawy yang! f)chua (colloq.) better, better
than before ค่อยยังชั่ว

l)khaʔ·l)yaʔ! n. trash ขยะ

l)khaʔ·r)yai v. expand, enlarge ขยาย

l)khaʔ·r)yan! adj. diligent, hard-working ขยัน

l)khaʔ·l)yaoʔ v. shake (as contents of a bottle)
เขย่า

f)khee n. excrement, waste material in general ขี้

l)khee v. ride (an animal, bicycle or other non-motorized means of transport) ขี่

f)khee-l)kiat (colloq.) lazy ขี้เกียจ

f)khee leum absent-minded, forgetful ขี้ลืม

kheem n. pliers คีม

f)khee r)neeo (colloq.) stingy ขี้เหนียว

h)kheeo v. chew เคี้ยว

r)kheeo [r)see r)kheeo] green (color) เขียว (สีเขียว)

l)kheet f)sen draw a line ขีดเส้น

l)kheet f)sen f)tai! v. underline ขีดเส้นใต้

khem! salty (in taste) เค็ม

r)khem! n. needle เข็ม

r)khem! h)chee h)thit, r)khem! h)thit! n. compass เข็มทิศ, เข็มทิศ

r)khem!-l)khat! n. belt (for trousers) เข็มขัด

r)khem!-l)klat! n. safety-pin เข็มกลัด

r)khem! l)moot! n. pin, straight pin เข็มหมุด

f)kheu!-f)nguat adj. strict, rigid เข้มงวด

l)khet n. area, jurisdiction, zone เขต

kheu that is, that is to say (also used as a "be" verb, in certain cases) คือ

l)kheuan n. dam เขื่อน

kheun n. night คืน

kheun, kheun f)hai! v. return, give back คืน, คืนให้

f)kheun! up, more...., ...er [as in "hotter" = "h)rawn f)kheun!"] ขึ้น

kheun h)nee tonight คืนนี้

h)khew! n. eyebrows คิ้ว

r)khian v. write เขียน

h)khit! v. think คิด

h)khit!, h)khit ra-kha charge a price คิด, คิดราคา

h)khit! f)thao!-rai! How much? How much will you charge? คิดเท่าไร

h)khit! r)theung! v. think about, miss [as in "h)kbit! r)theung! f)ban" = be homesick] คิดถึง

khlawng (klong) n. canal คลอง

f)khlawt v. give birth คลอด

khlee-nik (med.) private medical clinic คลินิค

f)khleuan r)wai! v. move around, have activities เคลื่อนไหว

f)khleun n. waves (of sea, air, radio) คลื่น

khlon n. mud โคลน

khloom!, khloom! h)wai! v. cover up คลุม, คลุมไว้

khom! adj. sharp (not dull) คม

khom! (suffix used in full name of months with 31 days.-often omitted) คม

r)khom! adj. bitter ขม

l)khom! r)kheun v. rape ข่มขืน

khon! person, people (much used as a prefix to show a person who does something, like the "....er" construction in Eng.; also much used before names of countries, nationalities, cities to mean "person or people of that place") คน

khon! v. stir คน

f)khon! adj. thick, concentrated ข้น

h)khon!, h)khon! r)ha   v. look for, search ค้น, ค้นหา

r)khon!   n. hair (of body, not of head; hair, bristles, fur of animals) ขน

r)khon! v. load, transport ขน

khon! h)chai! n. servant คนใช้

khon! deeo   alone, one person only, by oneself คนเดียว

khon! duhn h)to! n. waiter คนเดินโต๊ะ

khong!, khong! l)ja! probably, most likely คง, คงจะ

h)khong adj. bent, curved โค้ง

khon! f)khai!   (med.) patient (of a doctor etc.)
คนไข้

khon! f)khao!-meuang ก. immigrant   คนเข้าเมือง

khon! l)khəp! h)rot! n. driver, chauffeur คนขับรถ

khon! h)liang l)dek! n   nursemaid, baby ayah
คนเลี้ยงเด็ก

khon! ngan n servant, worker, employee คนงาน.

khon! h)sak! f)pha n. washwoman คนซักผ้า

khon! h)sak! f)reet n. washwoman (who also
does ironing) คนซักรีด

r)khon! l)sat! n. fur, hair, bristles (of animals)
ขนสัตว์

r)khon! l)song! v. transport, send goods ขนส่ง

khon! r)suan, khon! tham! r)suan n. gardener
คนสวน, คนทำสวน

r)khon! ta n. eyelashes ขนตา

khon! thai! Thai person, Thai people คนไทย

khon! tham! i)kap!-f)khao, khon! tham! khrua [f)mae
khrua] n. cook คนทำกับข้าว, คนทำครัว (แม่ครัว)

khon! yam [khon! f)fao! yam] n. watchman,
. guard คนยาม (คนเฝ้ายาม)

f)khoo n. pair, couple คู่

l)khoo v. threaten ขู่

h)khook! n. jail (gaol) คุก

khoom! kam!-l)nuht practice birth control คุมกำเนิด

khoon! you (also often used before first names, for politeness, and before names of relatives, for respect) คุณ

khoon v. multiply (arithmetic) คูณ

khoon!-f)kha n. value, worth คุณค่า

khoon!-na!-f)phap n. quality คุณภาพ

f)khoo h)rak! n. sweetheart คู่รัก

l)khoot! v. dig ขุด

khooy v. chat คุย

kho-sa-na v. advertise โฆษณา

kho-sa-na chuan f)cheua propagandize โฆษณา ชวนเชื่อ

l)khot! n. coil, roll of something ขด

khrai! who? whom? anyone, someone ใคร

khrai! f)kaw! f)dai! anybody will do, anybody will be all right ใครก็ได้

khrai! khon l)neung! someone, a certain person ใครคนหนึ่ง

h)khrang! time, times [as in "r)sawng h)khrang!" = two times, twice] ครั้ง

h)khrang! h)la!.... ....at a time, ...per time ครั้งละ..

khrao n. occasion, time (certain time) คราว

khrao f)na next time คราวหน้า

h)khrap! (spoken by males only) sir, ma'am,
  yes, yes sir, yes ma'am ครับ

f)khrat n., v. rake คราด

f)khrawp-khrua n. family ครอบครัว

khreem n. cream [as in shaving cream = "khreem
  kon l)nuat"] ครีม

f)khreuang n. machine, motor, engine, machinery, device เครื่อง

f)khreuang aer (colloq.) air-conditioner เครื่องแอร์

f)khreuang l)ah!-l)lai! n. spare parts เครื่องอะไหล่

f)khreuang l)at! r)sam!-nao! mimeograph or other
  duplicating machine เครื่องอัดสำเนา

f)khreuang l)baep   n. uniform (for soldiers,
  students etc.) เครื่องแบบ

f)khreuang-bin! n. airplane เครื่องบิน

f)khreuang bin! ai!-f)phon! n. jet plane เครื่องบิน
  ไอพ่น

f)khreuang-bin! f)kheun! airplane takeoff เครื่องบิน
  บิน

f)khreuang bin! long! airplane landing เครื่องบินลง

f)khreuang-bin! h)thing! h)ra!-l)buht n. bomber
(a!rplane) เครื่องบินทิ้งระเบิด

f)khreuang-bin! l)tok! airplane crash เครื่องบินตก

f)khreuang l)deum n drinks, refreshments
เครื่องดื่ม

f)khreuang l)jak!, f)khreuang`kon!-kai! n. machinery
เครื่องจักร, เครื่องกลไก

f)khreuang kham!-nuan n. computer เครื่องคำนวณ

f)khreuang l)kha!-r)yai r)siang n. loudspeaker,
amplifier เครื่องขยายเสียง

f)khreuang r)khian n. stationery, writing supplies
เครื่องเขียน

f)khreuang-r)mai n. badge, mark, sign เครื่องหมาย

f)khreuang-meu n. tools เครื่องมือ

f)khreuang phim!-l)deet n. typewriter เครื่องพิมพ์ดีด

f)khreuang plaeng fai! (elect.) transformer

f)khreuang l)prap ah-l)kat n. air-conditioner
เครื่องปรับอากาศ

f)khreuang reuan n. furniture เครื่องเรือน

f)khreuang h)rot!-yon!. n. vehicle engine เครื่อง
รถยนต์

f)khreuang l)soop h)nam! n. water pump เครื่องสูบน้ำ

f)khreuang l)taeng kai n. clothes and accessories
เครื่องแต่งกาย

f)khreuang tham! khwam yen n. air-conditioner
เครื่องทำความเย็น

f)khreuang yon! n. engine, motor เครื่องยนต์

f)khreuang h)yot! n. rank, insignia (worn on
uniforms) เครื่องยศ

f)khreung!, f)khreung! l)neung half, one half
ครึ่ง, ครึ่งหนึ่ง

khrong-kan n. project, program โครงการ

khroo n. teacher ครู

l)khroo!-l)khra! adj. rough, bumpy ขรุขระ

h)khrop! adj. complete, in full amount ครบ

khrua n. kitchen ครัว

khuan ought to, should ควร

l)khuan v. scratch, claw (with nails or claws)
ข่วน

l)khuap n. year (for ages of small children)
ขวบ

f)khuap-khoom! v. supervise, control ควบคุม

l)khuat n. bottle ขวด

khuhy have ever (done something, gone somewhere, in the past) เคย

khuhy chin!   accustomed to, used to something
เคยชิน

r)khwa, r)khwa meu   right-hand side, on the
right   ขวา, ขวามือ

r)khwaen v. hang up   แขวน

khwai n. water buffalo   ควาย

khwam   n.   (prefix used to form abstract &
other nouns, as in khwam h)rak! = love) ความ

f)khwam! turn over, overturn, upside down คว่ำ

khwam cham!-nan   n. skill (from experience)
ความชำนาญ

khwam f)chuay-r)leua   n. aid, assistance, help
ความช่วยเหลือ

khwam dan! n. pressure   ความดัน

khwam dan! lo-l)hit! n. blood pressure ความดันโลหิต

khwam r)hen n. opinion   ความเห็น

khwam r)hew! n. hunger, appetite   ความหิว

khwam jing! n. truth, the truth   ความจริง

khwam h)khit! n. thought, idea   ความคิด

khwam h)lap! n. secrets, classified information
ความลับ

khwam-r)mai n. meaning, significance ความหมาย

khwam h)rak! n. love   ความรัก

khwam h)rawn n. heat, temperature ความร้อน

khwam reh-oh! n. speed ความเร็ว

khwam h)roo n. knowledge ความรู้

khwam l)sa!-l)duak n. convenience, ease ความสะดวก

khwam r)sa-f)mat n. ability, competence ความ
สามารถ

khwam r)sam!-l)ret! n. success ความสำเร็จ

khwam l)sa!-l)ngop! n. peace ความสงบ

khwam l)sook! n. happiness ความสุข

khwam f)yoong!-f)yak n. trouble, difficulty ความ
ยุ่งยาก

khwan! n. smoke ควัน

r)khwan n. axe ขวาน

f)khwang v. throw ขว้าง

r)khwang v. lie across, obstruct ขวาง

kin! v. eat, drink, consume, take (medicine) กิน

kin! f)khao eat, have a meal กินข้าว

kin! f)lao! drink alcoholic beverages กินเหล้า

kin! h)liang (colloq.) dinner party กินเลี้ยง

h)kip! r)phom! n. hairpin กิ๊บผม

l)kit!-l)ja!-kam! n. special activities, extra-cur-
ricular activities กิจกรรม

l)kit!-l)ja!-kan n. business activities กิจการ

l)kit! h)thoo!-h)ra! n. affairs, business (in general) กิจธุระ

f)kla adj. bold, brave กล้า

f)klaeng v. make a pretence, do on purpose, do deliberately แกล้ง

f)kla-r)han adj. brave, courageous กล้าหาญ

klai! distant, far away ไกล

f)klai!, f)klai! f)klai! ŋear, nearby ใกล้, ใกล้ ๆ

klai pen! v. become กลายเป็น

l)klan! v. refine, distill กลั่น

klaŋ center, centre, middle, neutral กลาง

klaŋ f)jaeng outdoors, in the open air กลางแจ้ง

klaŋ kheun at night, nighttime กลางคืน

klaŋ wan! daytime, in the daytime กลางวัน

l)klao v. state, say, tell กล่าว

l)klao r)ha (v., leg.) accuse, make an accusation กล่าวหา

l)klao r)theung! v. mention, refer to กล่าวถึง

l)klap! backwards, turn around, turn upside down กลับ

l)klap!, l)klap! pai! v. go back, return, return home (after day's work or school), turn back กลับ, กลับไป

l)klap! f)ban return home, go back home กลับบ้าน

l)klap! jai! change one's mind กลับใจ

l)klap! ma come back กลับมา

l)klap! pai! go back กลับไป

l)klap! h)rot! turn a car around กลับรถ

l)klap! tua reform oneself, turn over a new leaf กลับตัว

klawn n. bolt กลอน

f)klawng n. pipe (for smoking) กล้อง

l)klawng n. box (small), case, carton กล่อง

f)klawng l)thai f)roop n. camera กล้องถ่ายรูป

kleua n. salt เกลือ

kleun v. swallow กลืน

l)kliat, l)kliat chang! v. hate เกลียด, เกลียดชัง

l)klin! n. smell, odor, scent กลิ่น

klom! adj. round, circular กลม

f)kloom!, f)kloom! jai! adj. worried, depressed กลุ้ม, กลุ้มใจ

klua v. fear, be afraid of กลัว

f)klua khaw v. gargle กลั้วคอ

kluang adj. hollow กลวง

f)kluay, f)kluay r)hawm n. bananas กล้วย, กล้วยหอม

f)kluay h)mai! n. orchid plants กล้วยไม้

ko-l)hok! v., n. lie, tell a lie โกหก

f)kom! v. bend over, stoop down ก้ม

kon, kon l)nuat v. shave (beard) โกน, โกนหนวด

f)kon! n. bottom, end, rectum ก้น

kong v. cheat โกง

koo I, me (very coarse speech, may be offensive) กู

f)koo, f)koo nguhn borrow, borrow money กู้, กู้เงิน

koo-l)lap n. rose กุหลาบ

koom-pha, koom-pha-phan February กุมภา, กุมภาพันธ์

f)koong! n. lobster, prawn, shrimp กุ้ง

koon!-jae n. key, hand wrench กุญแจ

l)kot! v. press, mash กด

l)kot ai-ya-kan l)seuk! n. martial law กฎอัยการศึก

l)kot! l)khee v. oppress กดขี่

l)kot!-r)mai n. law กฎหมาย

l)kra!-l)bawk l)soop n. cylinder (of engine) กระบอกสูบ

l)kra!-f)beuang n. tiles (roof, floor, etc.) กระเบื้อง

l)kra!-dai! n. stairway, ladder กระไ

l)kra!-dan n. board (of wood), plank   กระดาน

l)kra!-dan dam! n. blackboard   กระดานดำ

l)kra!-l)dat n. paper   กระดาษ

l)kra!-l)dat cham!-h)ra!   n. toilet tissue (paper)
กระดาษชำระ

l)kra!-l)dat h)chet! meu n. paper towels   กระดาษ
เช็ดมือ

l)kra!-den! v. bounce, splash   กระเด็น

l)kra!-ding! n. bell, buzzer   กระดิ่ง

l)kra!-l)dook n. bone   กระดูก

l)kra!-doom! n. button   กระดุม

l)kra!-l)dot v. jump, leap   กระโดด

l)kra!-r)hai h)nam! thirsty (for water)   กระหายน้ำ

l)kra!-jai v. scatter, disperse   กระจาย

l)kra!-jai r)siang v. broadcast (radio)   กระจายเสียง

l)kra!-l)jok! n. mirror, window-pane, sheet of
glass   กระจก

l)kra!-l)jok! f)na n. windshield (of a car)   กระจก
หน้า

l)kra!-jom n. tent   กระโจม

l)kra!-r)pao! n. pocket, purse, handbag, suitcase;
ticket-seller (boy or girl) on busses   กระเป๋า

l)kra!·r)pao! duhn thang n. suitcase, luggage
กระเป๋าเดินทาง

l)kra!·r)pao! l)ck-l)ka!·r)san n. briefcase, attache
case กระเป๋าเอกสาร

l)kra!-r)pawng n. can, tin, tincan กระป๋อง

l)kra!-h)phaw! ah-r)han n. stomach กระเพาะอาหาร

l)kra!-prong n. skirt, dress (for females) กระโปรง

l)kra!-prong h)thai h)rot! n. trunk (of an auto)
กระโปรงท้ายรถ

l)kra!-f)rawk n. squirrel กระรอก

l)kra!·r)sae fai!-h)fa n. electric current กระแส
ไฟฟ้า

l)kra!·r)sae h)nam! n. water current กระแสน้ำ

l)kra!-l)sawp n. gunnysack กระสอบ

l)kra!-h)sip! v. whisper กระซิบ

l)kra!·r)soon!, l)kra!·r)seon! peun n. bullet, ammunition กระสุน, กระสุนปืน

l)kra!-suang n. govt. ministry กระทรวง

l)kra!·l)tai n. animal กระต่าย

l)kra!-h)tha! n. frying-pan, skillet กระทะ

l)kra!-than! r)han! sudden, suddenly กระทันหัน

l)kra!-thiam n. garlic กระเทียม

l)kra!-r)thon n. cuspidor, night-jar, urinary pan กระโถน

l)kra!-l)tik!, l)kra!-l)tik h)nam! n. canteen, thermos bottle กระติก, กระติกน้ำ

krawng v. strain, filter กรอง

l)krawp adj. crisp (in taste) กรอบ

kreng jai! be considerate, have deference for someone else เกรงใจ

l)kring! n. bell, buzzer กริ่ง

krom! n. dept. (subdiv. of a govt. ministry) กรม

krom!, krom! h)tha!-r)han n. (mil.) regiment กรม, กรมทหาร

krom! [l)lao!] na-wi-ka-yo-thin n. (mil.). Marines กรม (เหล่า) นาวิกโยธิน

kron! v. snore กรน

krong! n. cage กรง

kroong! n. city กรุง

kroong! f)thep, kroong! f)thep h)ma!-r)ha h)na!-khawn Bangkok, Bangkok Metropolis กรุงเทพฯ, กรุงเทพมหานคร

l)krot adj. angry, bitter โกรธ

r)kuay-r)teeo n. Chinese noodles ก๋วยเตี๋ยว

kuhn, kuhn pai! too much, over (more than enough) เกิน, เกินไป

l)kuht born, to be born เกิด

l)kuht f)kheun! v. happen เกิดขึ้น

l)kwa more, than, more than, over [used to show comparative form of adj. and adv., as in "r)suay l)kwa" = prettier] กว่า

f)kwang adj. broad, wide กว้าง

f)kwang-r)khwang adj. widespread, (colloq., for people) well-known, popular กว้างขวาง

kwang-f)toong! Canton, Cantonese กวางตุ้ง

l)kwat v. sweep กวาด

kwian n. oxcart เกวียน

la v. say farewell, take leave or be absent from work ลา

h)la! etc., and so on ฯลฯ

h)la! per [as in "wan h)la! r)sam h)khrang!" = 3 times per day] ละ

r)la n. yard (3 feet) หลา

fa!-ai adj. ashamed ละอาย

la l)awk v. resign (from a position etc.) ลาออก

h)lae!, h)lae! f)kaw!, h)laeo f)kaw and, and then (connecting words) และ, และก็, แล้วก็

h)laek h)chek! cash a check (cheque) แลกเช็ค

h)laek l)plian v. exchange แลกเปลี่ยน

r)laem n. cape (of land); adj. sharp-pointed แหลม

f)laen v. (for boats and vehicles) run, move along, sail along แล่น

h)laeng dry, lacking rain, arid แล้ง

h)laeo already (also used to show a completed action) แล้ว

h)laeo f)kaw! and then, after that แล้วก็

h)laeo l)tae as you like, it's up to you (her, him) แล้วแต่

f)lai! v chase away ไล่

l)lai! n. shoulder ไหล่

r)lai! v. flow, run (as water) ไหล

r)lai adj. many หลาย

h)la!-l)iat adj. detailed, fine, delicate ละเอียด

f)lai! l)awk discharge from employment, "fire" ไล่ออก

lai meu n. handwriting ลายมือ

lai meu, lai meu phim! n. fingerprints ลายมือ, ลายมือพิมพ์

lai sen! n. signature ลายเซ็น

f)lak v. pull, drag, haul, tow ลาก

l)lak! n. post or stake (used as a marker), fundamentals of something หลัก

la l)kawn farewell, goodbye for now ลาก่อน

la-khawn n. play, drama ละคร

la-khawn l)sat! n. circus ละครสัตว์

lak-sa-na! n. features, characteristics ลักษณะ

l)lak! h)sap! (fin.) securities หลักทรัพย์

l)lak!-l)soot (educ.) curriculm, course หลักสูตร

f)lak!-r)than (leg.) proof, evidence หลักฐาน

la!-lai v. dissolve, melt ละลาย

lam! [classifier noun for ships and long round objects, as "reua r)sawng lam!" = 2 ships] ลำ

f)lam n. interpreter ล่าม

lam!-l)bak troublesome, difficult ลำบาก

lam!-l)dap! in order, orderly arrangement by precedence ลำดับ

lam!-khaw n. throat (of body) ลำคอ

lam!-f)sai! n. bowels, intestines ลำไส้

la!-muh talk in one's sleep ละเมอ

h)lan (h)lan l)neung!. l)neung! h)lan] million, one million ล้าน (ล้านหนึ่ง, หนึ่งล้าน)

r)lan grandchild, nephew, niece หลาน

r)lan chai grandson, nephew หลานชาย

lang n. large box, crate ลัง

h)lang v. wash (with water, for things other than hair or clothes) ล้าง

r)lang! n. back (of body); [classifier for houses, as in "f)ban 2)sawng r)lang! = 2 houses] หลัง

h)lang cham wash the dishes ล้างชาม

h)lang fim develop film (photography) ล้างฟิล์ม

r)lang! l)jak [h)nan!] after, afterwards หลังจาก(นั้น)

lang!-ka Ceylon, Sri Lanka ลังกา

r)lang!-kha n. roof หลังคา

r)lan r)sao granddaughter, niece หลานสาว

lao Laos, Laotian ลาว

f)lao! liquor, whiskey, alcoholic beverages เหล้า

f)lao!, f)lao! f)hai! fang! v. tell, narrate, relate เล่า, เล่าให้ฟัง

h)lao! n. pen (for pigs and fowl) เล้า

l)lao! n. branch (of mil. service), group of things เหล่า

r)lao! din!-r)saw sharpen a pencil เหลาดินสอ

h)lap! secret, classified information ลับ

l)lap! sleep, asleep หลับ

h)lap! f)meet sharpen a knife ลับมีด

l)lap! ta close the eyes หลับตา

l)la l)sat! v. hunt (animals) ล่าสัตว์

h)la! h)thing! v. desert, abandon, neglect ละทิ้ง

h)law, h)law f)len v. tease, mock, make fun of
ล้อ, ล้อเล่น

h)law n. wheel ล้อ

l)law adj. handsome (said of men) หล่อ

f)lawk v. copy (usually by hand) ลอก

f)lawk l)baep, lian l)baep v. copy, imitate ลอกแบบ,
เลียนแบบ

h)lawm v. surround ล้อม

lawng, lawng doo v. try out, test ลอง, ลองดู

f)lawp jom-tee v. ambush ลอบโจมตี

l)lawt n. tube หลอด

l)lawt, l)lawt l)kra!-l)dat, l)lawt l)doot! n. drinking
straw, soda straw หลอด, หลอดกระดาษ, หลอดดูด

l)lawt fai! n. light bulb หลอดไฟ

l)lawt wit-tha-yoo! n. radio tube, electron tube
หลอดวิทยุ

lawy v. float (on water, in air etc.) ลอย

lawy l)kra!-thong! the Loy' Krathong Festival
ลอยกระทง

l)leek v. get out of the way, dodge, avoid, evade
หลีก

l)leek f)liang v. avoid, evade หลีกเลี่ยง

l)leek thang v. move out of the way, make way
หลีกทาง

h)leeo v. turn (to left or right) เลี้ยว

h)leeo r)khwa turn right เลี้ยวขวา

h)leeo h)sai turn left เลี้ยวซ้าย

h)leet!, h)lit! liter, litre (1,000 c.c.) ลิตร

h)lek! adj. little, small เล็ก

l)lek! n. iron (the metal) เหล็ก

le-kha-noo-kan n secretary (office) เลขานุการ

le-kha-thi-kan n. secretary-general เลขาธิการ

f)lek-kha-nit! n. arithmetic เลขคณิต

l)lek! f)kla n. steel (the metal) เหล็กกล้า

h)lek! h)nawy a little bit, not much เล็กน้อย

f)lek f)thee number (of something or ordinal
number) เลขที่

lem! v. trim (as the hair) เล็ม

f)lem n. book, volume [classifier noun for
books, knives, and some other objects, as in
"r)nang-r)seu l)paet f)lem = 8 books] เล่ม

f)len v. play เล่น

f)len bo-f)ling! v. bowl (the sport) เล่นโบว์ลิ่ง

leng! v. aim (a weapon), take aim เล็ง

f)len kan pha!-nan! v. gamble เล่นการพนัน

f)len kon! v. do tricks and stunts, perform
magic acts เล่นกล

f)len la-khawn v. give dramatic performances
เล่นละคร

f)len f)phai! play cards เล่นไพ่

leo (leh-o), lee sam adj. bad (morally), evil,
corrupted เลว, เลวทราม

h)lepl-meu n. fingernails เล็บมือ

h)lepl-h)thaol n. toenails เล็บเท้า

r)leua v. be remaining, left over, have left เหลือ

f)leuak, f)leuak ao! v. choose, select เลือก, เลือกเอา

f)leuak f)tang! v. elect เลือกตั้ง

f)leuan v. move, move along, slide เลื่อน

f)leuan, f)leuan pai! v. postpone เลื่อน, เลื่อนไป

f)leuan h)chan!, f)leuan f)khin!, f)leuan f)kheun!
v. promote or be promoted in rank or position
เลื่อนชั้น, เลื่อนขั้น, เลื่อนขึ้น

r)leuang [r)see r)leuang] yellow (color) เหลือง
(สีเหลือง)

f)leuat n. blood เลือด

f)leuat l)awk v. bleed เลือดออก

f)leuay, f)leuay h)mai! v. saw, saw wood; n. saw,
wood saw เลื่อย, เลื่อยไม้

f)leuay l)lek! v. saw metal; n. metal saw, hack-saw เลื่อยเหล็ก

h)leuk! adj. deep ลึก

h)leuk!-h)lap! adj. mysterious ลึกลับ

leum. leum pai!, leum r)sia v. forget ลืม, ลืมไป, ลืมเสีย

leum ta open the eyes ลืมตา

leum....h)thing! h)wai! accidentally leave some-thing somewhere (because of forgetfulness) ลืม....ทิ้งไว้

f)leun v., adj. skid, slip, slide, slippery ลื่น

lia v. lick (with tongue) เลีย

lian l)baep v. imitate เลียนแบบ

h)liang v. feed an animal, raise an animal, raise or take care of a child, treat someone to a meal เลี้ยง

h)liang l)dek! take care of a baby or a child (as a mother, babysitter, baby ayah etc.) เลี้ยงเด็ก

lift n. lift, elevator ลิฟท์

li!-keh n. Thai musical folk drama ลิเก

h)lin! n. tongue (of body, machine etc.) ลิ้น

h)lin!-h)chak! n. drawer (of cabinet, desk etc.) ลิ้นชัก

ling! n. monkey ลิง

h)lit!, h)leet! n. litre ลิตร

r)lo [r)lo l)neung', l)neung! r)lo] dozen, a dozen,
   one dozen โหล (โหลหนึ่ง, หนึ่งโหล)

lo-l)ha! n. metal (in general) โลหะ

lo-l)hit! n. blood โลหิต

lo-l)hit! jang n. anemia โลหิตจาง

f)lok n. world, the earth โลก

lom! n. wind, breeze ลม

h)lom! v. fall down (physically, accidentally)
   ล้ม

lom! r)hai-jai! n. breath (of body) ลมหายใจ

h)lom! la!-lai bankrupt, go bankrupt ล้มละลาย

lom! h)phat! the wind is blowing, blowing wind
   ลมพัด

lom! pha-h)yoo! n. windstorm ลมพายุ

long! v. come down, descend, get down, get off,
   land (as an airplane) ลง

r)long! v. become infatuated, be deceived or
   beguiled หลง

long! f)cheu sign one's name ลงชื่อ

r)long! f)cheua be deceived หลงเชื่อ

long! kha-naen v. vote (with ballot) ลงคะแนน

---

long! meu v. begin to do something (as a task) ลงมือ

long! f)paeng v. starch, use starch (in washing clothes) ลงแป้ง

r)long! h)rak! v. fall in love หลงรัก

long! tha-bian v. register ลงทะเบียน

r)long! thang v. be lost, get lost, lose one's way หลงทาง

long! thoon! invest, make investments ลงทุน

long! wan!-f)thee dated, put down the date, date something ลงวันที่

long! wan!-f)thee f)luang-f)na v. postdate ลงวันที่ ล่วงหน้า

f)look n. berry, fruit, round object [classifier noun for fruit, mountains, balls, certain round or small objects, etc., as in f)som! r)sawng f)look = 2 oranges] ลูก

f)look n. child (son or daughter); offspring of animals ลูก

h)look!, h)look! f)kheun! v. arise, get up ลุก, ลุกขึ้น

f)look bawn n. ball (plaything) ลูกบอล

f)look boon!-tham! n. adopted child ลูกบุญธรรม

f)look chai n. son ลูกชาย

f)look l)faet n. twins (children) ลูกแฝด

f)look kaml-h)phra n. orphan ลูกกำพร้า

h)look! f)kheun! v. get up, arise ลูกขึ้น

f)look h)khit! n abacus ลูกคิด

f)look r)khuhy son-in-law ลูกเขย

f)look koon!-jae n. key ลูกกุญแจ

f)look l)kra!-r)soon! n. cartridge, unfired bullet
ลูกกระสุน

f)look r)lan n. one's descendants (children,
grandchildren etc.) ลูกหลาน

f)look h)liang n. stepchild ลูกเลี้ยง

f)look r)ma n. puppy ลูกหมา

f)look maeo n. kitten ลูกแมว

f)look r)men! n. mothballs ลูกเหม็น

f)look f)nee n. debtor ลูกหนี้

f)look peun n. bullet ลูกปืน

f)look f)phee f)look h)nawng n. cousins ลูกพี่ลูกน้อง

f)look l)pong n. balloon ลูกโป่ง

f)look h)ra!-l)buht n. bomb ลูกระเบิด

f)look f)rawk n. pulley ลูกรอก

f)look r)sao n. daughter ลูกสาว

f)look r)seua n. tiger cub, Boy Scout (Thailand)
ลูกเสือ

f)look wua n. calf ลูกวัว

r)loom! n. hole (in ground), hole of a golf course หลุม

r)loom! r)fang! l)sop! n. grave หลุมฝังศพ

loong! n. uncle (elder brother of father or mother) ลุง

l)loot!, l)loot! l)awk v. slip off, become detached, slip out, fall off หลุด, หลุดออก

h)lop!, h)lop! l)awk v. erase, subtract ลบ ลบออก

l)lop! v. dodge, move out of way หลบ

h)lot!, h)lot! long! v. decrease, reduce ลด, ลดลง

h)lot! long!, h)lot! h)nawy long! v. lessen ลดลง, ลดน้อยลง

h)lot! ra-kha reduce prices, have a sale ลดราคา

r)luam adj. loose, not snug หลวม

luang v. deceive ลวง

r)luang adj. royal, state (of state or govt.), legal or main one [as in "mia r)luang" = first wife or legal wife, in contrast to "mia h)nawy" = minor wife] หลวง

h)luang l)kra!-r)pao! pick someone's pocket ล้วงกระเป๋า

f)luang f)na in advance, ahead of time ล่วงหน้า

f)luat n. wire ลวด

f)luat r)nam n. barbed-wire ลวดหนาม

f)luhk v., adj. stop, quit, over, finished เลิก

f)luhk kan! v. divorce, separate (stop living together) เลิกกัน

luhy (adj., adv., v.) at all, beyond, past, on past a place; and then, so then, consequently (also used for emphasis after verbs and phrases, sometimes with no exact meaning that can be translated) เลย

ma v. come [also shows action toward location of speaker, when used with other verbs, as in "f)khao! ma" = come in, enter; also shows a "time-sense" idea of "from the past until the present", when used with some verbs, adjectives, and adverbs, as in "l)sa!-r)muh ma" = always, up to now] มา

h)ma n. horse ม้า

r)ma n. dog หมา

f)mae n. mother แม่

h)mae, h)mae f)wa even, even if, even so แม้, แม้ว่า

f)mae h)kha n. woman vendor แม่ค้า

f)mae-r)khong Mekong River and name of popular brand of Thai whiskey แม่โขง

f)mae khrua n. cook (female) แม่ครัว

f)mae koon!-jae n. lock แม่กุญแจ

f)mae h)liang n. stepmother แม่เลี้ยง

f)mae h)mot! n. witch แม่มด

f)mae-h)nam! n. river แม่น้ำ

maeng-da n. (sl.) pimp, pander แมงดา

maeng, h)mal-laeng n. insect, bug แมง, แมลง

maeng-ka-phroon n. jellyfish แมงกะพรุน

maeng moom!, n. spider แมงมุม

maeng l)pawng n. scorpion แมงป่อง

maeng [h)mal-laeng] l)sap n. cockroach แมง (แมลง) สาบ

maeng [h)mal-laeng] wan! n. fly (insect) แมง (แมลง) วัน

maeo n. cat แมว

f)mae r)phua, f)mae r)sa-mee n. mother-in-law (mother of husband) แม่ผัว, แม่สามี

f)mae-raeng n. jack (as a car-jack) แม่แรง

f)mae h)thap! (mil., colloq.) high military commander แม่ทัพ

f)mae yai n. mother-in-law (maternal) แม่ยาย

h)ma!-r)ha l)sa!-l)moot! n. ocean   มหาสมุทร

h)ma!-r)ha wit!-tha!-ya-lai! n. university มหาวิทยาลัย

f)mai! no, not ไม่

f)mai! v.i. burn ไหม้

f)mai [f)mae f)mai] n. widow หม้าย (แม่หม้าย);
 f)phaw f)mai! widower พ่อหม้าย

h)mai! n. wood, stick ไม้

l)mai! adj. new ใหม่

r)mai! (used to show interrogation at end of
 word or sentence) ไหม

r)mai! [f)pha r)mai!] silk, silk cloth ไหม

f)mai! ao! not to want, not to agree, not to
 take, not to accept, refuse ไม่เอา

h)mai! l)at! n. plywood ไม้อัด

h)mai! ban!-h)that! n. ruler (for measuring)
 ไม้บรรทัด

f)mai! h)cha [nai! f)mai! h)cha] soon, shortly, in
 the near future ไม่ช้า (ในไม่ช้า)

f)mai! f)chai! no, that's not right; not (before
 a noun or pronoun) ไม่ใช่

f)mai! f)dai! cannot (prohibition or refusal to
 grant permission); cannot (unable to do,
 cannot be done) ไม่ได้

f)mai! dee not good, bad ไม่ดี

f)mai! jam!-pen! not necessary ไม่จำเป็น

h)mai! f)jim! fan! n. toothpick ไม้จิ้มฟัน

h)mai! kang-r)khehn n. cross (for Christians) ไม้กางเขน

f)mai! khae (colloq.) not to care, be impassive, be unconcerned ไม่แคร์

f)mai! f)khawy not very, hardly, not quite ไม่ค่อย

h)mai! l)kheet (fail) n. matches (for lighting) ไม้ขีด (ไฟ)

f)mai! khuhy never, not ever, never have ไม่เคย

h)mai! r)khwaen f)seua n. coat-hanger, clothes-hanger ไม้แขวนเสื้อ

r)mai khwam, r)mai khwam f)wa v. mean, have a certain meaning, it or that means.... หมายความ, หมายความว่า

h)mai l)kra!-dan n. board (of wood) ไม้กระดาน

h)mai l)kwat n. broom (for sweeping) ไม้กวาด

r)mai f)lek number (in general) หมายเลข

r)mai f)lek tho-ra-sap! (buh tho-ra-sap!) telephone number หมายเลขโทรศัพท์ (เบอร์โทรศัพท์)

f)mai! mee don't have, there is none, there aren't any ไม่มี

f)mai! mee a-rai nothing, there's nothing, nothing wrong ไม่เนอะไร

f)mai! mee nguhn "broke", no money ไม่มีเงิน

f)mai! mee l)reuang There is no trouble (no problem etc.) ไม่มีเรื่อง

f)mai! mee l)sai-tang "broke", without money ไม่มีสตางค์

f)mai! nan not a long time ไม่นาน

f)mai! pen!-rai! never mind, that's all right, you're welcome (in response to "thank you"), it's nothing, don't mention it ไม่เป็นไร

h)mai!-l)phai! n. bamboo ไม้ไผ่

f)mai! h)roo not to know, don't know ไม่รู้

f)mai! h)roo f)reuang not to know about something, be completely ignorant of something or about what's going on, not understand at all ไม่รู้เรื่อง

f)mai! l)sai-l)bai not well, sick, ill ไม่สบาย

h)mai! l)sak! n. teak, teakwood ไม้สัก

f)mai! f)sap not to know (something) ไม่ทราบ

f)mai! f)tawng not necessary ไม่ต้อง

f)mai! thai-l)nat! awkward, not convenient to do ไม่ถนัด

h)mai! h)thao! n. walking-stick ไม้เท้า

f)mai!....f)thao!-rai! not so.... ไม่....เท่าไร

h)mai! r)thoo f)ban n. mop (for housecleaning) ไม้ถูบ้าน

mai!-tree friendly, friendship ไมตรี

f)mai! l)yoo absent, not in (a place), not present ไม่อยู่

f)mak, f)mak f)mak much, very much, many, very many มาก, มาก ๆ

l)mak n. betel-nut หมาก

l)mak l)fa!-l)rang! n. chewing-gum หมากฝรั่ง

h)ma!-r)kheua-f)thet n. tomato มะเขือเทศ

f)mak f)kheun! more, become more, increase มากขึ้น

f)mak l)kwa more (than), more than...., rather, preferable มากกว่า

f)mak-mai very much, very many มากมาย

f)mak pai!, f)mak kuhn pai! too much มากไป, มาก เกินไป

f)mak phiang phaw ample, adequate, just enough มากเพียงพอ

l)mak-h)rook! chess (the game) หมากรุก

h)ma!-laeng (maeng) n. insect, bug แมลง (แมง)

h)ma!-laeng paw n. dragonfly แมลงปอ

ma!-la!-kaw n. papaya มะละกอ

ma!-la-ria [f)khai! l)jap!-l)san!] n. malaria มาลาเรีย (ไข้จับสั่น)

ma!-la-yoo Malay, Malaya, Malayan มลายู

ma-le-sia Malaysia, Malaysian มาเลเซีย

ma!-h)let! [h)met!] n. seed เมล็ด (เม็ด)

h)mam n. spleen ม้าม

ma!-f)muang n. mango มะม่วง

man! pron it (sometimes "he, she, him, her", but should be used cautiously) มัน

man! (pen! man!) shiny, oily, good taste, (sl.) enjoyable มัน (เป็นมัน)

f)man!, f)man! h)laeo become engaged, be engaged (to be married) หมั้น, หมั้นแล้ว

f)man [f)pha f)man!] n. curtain ม่าน (ผ้าม่าน)

h)ma f)nang! n. bench, stool ม้านั่ง

ma!-nao n. lemon, lime มะนาว

man-da [f)mae] n. mother มารดา (แม่)

man! l)fa!-l)rang! n. potato (Irish potato) มันฝรั่ง

mang!-h)khoot! mangosteen (a Thai fruit) มังคุด

f)man!-khong! adj. stable, solid มั่นคง

l)man! f)sai! be disgusted, disgusting มันไส้

man! f)thet n. sweet potato มันเทศ

mao! adj. drunk, intoxicated, motion-sick เมา

mao! f)khleun adj. seasick เมาคลื่น

mao! f)khreuang-bin! adj. airsick เมาเครื่องบิน

mao! h)rot! adj. carsick เมารถ

h)ma!-h)phrao n. coconut มะพร้าว

h)ma!-reng! n. cancer มะเร็ง

h)ma!-reun-h)nee day after tomorrow มะรืนนี้

l)mat! n. flea หมัด

ma r)theung! v. arrive มาถึง

f)maw n. pot หม้อ

r)maw n. medical doctor หมอ

r)maw doo n. fortune-teller หมอดู

f)maw-fai! n. large battery หม้อไฟ

f)maw fan! n. dentist หมอฟัน

l)mawk n. fog, mist หมอก

r)mawn n. pillow หมอน

mawng, mawng doo v. look at มอง, มองดู

mawng, mawng r)hen! v. look at (and see) มอง, มองเห็น

mawng doo v. watch closely มองดู

mawng r)ha v. look for มองหา

f)mawp v. entrust, assign, delegate, deliver มอบ

f)maw plaeng-fai! (elect.) transformer หม้อแปลงไฟ

f)mawp tua turn oneself in, surrender to authorities (as an outlaw, terrorist etc.) มอบตัว

r)maw r)sawn sat-sa-na n. missionary หมอสอนศาสนา

l)maw!-r)som! adj. suitable, appropriate เหมาะสม

f)mawt n. mothlike insects มอด, มอต

r)maw tam!-yae n. midwife (old-fashioned) หมอ
ตำแย

r)maw tham! fan! n. dentist หมอทำฟัน

r)maw l)thenan n. quack doctor, illegal doctor
หมอเถื่อน

mee have, there is, there are มี

r)mee n. bear หมี

mee-na-khom! March มีนาคม

f)meet [or f)meed] n. knife มีด

mee h)thawng, mee khan! adj. pregnant มีท้อง,
มีครรภ์

f)meet kon n. razor มีดโกน

f)mek n. cloud เมฆ

r)men! v. smell (bad smell) เหม็น

r)men! l)boot v. stink (very bad smell) เหม็นบูด

me-r)sa-yon! April เมษายน

h)met! n. seed, pill, gem button [also classifier noun for such items as the foregoing, as in "l)kra!-doom! r)sawng h)met! = 2 buttons] เม็ด

f)met n. metre เมตร

meu n. hand มือ

f)meua when, ago, at a certain time; since, as เมื่อ

f)meua l)kawn formerly เมื่อก่อน

f)meua f)kee h)nee just a moment ago เมื่อกี้นี้

f)meua kheun last night เมื่อคืน

f)meua....ma h)laeo ....ago เมื่อ....มาแล้ว

r)meuan v. look like, be the same or similar เหมือน

meuang n. land, country, town เมือง

meuang r)luang n. capital (city) เมืองหลวง

r)meuang f)rae n. mine (for mining) เหมืองแร่

r)meuang f)rae dee-l)book! tin mine เหมืองแร่ดีบุก

r)meuan kan! alike, the same, likewise เหมือนกัน

f)meua-rail? when เมื่อไร

r)meua-rail! f)kaw! f)dai! at any time, any time will do เมื่อไรก็ได้

f)meua reh-o! reh-o! h)nee recently เมื่อเร็วๆนี้

f)meua l)ta!-f)kee just now, just a moment ago เมื่อตะกี้

f)meua wan yesterday เมื่อวาน

f)meuay adj. stiff, sore, tired เมื่อย

l)meuk! n. ink หมึก

l)meun [l)neung! l)meun, l)meun l)neung!] ten thousand (10,000) หมื่น, (หนึ่งหมื่น, หมื่นหนึ่ง)

f)meut adj. dark (no light) มืด

mia n. wife เมีย

mia r)luang legal wife, major wife (or first legal wife) เมียหลวง

mia h)nawy minor wife, mistress เมียน้อย

mi!-thoo!-na-yon! June มิถุนายน

mo-r)ho angry (suddenly) โมโห

mok-ka-ra-khom January มกราคม

mong o'clock (for telling time) โมง

mon!-rat!, mon!-lal-rat! n state (of USA) มลรัฐ

l)moo, l)moo tha!-r)han (mil.) squad หมู่, หมู่ทหาร

r)moo n. pork, pig หมู

l)moo-f)ban n. village (subdiv. of tambon) หมู่บ้าน

r)moo haem n. ham หมูแฮม

r)moo khem!, r)moo beh-khawa n. bacon หมูเค็ม, หมูเบคอน

f)moo-f)lee n. blinds (venetian, bamboo) มู่ลี่

moom! n. corner, angle มุม

moom! l)chak right angle (90˚) มุมฉาก

r)moon!, r)moon! wian v. turn, rotate, go around, circulate (as money) หมุน, หมุนเวียน

h)moong! n. mosquito-net มุ้ง

h)moong!-f)luat n. window-screens มุ้งลวด

r)moon! r)mai-f)lek (buh) tho-ra-sap! dial a telephone number หมุนหมายเลขโทรศัพท์

h)mot! n. ant มด

l)mot!, l)mot! h)laeo finished, used up, all gone หมด, หมดแล้ว

l)mot! ah-h)yoo! expired, out of date หมดอายุ

l)muak n. hat หมวก

h)muan v. roll, roll up, wind up; n. roll or reel of something [also used as classifier noun for cigarettes and certain other objects, as in "boo-l)ree r)sawng h)muan" = 2 cigarettes] ม้วน

f)muang [r)see f)muang] purple (color) ม่วง (สีม่วง)

l)muat (mil.) platoon หมวด

muay f)plam! n. wrestling มวยปล้ำ

na, f)rai!-na n. rice-field, rice-farm นา, ไร่นา

f)na, bai! f)na n. face (of a person) หน้า, ใบหน้า

f)na n. page (of book etc.), in front (of) หน้า

f)na ....able, tempting to น่า [as in "f)na h)rak!"
= lovable, "f)na pai!" = tempting to go]

f)na next....หน้า [as in "ah-h)thit! f)na" = next
week]

h)na! please (polite word used at end of requests, etc.--often not translated) นะ

h)na n. aunt, uncle (maternal, younger than
one's mother) น้า

r)na adj. thick หนา

f)na l)beua boring, tiresome น่าเบื่อ

f)na chom!-chuhy admirable, praiseworthy น่า
ชมเชย

f)na daeng blush (red-faced), turn red หน้าแดง

f)nae, f)nae jai!, f)nae nawn certain, sure, certainly แน่, แน่ใจ, แน่นอน

f)naen, f)naen f)naen tight, tightly แน่น, แน่นๆ

h)nae!-nam! v. recommend, suggest, advise
แนะนำ

h)nae!-nam!, h)nae!-nam! f)hai! h)roo-l)jak! introduce (someone to someone else) แนะนำ, แนะนำ
ให้รู้จัก

f)na r)fon! rainy season หน้าฝน

f)na r)hua-h)raw! laughable, funny น่าหัวเราะ

nai! in, on (a day of the week) ใน

nai Mister (Mr.) boss, chief, master นาย

nai, nai f)jang boss, chief, employer นาย, นายจ้าง

r)nai!? where? which? which one? ไหน

nai am-phuh nai amphoe, district officer นาย
อำเภอ

nai! ah-na-khot! in the future ในอนาคต

nai! l)dap (mil.) warrant officer นายดาบ

nai! r)luang (colloq., respectful) the King ในหลวง

nai! f)mai! h)cha soon, in the near future ในไม่ช้า

nai f)na (comr.) broker, commission agent
นายหน้า

nai! f)phaet doctor, M.D. นายแพทย์

nai! phai-r)lang! afterwards, later on ในภายหลัง

nai! phon! (mil.) general นายพล

nai! h)ral-l)wang among, during, between ใน
ระหว่าง

nai! reh-o! reh-o! h)nee soon, in the near future
ในเร็ว ๆ นี้

nai reua ship captain นายเรือ

nai tha-r)han military officer นายทหาร

nai tha-r)han ah-l)kat air-force officer นายทหาร
อากาศ

nai tha-r)han l)bok! army officer นายทหารบก

nai tha-r)han h)chan! r)san!-ya-l)bat! (mil.) commissioned officer นายทหารชั้นสัญญาบัตร

nai tha-r)han h)chan! l)pra-thuan (mil.) NCO
นายทหารชั้นประทวน

nai tha-r)han l)fai na-wi-ka-yo-thin! (mil.) marine-
corps officer นายทหารฝ่ายนาวิกโยธิน

nai tha-r)han reua (mil.) naval officer นายทหารเรือ

nai tha!-na-khan n. banker นายธนาคาร

nai! f)thee l)soot! at last, finally, in the end
ในที่สุด

nai! we-la, nai! we-la f)thee while, meanwhile
ในเวลา, ในเวลาที่

h)nak! so much, so very [much used as a prefix
to show a person who does a certain kind of
activity very much, as in "h)nak! rian" =
student, "h)nak! bin" = pilot] นัก

l)nak! adj., adv. heavy, hard [as in "tham! ngan
h)nak!" = work hard] หนัก

h)nak! bin! n. pilot (airplane) นักบิน

h)nak! don-tree n. musician นักดนตรี

aa!·khawn n. city นคร

h)nak! kan-meuang n. politician นักการเมือง

h)nak! kee-la n. athlete นักกีฬา

h)nak! r)khian, h)nak! l)pra!-phan! n. author, writer นักเขียน, นักประพันธ์

f)na l)kliat ugly, despisable น่าเกลียด

h)nak! muay n. boxer นักมวย

h)nak! h)rawng n. singer นักร้อง

h)nak! rian n. student นักเรียน

h)nak! sa!-daeng n. actor, actress นักแสดง

h)nak! l)seuk!-r)sa n. university student นักศึกษา

h)nak! l)ta!-l)lok! n. comedian, joker นักตลก

h)nak! f)thawng f)theeo n. tourist นักท่องเที่ยว

h)nak! f)thot n. prisoner, convict นักโทษ

h)nak! wi-tha-ya-l)sat n. scientist นักวิทยาศาสตร์

f)na h)laeng the dry season หน้าแล้ง

na-li-ka n. clock, watch, o'clock (for 24-hour system) นาฬิกา

na-li-ka f)khaw meu n. wristwatch นาฬิกาข้อมือ

na-li-ka l)plook n. alarm clock นาฬิกาปลุก

nam!, nam! ma, nam! pai! v. lead, bring or take someone or something somewhere นำ, นำมา, นำไป

nam n. name [usually for words and terms other than first name, which is normally "f)cheu"] นาม

r)nam n. thorn, barb หนาม

h)nam! n. water, juice, liquid น้ำ

nam l)bat! n. name-card, business card นามบัตร

h)nam! l)baw n. well water น้ำบ่อ

h)nam! cha n. tea น้ำชา

h)nam! l)deum n. drinking water น้ำดื่ม

h)nam! r)fon n. rainwater น้ำฝน

h)nam! r)hawm n. perfume น้ำหอม

h)nam! l)jeut n. fresh water (not salt water) น้ำจืด

h)nam! f)jim! mas-tad n. prepared mustard น้ำจิ้ม มาสตาด

h)nam! r)khaeng! n. ice น้ำแข็ง

h`nam! khem! n. salt water, sea water น้ำเค็ม

h)nam! l)kin! n. drinking water น้ำกิน

h)nam! l)klan! n. distilled water น้ำกลั่น

h)nam! l)krot! n. acid น้ำกรด

h)nam!-lai n. saliva, spit น้ำลาย

h)nam! h)ma!-r)kheua-f)thet n. tomato juice น้ำ
มะเขือเทศ

h)nam!-man! n. oil, gasoline, petrol, grease น้ำมัน

h)nam! h)ma!-nao n. lemonade, limeade น้ำมะนาว

h)nam!-man! h)kat n. kerosene น้ำมันก๊าด

h)nam!-man f)khreuang n. motor oil, engine oil
น้ำมันเครื่อง

h)nam!-man! r)moo n. shortening, lard น้ำมันหมู

h)nam! l)meuk! n. ink น้ำหมึก

h)nam! l)nak n. weight น้ำหนัก

h)nam! nguhn [r)see h)nam! nguhn]   dark blue
(color) น้ำเงิน (สีน้ำเงิน)

h)nam! f)pheung! n. honey น้ำผึ้ง

h)nam! r)phon!-la!-h)mai! n. fruit juice น้ำผลไม้

h)nam! h)phoo! n. fountain, natural spring น้ำพุ

h)nam! h)phrik! n. pepper sauce (a Thai acces-
sory dish at mealtime) น้ำพริก

h)nam! pla n. fish soy, fish sauce น้ำปลา

h)nam! l)pra!-pa n. city water, water supply น้ำ
ประปา

nam l)sa!-koon! n. last name, family name, surname นามสกุล

h)nam! so-da n. soda, soda water น้ำโซดา

h)nam! f)som! n. orange juice น้ำส้ม

h)nam!-ta n. tears (from the eyes) น้ำตา

h)nam!-tan n. sugar น้ำตาล

h)nam!-tan [r)see h)nam!-tan] n. brown (color) น้ำตาล (สีน้ำตาล)

h)nam!-tan daeng n. brown sugar น้ำตาลแดง

h)nam!-tan sai n. granulated sugar น้ำตาลทราย

nam! thang v. guide, lead the way นำทาง

nam! f)theeo v. guide, take around on tours นำเที่ยว

h)nam! f)thuam n., v. flood น้ำท่วม

h)nam! l)tok! n. waterfall น้ำตก

h)nam! f)tom!, h)nam! f)tom! h)laeo boiled water น้ำต้ม, น้ำต้มแล้ว

h)nam! yen! cold water, cool water น้ำเย็น

nan, nan nan a long time, for a long time นาน, นานๆ

h)nan! adj. that นั้น

f)nan! there, at that place นั่น

f)na r)nao winter, the cold season (cool season, in Thailand) หน้าหนาว

nang Mrs., married woman, woman in general นาง

f)nang! v. sit, ride (in or on a conveyance) นั่ง

r)nang! n. leather, skin, hide; (colloq.) movie, film, cinema หนัง

nang l)baep n. model (female) นางแบบ

f)nang! long! v. sit down นั่งลง

nang pha!-ya-ban n. nurse นางพยาบาล

nang r)sao miss (females 15 or over) นางสาว

r)nang! l)sat! n. leather, animal skin หนังสัตว์

r)nang!-r)seu n. book, document หนังสือ

r)nang!-r)seu duhn thang n. passport หนังสือเดินทาง

r)nang!-r)seu-phim! n. newspaper หนังสือพิมพ์

nan f)thao!-rai!? how long (in time) นานเท่าไร

f)nao! adj. rotten, spoiled, decayed เน่า

r)nao adj. cold หนาว

f)na-l)ok! n. chest (of body), breasts หน้าอก

h)nap! v. count (numerically) นับ

f)na-l)phak n. forehead หน้าผาก

h)nap!-r)theu v. respect, believe in (as a religion) นับถือ

f)na h)rak! adj. cute, lovable, lovely น่ารัก

f)na ram!-khan adj. annoying, irritating น่ารำคาญ

f)na h)rawn n. summer, the hot season หน้าร้อน

h)na!-h)rok! n. hell นรก

f)na r) sia-dai regrettable, too bad, what a pity
น่าเสียดาย

f)na r)song-r)san pitiful, unfortunate น่าสงสาร

f)na r)son!-jai! interesting น่าสนใจ

f)na-l)tang n. window หน้าต่าง

na-thee n. minute (of time) นาที

f)na-f)thee n. duty, function หน้าที่

na-wa-ah-l)kat l)ek (mil.) AF col., group capt.
นาวาอากาศเอก

na-wa ah-l)kat tho (mil.) AF lt.-col., wing cmdr.
นาวาอากาศโท

na-wa ah-l)kat tree (mil.) AF maj., sqdn. leader
นาวาอากาศตรี

na-wa l)ek (mil.) capt. (navy) นาวาเอก

na-wa-ni-yai n. novel (literature) นวนิยาย

na-wa tho (mil.) cmdr. (navy) นาวาโท

na-wa tree (mil.) lt.-cmdr. (navy) นาวาตรี

na-wee, rat-cha-na-wee n. navy, naval, Royal
Thai Navy นาวี, ราชนาวี

na-wi-ka-yo-thin (mil.) marines นาวิกโยธิน

f)nawk out, outside, (colloq.) abroad นอก

f)nawk-chan n. porch, veranda นอกชาน

f)nawk l)jak [f)wa] except, unless นอกจาก (ว่า)

f)nawk l)jak h)nan! besides, in addition นอกจากนั้น

f)nawk f)reuang beside the point, off the subject นอกเรื่อง

l)naw h)mai bamboo shoots (edible) หน่อไม้

r)nawn n. worm หนอน

nawn, nawn l)lap! v. sleep, be asleep นอน, นอนหลับ

nawn, nawn long! v. lie down นอน, นอนลง

f)nawng n. calf (of leg) น่อง

h)nawng n. younger brother, sister, friend, cousin etc. น้อง

r)nawng, r)nawng h)nam! n. marsh, swamp, lake หนอง, หนองน้ำ

h)nawng chai younger brother, male cousin, male friend etc. น้องชาย

h)nawng r)khŏoy younger brother-in-law น้องเขย

r)nawng-nai! [f)rok r)nawng-nai!] n. gonorrhea, the "clap" หนองใน (โรคหนองใน)

h)nawng r)sao younger sister, female cousin, female friend etc. น้องสาว

h)nawng l)sa!-h)phai! sister-in-law (wife of one's younger brother) น้องสะใภ้

nawn kron! v. snore นอนกรน

nawn l)lap!, nawn l)lap! l)yoo asleep, be asleep นอนหลับ, นอนหลับอยู่

h)nawy little, not much, few, minor (as in "mia h)nawy" = minor wife) น้อย

l)nawy rather, a little, somewhat หน่อย

h)nawy l)kwa less than น้อยกว่า

h)nawy f)thee l)soot! the least, the smallest amount น้อยที่สุด

h)nee adj. this นี้

f)nee here, this place นี่

f)nee, f)nee-r)sin! n. debts, indebtedness หนี้, หนี้สิน

r)nee, r)nee pai!, r)nee pai f)dai! v. escape, run away หนี, หนีไป, หนีไปได้

r)neeo adj. sticky, tough (as meat) เหนียว

nek-thai! n. necktie เน็คไท

nen n. Buddhist novice (younger than monk) เณร

l)nep! cha numb, "asleep" (part of body) เหน็บชา

h)neua n. meat, flesh, skin เนื้อ

r)neua above, over, higher, north เหนือ

f)neuang, f)neuang l)jak owing to, due to เนื่อง, เนื่องจาก

h)neua-f)thee n. area เนื้อที่

l)neuay tired, fatigued เหนื่อย

h)neuk! v. think นึก

f)neung! v. steam (in cooking) นึ่ง

l)neung! one (1), a, an หนึ่ง

h)new!, h)new! h)foot! n. inch (measurement) นิ้ว, นิ้วฟุต

h)new!, h)new! meu n. finger นิ้ว, นิ้วมือ

h)new! h)thao! n. toe นิ้วเท้า

nga, nga h)chang n. ivory งา, งาช้าง

f)ngai adj. easy ง่าย

ngam adj. beautiful งาม

ngan n. work, job, ceremony, party งาน

ngan l)sop! n. cremation ceremony งานศพ

ngao! n. shadow เงา

ngaw v. bend, fold, curl งอ

l)ngeua n. perspiration, sweat เหงื่อ

l)ngeua l)awk v. perspire, sweat เหงื่อออก

l)ngeuak n. gums (of mouth) เหงือก

f)ngiap quiet, silent เงียบ

f)ngo foolish, stupid โง่

ngong! confused งง

ngoo n. snake งู

ngoo l)hao! n. cobra งูเห่า

ng๐o jong!-ang n. king cobra งูจงอาง

ngoo r)sam-l)liam n. banded krait snake งูสามเหลี่ยม

f)nguang nawn adj. sleepy ง่วงนอน

nguhn n. silver (the metal) เงิน

nguhn, nguhn tra n. money, currency เงิน, เงินตรา

nguhn deuan n. salary, wages เงินเดือน

nguhn l)sot! n. cash (currency) เงินสด

nguhn thawn n. change (money returned from a purchase) เงินทอน

nguhn f)yawy n. small bills, change (money) เงินย่อย

f)nim! adj. soft, delicate นิ่ม

nin! n. sapphire นิล

f)ning! adj. still, quiet นิ่ง

nin!-tha v. gossip นินทา

ni!-r)sai! n. habit นิสัย

h)nit!, h)nit! h)nit! a little, a little bit นิด, นิดๆ

h)nit! deeo only a little bit นิดเดียว

ni!-than n. fairy tale, fable, story นิทาน

h)nit! l)nawy a little bit นิดหน่อย

h)ni!-yom! popular, well-liked นิยม

h)nok! n. bird นก

h)nok! f)kaeo n. parrot นกแก้ว

h)nok! l)weet n. whistle นกหวีด

nom! n. milk, breasts นม

nom! r)phong! n. powdered milk นมผง

f)non, h)non over there, that one over there, yonder โน่น, โน้น

r)noo n. rat, mouse (also used to mean "I, me, you", for children, especially girls, when talking with elders) หนู

l)noom! young man, soft, youthful (for men) หนุ่ม

f)noong! v. dress, put on, wear นุ่ง

l)nuak r)hoo noise, noisy หนวกหู

f)nuat massage, get a massage, massage someone นวด

l)nuat n. moustache, beard หนวด

l)nuay n. unit, agency หน่วย

l)nuay r)san!-l)ti-f)phap U.S. Peace Corps หน่วย สันติภาพ

l)nuay tha!-r)han military unit หน่วยทหาร

nuhy n. butter, cheese เนย

nuhy l)awn, nuhy l)jeut, nuhy r)leh-o n. butter เนสสอน, เนยจค, เนยเลอ

nuhy r)khaeng, nuhy khem! n. cheese เนยแข็ง, เนยเคม

l)ok! n. chest, breasts อก

ๆ-l)kat n. chance, opportunity โอกาส

l)ok! l)hak! heart-broken, broken-hearted อกหัก

o. khe O.K. (okay) โอ.เค.

o-h)liang n. iced coffee (with sugar only) โอเลี้ยง

om! v. hold something in the mouth, suck on something อม

ong!-kan n. organization, govt. agency องค์การ

ong!-r)sa n. degree (angular or temperature), proof (alcohol), องศา

l)oo, l)oo reua n. dockyards อู่, อู่เรือ

l)oo, l)oo h)rot! n. repair shop, garage (for vehicles) อู่, อู่รถ

oo!-bat!-ti!-l)het n. accident อุบัติเหตุ

f)oom v. carry (in the arms, as a baby) อุ้ม

oo!-mong n. tunnel อุโมงค์

l)oon! v. warm, warm up อุ่น

oon!-ha!-phoom n. temperature อุณหภูมิ

l)oop!-l)pa!-kawn n. equipment อุปกรณ์

h)ooy!, h)ooy! tai (interj. used mostly by females for pain etc.) oh!, oh my! อุ้ย, อุ้ยตาย

l)op! v. bake อบ

l)op!-l)oon! warm, cozy อบอุ่น

l)ot! v. starve, do without food อด

l)ot! ah-r)han v. starve, do without food อดอาหาร

l)ot! tai v. starve to death อดตาย

l)ot!-thon! v. endure, bear อดทน

f)o-l)uat v. boast, brag โอ้อวด

pa v. throw ปา

f)pa n. aunt (elder sister of father or mother) ป้า

l)pa, l)pa h)mai n. forests, jungles ป่า, ป่าไม้

r)pa n. father (especially foreign fathers & elder fathers) ป๋า

l)pa-h)cha n. cemetery ป่าช้า

f)paeng n. flour, starch, powder แป้ง

f)paeng l)phat! f)na n. face powder แป้งผัดหน้า

l)paet eight (8) แปด (๘)

l)paet-l)sip! eighty (80) แปดสิบ (๘๐)

pai! v. go, attend, (also shows action away from speaker, as "pai! doo" = go to see) ไป

f)pai n. sign ป้าย

f)pai, f)pai h)rot! meh n. bus stop ป้าย, ป้ายรถเมล์

h)pai! Go away! (emphatic use of verb "go--pai!") ไป

pai! luhy go right on, go ahead ไปเลย

pai!... ma go somewhere and come back [usually as in "Where have you been?" = **pai! r)nai! ma?** = (literally) "go where come"] ไป....มา

pai! r)nai!? Where are you going? (friendly greeting in Thailand, roughly equivalent to "How're you?") ไปไหน?

pai! r)nai! ma? Where have you been? (friendly greeting) ไปไหนมา?

pai! nawn go to bed ไปนอน

pai! h)seu r)khawng go shopping ไปซื้อของ

pai! f)theeo go out, going out (for pleasure, sightseeing etc.) ไปเที่ยว

pai! h)thoo!-h)ra! go out on business (personal or otherwise) ไปธุระ

l)pak n. mouth ปาก

l)pak-ka n. pen (for writing) ปากกา

l)pak-ka f)look f)leun n. ballpoint pen ปากกาลูกลื่น

l)pak-ka l)meuk-seum! n. fountain pen ปากกาหมึกซึม

l)pak r)men! bad breath, halitosis ปากเหม็น

h)pam! h)nam!-man! n. gas station, petrol pump ปั๊มน้ำมัน

pan!-r)ha n. problem, puzzle, riddle ปัญหา

pan klang adj. medium, average ปานกลาง

pan!-ya n. wisdom, talent, mental abilities ปัญญา

f)pao!, f)pao!-r)mai n. target เป้า, เป้าหมาย

l)pao! v. blow (by mouth), play (musical instrument which requires blowing) เป่า

l)pa!-l)rawt n. thermometer ปรอท

l)pa! ri!-man n. quantity ปริมาณ

l)pat!, l)pat! l)foon! v. dust, wipe dust ปัด, ปัดฝุ่น

l)pa l)theuan adj. wild, savage, barbarous ป่าเถื่อน

l)pa!-r)thom! pha!-ya-ban (med.) first aid ปฐม พยาบาล

l)pa!-l)ti!-l)set v. deny, refuse, decline ปฏิเสธ

pa!-ti!-thin! n. calendar ปฏิทิน

l)pa!-l)ti!-h)wat! v. revolt ปฏิวัติ

l)pat!-r)sa-h)wa! (med.) urine, urinate ปัสสาวะ

paw n. jute, hemp ปอ

l)pawk, l)pawk l)pleuak v. peel (as a fruit) ปอก, ปอกเปลือก

pawn n. pound (16 ounces), pound sterling (British currency), loaf of bread ปอนด์

f)pawng-kan! v. prevent, defend, protect ป้องกัน

l)pawt n. lungs (of body), adj , v. (colloq.) afraid, fear

l)pawt buam (med.) pneumonia ปอดบวม

pee n. year ปี

l)peek n. wing ปีก

pee l)mai! new year, New Year's ปีใหม่

l)peep, h)peep n. bucket ปีบ, ปีป

h)pek! n. thumbtack เป๊ก

pen! v. be (existence), know how to do something, able to do something, have life, be afflicted with something เป็น

pen! f)bai! dumb (cannot speak) เป็นใบ้

pen! l)bit! (med.) have dysentery เป็นบิด

pen! r)fee (med.) have a boil เป็นฝี

pen! l)huang worry, worried เป็นห่วง

pen! f)jao!-r)khawng be the owner of เป็นเจ้าของ

pen! f)khai! (med.) have a fever เป็นไข้

pen! r)khawng.... v. belong to.... เป็นของ....

pen! f)lam interpret, be an interpreter เป็นล่าม

pen! lom! v. faint, become unconscious เป็นลม

pen! f)nee be in debt เป็นหนี้

pen! pai! f)dai! possible เป็นไปได้

pen! pai! f)mai! f)dai! impossible เป็นไปไม่ได้

pen! h)phit! adj. poisonous เป็นพิษ

pen! l)sa!-r)nim! adj. rusty เป็นสนิม

pen! l)sot adj. single, unmarried เป็นโสด

pea! l)wat! have a cold, catch cold เป็นหวัด

l)pet! n. duck เป็ด

f)peuan adj. stained, soiled เปื้อน

peun n. gun ปืน

peun kon! n. machine-gun ปืนกล

peun h)lek! small arms (weapons) ปืนเล็ก

peun h)lek! yao n. rifle ปืนเล็กยาว

peun h)phok! n. pistol ปืนพก

peun l)yai! (mil.) artillery ปืนใหญ่

peun yao n. rifle ปืนยาว

peun l)taw-f)soo ah-l)kat-sa-yan (mil.) anti-air-craft artillery ปืนต่อสู้อากาศยาน

pha, pha ma, pha pai! v. lead, take, escort [Note. "pha ma" indicates toward speaker; "pha pai!" = away from speaker.] พา, พามา, พาไป

f)pha n. cloth ผ้า

f)pha-bai! n. canvas ผ้าใบ

f)pha-h)chet!-men n. napkin ผ้าเช็ดมือ

f)pha-h)chet!-f)na n. handkerchief ผ้าเช็ดหน้า

f)pha-h)chet!-h)thao! n. floormat ผ้าเช็ดเท้า

f)pha-h)chet!-tua n. towel ผ้าเช็ดตัว

h)phae v. lose (be defeated) แพ้

h)phae ah-r)han be allergic to food แพ้อาหาร

h)phae ah-l)kat get ill because of the weather
    แพ้อากาศ

l)phaen n. sheet (of something) [as in "l)kra!-
    l)dat r)sawng l)phaen = 2 sheets of paper] แผ่น

r)phaen n. plan, scheme แผน

phaeng adj expensive, dear, costly แพง

l)phaen-r)siang n. phonograph record แผ่นเสียง

r)phaen-f)thee n. map แผนที่

l)phaet n. doctor, M.D. แพทย์

l)phaet l)sat! n. veterinarian แพทย์สัตว์

f)pha l)hom! n. blanket ผ้าห่ม

phai! n. danger ภัย

phai n.; v. paddle (a boat) พาย

f)phai! n. playing cards ไพ่

l)phai! n. bamboo ไผ่

phai-r)lang! after, afterwards ภายหลัง

phai-f)na in the future ภายหน้า

phai-f)nawk outside ภายนอก

phai!-h)raw! adj. beautiful (of sounds) ไพเราะ

f)phak n. region (of a country), semester (of school year) ภาค

h)phak!, h)phak! l)phawn v. rest พัก, พักผ่อน

h)phak!, h)phak! l)yoo v. stay, reside (temporarily or otherwise) พัก, พักอยู่

l)phak! n. vegetable ผัก

f)pha kan! f)peuan n. apron ผ้ากันเปื้อน

!)phak!-dawng n. pickles, pickled vegetables ผักดอง

f)pha f)khee-h)rew! n. rag ผ้าขี้ริว

h)phak! kan-meuang n. political party พรรคการเมือง

l)phak!-l)kat r)hawm n. lettuce ผักกาดหอม

h)phak! l)phawn v. rest พักผ่อน

pha!-la! l)seuk!-r)sa n. physical education พลศึกษา

l)phak!-l)lit! v. manufacture, produce ผลิต

h)pha! f)ma Burma, Burmese พม่า

f)pha r)mai! n. silk cloth ผ้าไหม

f)pha f)man n. curtain ม้าม่าน

f)pha-l)meuk! phim!-l)deet n. typewriter ribbon
ผ้าหมึกพิมพ์ดีด

phan! [l)neung! phan!, phan! l)neung] one thousand
(1,000) พัน (หนึ่งพัน, พันหนึ่ง)

phan! n. breed, kind, species พันธุ์

l)phan v. pass, pass by, pass through, experience ผ่าน

l)pha!-l)naek n. section (subdiv. of a div., in a
Thai-govt dept. of a ministry) แผนก

pha!-nak!-ngan n. employee, official, worker
พนักงาน

pha!-nak!-ngan tho-ra!-sap! n. telephone operator
พนักงานโทรศัพท์

pha!-nan! v. gamble พนัน

phan!-l)ek (mil) colonel พันเอก

phan!-l)ek phi!-l)set (mil.) special col. (equiv. to
brig.-gen.) พันเอก (พิเศษ)

pha-nit! n. commerce, trade พาณิชย์

phan!-l)ja ah-l)kat [tree, tho, l)ek] AF sgt. (s/sgt.,
t/sgt., m/sgt.) พันจ่าอากาศ (ตรี, โท, เอก)

phan!-l)ja-l)ek (navy) chief petty officer พันจ่าเอก

phan!-l)ja-tho (navy) petty-officer, 1st-class พัน
จ่าโท

phan!-l)ja-tree (navy) petty-officer, 2nd-class
พันจ่าตรี

phan! h)lan (l)neung! phan! h)lan] one billion
(one thousand million) พันล้าน (หนึ่งพันล้าน)
◦,○○○,○○○,○○○

phan!-na!-na v. describe พรรณนา

phan! r)phlae v. bandage พันแผล

phan!-ra!-ya n. wife (polite, more-formal term
for everyday term of "mia" or "faen") ภรรยา

phan rong n. janitor, building custodian การโรง

phan! tam!-l)ruat l)ek police colonel พันตำรวจเอก

phan! tam!-l)ruat l)ek phi!-l)set police special col.
(equiv. to brig.-gen.) พันตำรวจเอก (พิเศษ)

phan! tam!-l)ruat tho police lt.-col. พันตำรวจโท

phan! tam!-l)ruat tree police maj. พันตำรวจตรี

phan!-tho (mil.) lt.-col. พันโท

phan!-tree (mil.) maj. พันตรี

r)phao! v. burn, burn something เผา

r)phao! l)sop! v. cremate เผาศพ

f)phap n. picture, photo ภาพ

h)phap! v. fold พับ

f)pha phan! r)phlae n. bandage ผ้าพันแผล

f)pha phim!-l)deet n. typewriter ribbon ผ้าพิมพ์ดีด

f)pha l)phook khaw n. necktie ผ้าผูกคอ

f)pha poo f)thee-nawn n. bedspread, bedsheet
ผ้าปูที่นอน

f)pha poo h)to! n. tablecloth ผ้าปูโต๊ะ

f)phap-pha!-yon! n. movie, film, cinema ภาพยนตร์

f)phap-l)thai n. photo, picture ภาพถ่าย

pha-ra! n. burden ภาระ

pha-ra!-l)kit n. (mil.) mission การกิจ

pha-r)sa n. language ภาษา

pha-r)see n. taxes ภาษี

l)pha!-r)som! v. mix ผสม

l)pha!-r)som! l)sat! breed animals ผสมสัตว์

h)phat! v. blow gently (as the wind), fan (move air with fan) พัด

l)pha-l)tat! v. (med.) operate, perform surgery ผ่าตัด

h)phat!-lom! n. fan (for air circulation) พัดลม

h)phat!-l)sa!-l)doo! n. luggage, supplies, parcel post พัสดุ

phat!-ta-khan n. restaurant ภัตตาคาร

phat!-tha!-na v. develop, build up พัฒนา

phaw.... as soon as, just as, when.... พอ....

phaw, phaw h)laeo enough, that's enough พอ, พอแล้ว

f)phaw n. father พ่อ

phaw dee just enough, just right, just at the right (or wrong) moment พอดี

phaw-jai! satisfied, content พอใจ

f)phaw h)kha n. trader, merchant พ่อค้า

f)phaw khrua male cook, chef พ่อครัว

f)phaw h)liang n. stepfather, wealthy man (northern Thailand) พ่อเลี้ยง

r)phawm adj. thin (for persons, animals) ผอม

f)phaw f)mae n. parents (father, mother) พ่อแม่

f)phaw f)mai n. widower พ่อหม้าย

l)phawn l)song! v. pay for by installments ผ่อนส่ง

phaw. r)saw. B.E., the Buddhist era (543 years ahead of international year) พ.ศ.

pha!-ya-ban n. nurse พยาบาล

pha!-yan n. witness พยาน

pha!-ya-yam v. try พยายาม

pha-h)yoo! r)fon! rainstorm พายุฝน

pha-h)yoo l)yai! (tai!-foon!) n. typhoon พายุใหญ่ (ไต้ฝุ่น)

phe-dan n. ceiling (of a room) เพดาน

f)phee n. elder brother, sister, friend, cousin พี่

r)phee n. ghost, spirit ผี

f)phee-chai elder male relative (brother, cousin), elder male friend พี่ชาย

f)phee-r)khuhy elder brother-in-law (husband of one's older sister) พี่เขย

f)phee-h)nawng, brothers & sisters, close relatives พี่น้อง

f)phee-h)nawng chao-chai fellow Thais (said mostly by speakers) พี่น้องชาวไทย

f)phee-h)nawng h)thang!-r)lai brothers & sisters (said mostly by public speakers) พี่น้องทั้งหลาย

f)phee-r)sao elder relative (sister, cousin), elder female friend พี่สาว

f)phee sa!-h)phai! sister-in-law (wife of one's older brother) พี่สะใภ้

r)phee f)seua n. butterfly ผีเสื้อ

f)phet n. diamond เพชร

f)phet! adj. hot (spicy, hot in taste) เผ็ด

f)phet-phlawy n. jewelry, jewellery เพชรพลอย

f)pheua for, in order to, for the purpose of เพื่อ

f)pheuan a. friend เพื่อน

f)pheuan f)ban n. neighbor, neighbour เพื่อนบ้าน

h)pheun n. floor, surface พื้น

h)pheun-din! ground surface พื้นดิน

f)pheung! n. bee ผึ้ง

f)pheung! v. depend on, rely on; adv. just now, just recently พึ่ง

h)pheun-meuang adj native, local พื้นเมือง

h)pheun-f)thee n. area พื้นที่

f)pheut (phan!) n. plants, vegetation พืช (พันธุ์)

r)ohew n. surface ผิว

r)phew!, r)phew! r)nang! n. skin ผิว, ผิวหนัง

phiang only, just so much เพียง

phiang phaw just enough เพียงพอ

phi!-ja-ra-na v. consider พิจารณา

phi!-kan adj. crippled, abnormal, deformed พิการ

phim!, phim! r)nang!-r)sea v. print, publish พิมพ์, พิมพ์หนังสือ

phim!-l)deet v. typewrite พิมพ์ดีด

phi!-nai!-kam! n. will (legal document) พินัยกรรม

phi!-l)set adj. special พิเศษ

phi!-l)soot v. prove พิสูจน์

h)phit! n. poison พิษ

l)phit! adj. wrong ผิด

phi·thee, phi·thee-kan n. ceremony, protocol พิธี, พิธีการ

l)phit! l)kot!-r)mai break the law, il!-gal ผิด กฎหมาย

l)phit! f)phlat v. fail, make mistakes ผิดพลาด

l)phit! l)pok!-l)ka!-l)ti! adj. abnormal ผิดปกติ

l)phit! r)sang!-l)ket adj. odd, suspicious ผิดสังเกต

l)phit! l)taw.... against (in violation of)....ผิดต่อ....

l)phit! r)wang! disappoint, be disappointed ผิดหวัง

r)phlae n. wound, sore, ulcer แผล

r)phlae-pen! n. scar แผลเป็น

r)phlae h)phoo!-phawng! n. blister แผลพุพอง

l)phlak! v. push ผลัก

f)phlat v. miscalculate, fail, make mistakes พลาด

phlawy n. precious stone, gem, jewel พลอย

phleng n. song เพลง

phlia adj. weak (physically), tired เพลีย

h)phlik! v. turn over (as page of book) พลิก

f)phlua n. shovel พลั่ว

f)phlua meu n. trowel พลั่วมือ

phluhn adj. engrossed, absorbed เพลิน

r)phom! n. hair (of human head); I, me (male speakers only) ผม

phon! n. (mil.) troops พล

h)phon! v. get free, go beyond พ้น

r)phon! n. results, fruit (in general) ผล

phon! ah-l)kat l)ek (AF) air chief marshal (4-star gen.) พลอากาศเอก

phon! ah-l)kat l)jat!-l)ta!-wa (AF) air-commodore brig.-gen. พลอากาศจัตวา

phon! ah-l)kat tho (AF) air marshal, lt.-gen. พลอากาศโท

phon! ah-l)kat tree (AF) air vice-marshal, maj. gen. พลอากาศตรี

phon!-l)ek (mil.) 4-star (full) gen. พลเอก

r)phong n. powder ผง

r)phong! h)sak! f)pha, r)phong! h)sak! f)fawk n. washing powder ผงซักฟ้า, ผงซักฟอก

phon! l)jat!-l)ta!-wa (mil.) brig., brig.-gen. พลจัตวา

r)phon!-h)la-h)mai! n. fruit (to eat) ผลไม้

phon!-h)la!-meuang n. people, population พลเมือง

phon!-h)la!-reuan n. civilian (not military) พลเรือน

phon! h)nawy (mil.) brigade พลน้อย

r)phon! l)pra!-l)yot n. benefits, advantages ผลประโยชน์

phon! reua l)ek (navy) adm. (4-star) พลเรือเอก

phon! reua l)jat!-l)ta!-wa (navy) commodore พลเรือจัตวา

phon! reua tho (navy) vice-adm. พลเรือโท

phon! reua tree (navy) rear-adm. พลเรือตรี

f)phon! r)see v. spray-paint พ่นสี

phon! tha!-r)han (mil.) private, ordinary soldier พลทหาร

phon! tha-r)han reua (navy) seaman 3rd-class, ordinary seaman พลทหารเรือ

phon! tho (mil.) lt.-gen พลโท

phon! tree (mil.) maj-gen. พลตรี

f)phoo n. person (in general, used mostly as prefix) ผู้

l)phoo! adj. decayed ผุ

f)phoo ah-h)rak!-r)kha n. bodyguard, security guard (for VIP's) ผู้อารักขา

f)phoo am-nuay kan n. director ผู้อำนวยการ

f)phoo ban!-cha-kan (mil.) commander ผู้บัญชาการ

f)phoo ban!-cha-kan tha!-r)han r)soong l)soot! (mil.) supreme cmdr. ผู้บัญชาการทหารสูงสุด

f)phoo-chai n. man, male ผู้ชาย

f)phoo cham!-nan kan n. expert, skilled specialist ผู้ชำนาญการ

f)phoo cha!-na! n. winner, victor ผู้ชนะ

f)phoo f)chao! n. tenant, renter, lessee ผู้เช่า

f)phoo-f)chuay n. assistant ผู้ช่วย

f)phoo-f)chuay f)thoot (dipl.) attaché ผู้ช่วยทูต

f)phoo doy-r)san n. passenger ผู้โดยสาร

f)phoo duhn-h)thao! n. pedestrian ผู้เดินเท้า

f)phoo fang! n. audience, listeners ผู้ฟัง

f)phoo-l)jat!-kan n. manager ผู้จัดการ

l)phook v. tie, bind ผูก

f)phoo l)kaw kan h)rai (khawm-mew-nit) n. terrorist (communist) ผู้ก่อการร้าย (คอมมิวนิสต์)

f)phoo l)kep! nguhn n. bill-collector ผู้เก็บเงิน

phoo-r)khao! n. hill, mountain ภูเขา

phoom-jai be proud of, feel proud of ภูมิใจ

phoom-lam!-nao! home town, original home, place of origin ภูมิลำเนา

f)phoo nam! f)rawng n. pilot (of a ship, through a channel) ผู้นำร่อง

f)phoo nam!-f)theeo n. guide, tourist guide ผู้นำเที่ยว

f)phoo phi!-f)phak-r)sa n. judge ผู้พิพากษา

f)phoo l)pok!-khrawng n. parents, guardians ผู้ปกครอง

f)phoo h)rap! n. receiver, addressee ผู้รับ

f)phoo h)rap! r)phon! l)pra!-l)yot n beneficiary ผู้รับผลประโยชน์

f)phoo h)roo-l)jak! kan. n. acquaintance ผู้รู้จักกัน

f)phoo h)rook!-ran n. aggressor, invader ผู้รุกราน

f)phoo l)sa!-l)mak! n. applicant ผู้สมัคร

f)phoo l)sa!-l)mak! f)len n. amateur (sports etc.) ผู้สมัครเล่น

f)phoo l)sep-l)tit! n. addict (as drug addict etc.) ผู้เสพติด

f)phoo l)seu l)khao n. news reporter ผู้สื่อข่าว

f)phoot v. speak, talk พูด

h)phoot! [wan! h)phoot!] Wednesday พุธ (วันพุธ)

h)phoot!, h)phoot-h)tha! (rel.) Buddha, Buddhism พุทธ

f)phoot l)taeng n. author ผู้แต่ง

f)phoot ang!-l)krit speak English พูดอังกฤษ

f)phoo l)tat!-r)sin! n. judge, referee, umpire ผู้ตัดสิน

f)phoo-f)tawng-r)ha (n., leg.) the accused ผู้ต้องหา

f)phoo-thaen n. representative, agent, Thai M.P. (Member of Parliament) ผู้แทน

f)phoo-thaen jam!-l)nai n. (comr.) agent, distributor ผู้แทนจำหน่าย

f)phoo f)thee.... the person who/whom.... ผู้ที่....

f)phoo r)theu.... adherent of...., believer in.... (usually a religion) ผู้ถือ....

f)phoo r)theu f)hoon! (n., comr.) stockholder, shareholder ผู้ถือหุ้น

f)phoot f)len v. joke, speak jokingly or in fun พูดเล่น

f)phoot l)sa!-l)bot! v. swear, speak obscenely พูดสบถ

f)phoot l)ta!-l)lok! v. speak jokingly พูดตลก

f)phoot thai! speak Thai พูดไทย

h)phoot!-h)tha!-l)sak!-l)ka-rat the Buddhist era, B.E. (543 years ahead of international year) พุทธศักราช

h)phoot!-h)tha!-l)sat-l)sa!-r)na Buddhism พุทธศาสนา

f)phoot r)theung! v. mention, refer to พูดถึง

h)phoot!-f)tho (colloq.) Oh, my God! (exclamation of vague meaning) พุทโธ

f)phoot tho-ra!-l)sap! speak/talk on phone พูด
โทรศัพท์

f)phoot trong! pai! trong! ma speak bluntly, stra-
ightforwardly พูดตรงไปตรงมา

f)phoot l)yap speak vulgarly, crudely พูดหยาบ

f)phoo f)wa rat-cha!-kan jang!-l)wat! n. provincial
governor ผู้ว่าราชการจังหวัด

f)phoo-l)yai! n. adult, elder person, important
person ผู้ใหญ่

f)phoo-l)yai! f)ban n. village chief ผู้ใหญ่บ้าน

f)phoo-r)ying! n. woman, girl, female ผู้หญิง

f)phoo-r)ying! h)rap!-h.)chai! female servant ผู้หญิง
รับใช้

h)phop! v. find something, see someone, meet
someone พบ

phot-ja-na-noo-krom n. dictionary พจนานุกรม

h)phra! n. Buddhist priest, monk พระ

h)phra! ah-ram n. Buddhist temple พระอาราม

h)phra ah-h)thit! sun, the sun พระอาทิตย์

h)phra! ah-h)thit! f)kheun! sunrise พระอาทิตย์ขึ้น

h)phra! ah-h)thit! l)tok! sunset พระอาทิตย์ตก

f)phrae-r)lai spread out, widespread แพร่หลาย

h)phra!-jan! moon, the moon พระจันทร์

h)phra! f)jao!, h)phra! f)phoo pen! f)jao! God (a
vague term) พระเจ้า, พระผู้เป็นเจ้า

h)phra!·f)jao! l)yoo-r)hua n. the King, a king
พระเจ้าอยู่หัว

h)phra! jeh-dee n. pagoda, Buddhist pagoda พระ
เจดีย์

h)phra! kham!-phee n. the Bible, holy book พระ
คัมภีร์

phram n. Brahman, Brahmanism พราหมณ์

h)phra! h)na!-khawn [old name for Bangkok part
of Bangkok Metropolis, which is now known
as "kroong! f)thep h)ma!-r)ha h)na!-khawn]
พระนคร

h)phra! h)phoot!-h)tha!-f)jao! Buddha, Lord Buddha พระพุทธเจ้า

h)phra! h)phoot!-h)tha!-f)roop Buddha image or
statue พระพุทธรูป

h)phra! h)phoot!-h)tha!-l)sat-l)sa!-r)na Buddhism
พระพุทธศาสนา

h)phra! ra-chi!-nee (colloq., respectful) the Queen
พระราชินี

h)phra! f)rat-cha!-wang! n. royal palace พระราชวัง

h)phra! r)sang!-kha!-f)rat the Supreme Patriarch (of Thai Buddhism) พระสังฆราช

h)phra! l)sat-l)sa-da mo-l)ha!-l)mat! (rel.) Mohammed พระศาสดาโมหะหมัด

h)phraw! adj. beautiful (of sounds), politely (of words) เพราะ

h)phraw!, h)phraw! f)wa! because, because of เพราะ, เพราะว่า

h)phraw! l)cha!-h)nan! therefore เพราะฉะนั้น

h)phrawm ready, in readiness พร้อม

h)phrawm kan! at the same time, altogether พร้อมกัน

h)phra! yeh-soo Jesus Christ พระเยซู

phreu-l)ha! [wan! phreu-l)hat!] Thursday พฤหัส (วันพฤหัส)

phreut l)sa! l)ji!-ka-yon! November พฤศจิกายน

phreut-l)sa!-pha-khom! May พฤษภาคม

h)phrik!, h)phrik! thai! n. pepper พริก, พริกไทย

h)phrik! f)khee-r)noo n. chili peppers พริกขี้หนู

phrom! n. carpet, rug พรม

phrom! h)chet!-h)thao! n. foot-rug, scatter-rug พรมเช็ดเท้า

phrom! daen n. border, frontier พรมแดน

phrom! h)nam!-man! n. linoleum พรมน้ำมัน

f)phroong-h)nee tomorrow พรุ่งนี้

r)phua n. husband [ordinary term; more-formal term is "r)sa-mee"] ผัว

f)phuak n group (things or people) พวก

f)phuak rao! we, us พวกเรา

phuang ma-lai! n. steering wheel (of vehicle), garland (of flowers) พวงมาลัย

f)phuhm, f)phuhm f)kheun! v. increase, add to เพิ่ม, เพิ่มขึ้น

f)phuhm tuhm additional, in addition เพิ่มเติม

f)phuhng [f)pheung!] just.... (completed action), very recently, just now เพิ่ง (พึ่ง)

r)phuhy v. reveal เผย

r)phuhy f)phrae v. publicize เผยแพร่

l)piak adj. wet เปียก

l)pik!-h)ap! n. phonograph ปิคอัพ

l)pin! v. climb ปีน

f)ping! v. toast (as bread) ปิ้ง

l)pit!, l)pit! h)wai! v. close, turn off, shut, stick, stick to, attach to, cover up, seal ปิด, ปิดไว้

l)pit! fai! turn off a light ปิดไฟ

l)pit! l)pra!-choom! close a meeting, adjourn ปิดประชุม

pla n fish ปลา

pla l)chai-r)lam n. shark ปลาฉลาม

plae v. translate แปล

l)plaek, l)plaek l)prai-l)lat adj. strange, unusual
แปลก, แปลกประหลาด

l)plaek jai! adj. surprised, amazed แปลกใจ

plaeng v. change, transform แปลง

plae f)wa.... that means.... (by translation or by
inference) แปลว่า

plai n. end, tip ปลาย

plai l)sapl-pal-da n. weekend ปลายสัปดาห์

l)pla l)meuk! n. squid, cuttlefish ปลาหมึก

l)plao! no, nothing, not so, nothing at all (usually in answer to a question) เปล่า

l)plao! l)pleeo adj. lonely, deserted เปล่าเปลี่ยว

plas-tuh n. adhesive tape (plaster) ปลาสเตอร์

l)plawk khaw n. collar (of clothing) ปลอกคอ

plawm n., v. fake, not genuine ปลอม

l)plawt phai! adj. safe, without danger ปลอดภัย

l)plawy v. free, set free, release ปล่อย

ple (pleh) n. cradle, hammock, stretcher, litter
เปล

l)pleuak n. peeling, peel, crust, rind, skin (of fruit) เปลือก

l)pleuak, l)pleuak l)khai n. eggshell เปลือก, เปลือกไข่

pleuang v. waste เปลือง

pleuay, pleuay kai adj. naked, no clothes on เปลือย, เปลือยกาย (Note. "pleuay" is often pronounced "pluhy".)

f)pleum-jai! adj. delighted, greatly pleased ปลื้มใจ

plew! v. float (usually in the air) ปลิว

l)plian, l)plian-plaeng v. change เปลี่ยน, เปลี่ยนแปลง

l)plian jai! v. change one's mind เปลี่ยนใจ

pling! n. water leech ปลิง

l)plook!, l)plook! f)hai! l)teun v. awaken, wake up ปลุก, ปลุกให้ตื่น

l)plook v. plant, grow, build ปลูก

l)plook f)ban build a house ปลูกบ้าน

l)plook r)fee v. vaccinate ปลูกฝี

l)plot! l)kra!-doom! unbutton ปลดกระดุม

l)plot! l)plawy v. free, release, liberate ปลดปล่อย

l)pluak n. termite, white ant ปลวก

pluhy (See PLEUAY.)

l)pok!, l)pok! r)nang!-r)seu n. cover (of book) ปก, ปกหนังสือ

l)pok!-l)ka!-l)ti! adj. normal, usual, routine, regular ปกติ

l)**pok!** khrawng v. govern, supervise people
ปกครอง

pom!-f)dawy n. inferiority complex ปมด้อย

pon! kan! mix up, mixed up ปนกัน

poo n. crab (seafood) ปู

l)poo n. grandfather (paternal) ปู่

poon see-men n. cement ปูนซีเมนต์

poo tiang, poo f)thee-nawn make up a bed, put
sheets and/or bedspread on a bed ปูเตียง,
ปูที่นอน

poo h)to! put a tablecloth on a table ปูโต๊ะ

r)pooy n. fertilizer ปุ๋ย

pra!-cha-chon! people, the public ประชาชน

pra!-cha-r)song!-h)khraw! n. public welfare ประชา
สงเคราะห์

pra!-cha-thi!-pa!-tai! n. democracy ประชาธิปไตย

pra! choom!, pra!-choom! kan! meet, hold or have
a meeting ประชุม, ประชุมกัน

l)pra!-l)dap! v. decorate ประดับ

l)pra!-l)dap! kai dress up with ornaments, jewelry ประดับกาย

l)pra!-r)deeo just a minute, wait just a minute
ประเดี๋ยว

praeng n.v. brush แปรง

praeng praeng r)phom! n. hairbrush แปรงๆ ผม

praeng r)see fan! n. toothbrush แปรงสีฟัน

prai!-sa!-nee post, postal, post office ไปรษณีย์

prai!-sa!-nee ah-l)kat n. airmail ไปรษณีย์อากาศ

prai!-sa!-nee klang G.P.O. (General Post Office)
ไปรษณีย์กลาง

prai!-sa!-nee-ya!-bat! n. postcard ไปรษณียบัตร

prai! sa!-nee-ya-kawn n. postage stamps ไปรษณียากร

pra!-jam! adj. permanent, regular ประจำ

pra!-jam! deuan monthly (as a periodical), monthly menstrual period ประจำเดือน

pra!-jam! pee annual, yearly ประจำปี

pra!-kan! v. guarantee, insure ประกัน

pra!-kan n. kind, sort, thing, item, point ประการ

pra!-kan! chee-wit life insurance ประกันชีวิต

pra!-kan! oo!-bat!-til-het accident insurance ประกัน
อุบัติเหตุ

pra!-kan! phai! n.v. insurance, insure ประกันภัย

pra!-kan! tua (leg.) bail out (from court, jail)
ประกันตัว

l)pra!-l)kat v. announce ประกาศ

i)pra!-l)kat-l)sa!-nee-ya!-l)bat! n. certificate ประกาศนียบัตร

l)pra!-l)kawp assemble, consist of ประกอบ

l)pra-l)kot! v. appear, become clear ปรากฏ

l)pra!-l)kuat khwam ngam beauty contest ประกวดความงาม

l)pra!-l)lat adj. strange ประหลาด

l)pra!-l)lat jai! adj. surprised ประหลาดใจ

l)pra!-man about, approximately ประมาณ

l)pra!-nee l)pra!-nawm v. compromise ประนีประนอม

l)prap! v. fine (inflict a fine) ปรับ

l)prap! ah-l)kat v. air-condition ปรับอากาศ

l)pra!-pheh-nee n. traditions ประเพณี

l)pra!-h)phreut! n., v. conduct, behavior ประพฤติ

l)prap-pram v. suppress ปราบปราม

l)prap!-proong! v improve, adjust ปรับปรุง

l)pra!-r)san, l)pra!-r)san kan v. coordinate ประสาน, ประสานกัน

l)pra!-l)sat n. nerves (of body) ประสาท

l)pra!-r)song! v. wish, desire ประสงค์

l)pra!-than, l)pra!-than kam!-ma!-kan n. chairman ประธาน, ประธานกรรมการ

l)pra!-tha-na-thi!-baw-dee n. president (of a country) ประธานาธิบดี

l)pra!-h)thap! tra seal (officially with a seal) ประทับตรา

l)pra!-f)thet n. country, nation ประเทศ

l)pra!-f)thet thai! Thailand ประเทศไทย

l)pra!-too n. door, gate ประตู

l)prat-l)sa!-l)jak without ปราศจาก

l)prat-l)tha!-r)na v. desire, wish ปรารถนา

l)pra!-l)wat!-l)sat n. history ประวัติศาสตร์

l)pra!-l)yat! save, economical, economize ประหยัด

l)pra!-l)yok n. sentence (of words) ประโยค

l)pra!-l)yot n. usefulness, benefits ประโยชน์

f)preeo adj. sour เปรี้ยว

l)preuk!-r)sa v consult ปรึกษา

l)priap, l)priap f)thiap v. compare เปรียบ, เปรียบเทียบ

prin!-ya n. degree (academic) ปริญญา

prin!-ya l)ek Ph.D. degree ปริญญาเอก

prin!-ya tho master's degree ปริญญาโท

prin!-ya tree bachelor's degree ปริญญาตรี

l)prong, l)prong! r)sai airy, transparent, rangy (of body) โปร่ง, โปร่งใส

proong!, proong! h)rot! v. season, flavor (foods) ปรุง, ปรุงรส

proong ah-r)han cook, prepare food ปรุงอาหาร

l)prot please, kindly โปรด

l)puat v. ache ปวด

l)puat fan! (have a) toothache ปวดฟัน

l)puat r)hua, l)puat r)see!-l)sa! (have a) headache ปวดหัว, ปวดศีรษะ

l)puat r)lang! (have a) backache ปวดหลัง

l)puat l)pat!-r)sa-wa! have urge to urinate ปวด ปัสสาวะ

l)puat h)thawng (have a stomachache), have the urge to have a bowel movement ปวดท้อง

l)puat [h)thawng] f)yeeo (colloq.) have urge to urinate ปวด (ท้อง) เยี่ยว

l)puay be ill ป่วย

l)puht v. open, turn on เปิด

l)puht, l)puht l)awk v. uncover, open up เปิด, เปิดออก

l)puht fai! v. turn on a light เปิดไฟ

l)puht r)phuhy v. reveal เปิดเผย

ra n. mold, fungus รา

ra!-bai v. drain away ระบาย

ra! l)bat v. break out (as disease, war) ระบาด

ra!-l)bawp n. system ระบอบ

ra!-l)biap n. order, system, procedures ระเบียบ

ra!-l)biap f)riap-h)rawy in good order ระเบียบ
เรียบรอย

ra!-bom! adj. bruised ระบม

ra!-l)bop! n. system ระบบ

ra!-l)buht v. burst, explode ระเบิด

ra!-l)dap! n. level surface, a certain level ระดับ

ra!-l)dap! h)nam! [tha!-leh] sea level, carpenter's
level ระดับน้ำ(ทะเล)

f)rae n minerals, ore แร่

f)raek first, be first แรก

raeng n., adj. force, energy, strong, power,
strength แรง

raeng fai!-h)fa (elect.) voltage แรงไฟฟ้า

raeng h)ma (engr.) horsepower แรงม้า

rai by the...., ...ly (as in rai-wan! = daily, by
the day); n., case, instance, party ราย

rai, rai-kan n. item, entry (in lists, accounts)
ราย, รายการ

f)rai! n. farm (usually not rice), plantation;
"rai" (land-area measurement equiv. to 1,600
sq. metres or approx. 2/5 acre) ไร่

h)rai adj. bad, fierce, cruel, wicked ร้าย

rai-cheu n. roster, list of names รายชื่อ

rai-f)dai n. income รายได้

rai-kan list of items, program (radio, T.V.); item, entry (lists, accounts) รายการ

rai-kan ah-r)han n. menu รายการอาหาร

rai h)la!-l)iat n. details รายละเอียด

rai-ngan n.v report รายงาน

rai-ngan ah-l)kat n. weather report รายงานอากาศ

rai pee yearly รายปี

f)rak n. root (of plant, of gums etc.), root [math., as in "f)rak f)thee r)sawŋ" = square root] ราก

h)rak! v. love รัก

ra-kha n. cost, price, value. ราคา

ra!-khang! large bell (as in Buddhist temple) ระฆัง

h)rak!-r)sa v. treat, care for, maintain รักษา

h)rak!-r)sa r)hai v. (med.) cure, treat until well รักษาหาย

ra!-leuk!, ra!-leak! r)theung! v. think about, recall, reflect ระลึก, ระลึกถึง

ram!-khan feel annoyed (by something or somebody) รำคาญ

ram!-wong! n. popular Thai "circle" dance รำวง

h)ran, h)ran r)khai.... n. store, shop ร้าน, ร้านขาย....

h)ran ah-r)han n. food shop, ordinary restaurant
ร้านอาหาร

h)ran l)dat r)phom! n. beauty shop (hairdressing) ร้านตัดผม

rang! n. nest รัง

rang n. rail, track ราง

f)rang n., v. draft, make a draft of ร่าง

ra!-ngap! v. quell, stop, hold back ระงับ

rang!-kae v. deliberately annoy or irritate รังแก

f)rang-kai n. body (of a person) ร่างกาย

f)rang-kai phi!-kan crippled, deformed, abnormal
(of a person) ร่างกายพิการ

ang!-l)kiat v. mind, object to. dislike รังเกียจ

rang!-h)nok! bird's nest (also Chinese-food
delicacy) รังนก

rang! f)pheung! n. beehive รังผึ้ง

rang h)rot!-fai! n. railway tracks รางรถไฟ

rang-wan! n. prize, reward รางวัล

f)rang l)yai big-bodied, husky (of person) ร่าง
ใหญ่

h)ran r)khai ya n. drug store, pharmacy ร้าน
ขายยา

h)ran h)sak!-f)haeng n. dry-cleaners ร้านซักแห้ง

h)ran r)suhm r)suay n. beauty shop ร้านเสริมสวย

h)ran l)tat! r)phom! n. barbershop ร้านตัดผม

rao! we, us เรา

rao n. line, railing, bannister ราว

rao, rao rao approximately, about ราว, ราวๆ

h)rap! v. receive, pick up (as in a car), catch (as a ball) รับ

h)rap! chuhn accept an invitation รับเชิญ

h)rap! l)phit f)chawp be responsible, accept responsibility รับผิดชอบ

h)rap!-l)pra!-than v. dine รับประทาน

h)rap!-rawng v. recommend, vouch for, certify to, รับรอง

h)rap! f)sap v. acknowledge รับทราบ

h)rap! tho-ra!-l)sap! answer telephone รับโทรศัพท์

h)rat! n. state (of USA), state or nation in general รัฐ

h)rat!, h)rat! f)khao! v. tighten รัก, รัดเข้า

f)rat-cha!-kan govt. work, official business ราชการ

f)rat-sa!-dawn n. subjects, citizens ราษฎร

rat!-tha!-ban n. government รัฐบาล

rat!-tha!-mon!-tree govt. minister (chief of ministry) รัฐมนตรี

raw v. wait รอ

ra!-wang! Careful! Be careful! ระวัง

ra!-l)wang between, among, during ระหว่าง

ra!-wang! r)khawng l)tack Fragile! Handle with Care! ระวังของแตก

f)rawk n. pulley รอก

h)rawn hot (in temperature) ร้อน

rawng support, be underneath, deputy.... รอง

h)rawng v. shout, cry out, scream ร้อง

h)rawng f)hai! v. cry (tears) ร้องไห้

f)rawng h)nam! n. waterway, channel, canal ร่องน้ำ

h)rawng phleng v. sing (songs) ร้องเพลง

rawng h)thao! n. shoes รองเท้า

rawng h)thao! l)tae! shower slippers, open sandals รองเท้าแตะ

f)rawp, f)rawp f)rawp encircling, all around รอบ, รอบ ๆ

f)rawt, f)rawt ma, f)rawt ma f)dai! v. survive รอด, รอดมา, รอดมาได้

rawy, trace, mark, line, track รอย

h)rawy [l)neung! h)rawy, h)rawy l)neung!] one
hundred (100) ร้อย (หนึ่งร้อย, ร้อยหนึ่ง)

h)rawy l)ek (mil.) captain ร้อยเอก

h)rawy la!.... per cent [as in "h)rawy la! f)ha =
five per cent] ร้อยละ....

h)rawy tam!-l)ruat l)ek police capt. ร้อยตำรวจเอก

h)rawy tam!-l)ruat tho police lt., pol. 1st lt. ร้อย
ตำรวจโท

h)rawy tam!-l)ruat tree pol. sub-lt., pol. 2nd lt.
ร้อยตำรวจตรี

rawy h)thao! n. †footprint รอยเท้า

h)rawy tho (mil.) lt , 1st lt. ร้อยโท

h)rawy tree (mil.) sub-lt., 2nd lt. ร้อยตรี

ra!-ya! n. distance, interval, period (of time or
space) ระยะ

ra!-ya! thang n. distance ระยะทาง

ra!-ya! we-la n. period of time ระยะเวลา

f)reep, f)reep f)reep, f)reep l)nawy Hurry! Hurry
up! รีบ, รีบ ๆ, รีบหน่อย

f)reep h)rawn, f)reep f)reng in a hurry, in a rush
รีบร้อน, รีบเร่ง

ree raw, ree ree raw raw v. hesitate, vacillate
รีรอ, รี ๆ รอ ๆ

f)reet v. iron, press, lengthen by squeezing, milk (a cow) รีด

f)reet f)pha iron clothes รีดผ้า

f)reng v. accelerate, rush เร่ง

reo! (reh-o!), reo! reo!, reo! f)khao!, reo! reo! f)khao! fast, quickly, Hurry up! เร็ว, เร็วๆ, เร็วเข้า, เร็วๆเข้า

reo! (reh-o!) reo! h)nee soon, in the near future เร็วๆนี้

reo! f)thee l)soot! most quickly, as quickly as possible เร็วที่สุด

r)reu or (also used at end of sentence--not translated--to show a question) หรือ

reua n. boat, ship เรือ

reua ah-l)kat l)ek AF capt., flight-lt. เรืออากาศเอก

reua ah-l)kat tho AF 1st lt., flying-officer เรืออากาศโท

reua ah-l)kat tree AF 2nd lt., pilot officer เรืออากาศตรี

reua bai! n. sailboat เรือใบ

reua ban!-thook! f)khreuang-bin! n. aircraft-carrier เรือบรรทุกเครื่องบิน

reua bin! n. airplane, aircraft เรือบิน

reua l.bot! n. small boat เรือบด

reua dam! h)nam! n submarine เรือดำน้ำ

reua l)ek (navy) lt, lt. s.g. เรือเอก

reuan n. building เรือน

f)reuang n story, subject, title, heading เรื่อง

reuan jam! n. prison เรือนจำ

reua h)rop! n. warship เรือรบ

reua tho (navy) sub-lt., lt. j.g. เรือโท

reua tree (navy) ensign เรือตรี

f)reuay again and again, ever and ever เรื่อย

f)reuay f)reuay (colloq.) so-so, not so bad but
    not so good เรื่อย ๆ

reu!-doo n season (of year) ฤดู

reu!-doo bai!-h)mai! l)phli! spring (season) ฤดู
    ใบไม้ผลิ

reu!-doo bai!-h)mai! f)ruang autumn (season) ฤดู
    ใบไม้ร่วง

reu!-doo r)fon rainy season ฤดูฝน

reu!-doo h)laeng dry season ฤดูแล้ง

reu!-doo r)nao cool or cold season, winter ฤดูหนาว

reu!-doo h)rawn hot season, summer ฤดูร้อน

r)reu f)mai!? or not? (at end of questions)
    หรือไม่ ?

r)reu l)plao!? or not? (at end of questions) หรือเปล่า?

r)reu yang!? yet?.... or not yet? (used at end of questions) หรือยัง?

f)riak v. call เรียก

f)riak h)rawng v. claim (something due), demand เรียกร้อง

f)riak f)wa be called, be named เรียกว่า

f)riak f)wa ah!rai!? What do you call it? What's it called? เรียกว่าอะไร

rian v. learn, study เรียน

r)rian n. coins (money), dollars (US or other) เหรียญ

riang v. set up, line up, set type, put in order เรียง

riang phim! set type (printing) เรียงพิมพ์

rian r)sam!-l)ret! graduate, complete one's studies เรียนสำเร็จ

f)riap adj. smooth, even, smooth and level เรียบ

f)riap-h)rawy adj. orderly, neat, polite & well-mannered เรียบร้อย

rim! n. brim, edge, rim ริม

rim!-r)fee-l)pak lips (of mouth) ริมฝีปาก

h)rin! n. gnat, sandfly ริ้น

h)rit!-r)see-duang tha!-wan (med.) hemorrhoids (piles) ริดสดวงทวาร

f)rok n. disease, disease of...., illness of.... โรค

f)rok klua h)nam! n. hydrophobia, rabies โรค กลัวน้ำ

f)rok r)nawng-nai! n. gonorrhea, the "clap" โรค หนองใน

f)rok h)phit! l)soo!-ra n. alcoholism โรคพิษสุรา

f)rok f)phoo-r)ying! (euphemism) syphilis (contracted by men) โรคผู้หญิง

f)rok ra!-l)bat n. epidemic โรคระบาด

f)rok h)reuan n. leprosy โรคเรื้อน

f)rok l)tit!-l)law n. contagious disease โรคติดต่อ

f)rom! n. umbrella, shade ร่ม

rong, rong reuan n. building โรง, โรงเรือน

rong la!-khawn n. theatre (for drama) โรงละคร

rong f)leuay n. sawmill โรงเลื่อย

rong h)mai! n. lumbermill, lumberyard โรงไม้

rong r)nang!, rong f)phap-pha!-yon! n. moviehouse, cinema, motion-picture theatre โรงหนัง, โรง ภาพยนตร์

rong-ngan n. factory, plant, workshop โรงงาน

rong pha!-ya-ban n. hospital โรงพยาบาล

rong raem n. hotel โรงแรม

rong h)rap! jam!-nam! n. pawnshop โรงรับจำนำ

rong-rian n. school โรงเรียน

rong-rian ah!-noo!-ban n. kindergarten โรงเรียน
อนุบาล

rong-rian nai h)rawy n. military academy โรงเรียน
นายร้อย

rong-rian nai h)rawy tam!-l)ruat n. police academy
โรงเรียนนายร้อยตำรวจ

rong-rian nai reua n. naval academy โรงเรียน
นายเรือ

rong-rian nai reua ah-l)kat n. AF academy โรงเรียน
นายเรืออากาศ

rong h)rot! n. garage (for parking vehicles)
โรงรถ

rong r)see [f)khao] n. rice-mill โรงสี (ข้าว)

roo n. hole รู

h)roo v. know (something) รู้

h)roo-l)jak! know someone or a place, make
someone's acquaintance รู้จัก

h)rook! v. attack, invade รุก

h)rook!-ran v. aggress รุกราน

f)roong! n. dawn, daybreak รุ่ง

h)roong! n. rainbow รุ้ง

f)roop n. picture รูป

f)roop, f)roop r)khian n. painting, drawing, picture รูป, รูปเขียน

f)roop, f)roop f)phap, f)roop l)thai n. photo รูป, รูปภาพ, รูปถ่าย

roo phrong n. cavity รูโพรง

f)roop l)law handsome (said of men) รูปหล่อ

f)roop f)pan!, f)roop l)sa!-l)lak! n. statue รูปปั้น, รูปสลัก

f)roop f)rang n. shape, appearance, form รูปร่าง

h)roo f)reuang (colloq.) know what's going on, understand what it's all about รู้เรื่อง

h)roo-l)seuk! v. feel, have feeling of รู้สึก

h)rop!, h)rop! kan (mil.) fight, have battles รบ, รบกัน

h)rop!-kuan v. annoy, bother รบกวน

h)rot! n. taste รส

h)rot! n. vehicle, land conveyance, car, wagon รถ

h)rot!, h)rot!-yon! n. auto รถ, รถยนต์

h)rot! ban!.thook!, h)rot! ko-dang n. truck, lorry รถบันทุก, รถโกดัง

h)rot! f)chat tasteful รสชาติ

h)rot! chon! kan! auto accident รถชนกัน

h)rot! doy-r)san, h)rot! meh n. passenger bus รถโดยสาร, รถเมล์

h)rot!-fai! n. train, railway train รถไฟ

h)rot! l)jak!-ra!-yan n. bicycle รถจักรยาน

h)rot! l)jak!-ra!-yan-yon!, h)rot! maw-tuh-sai! n. motorcycle รถจักรยานยนต์, รถมอเตอร์ไซค์

h)rot! l)kraw! (mil.) armored vehicles รถเกราะ

h)rot! h)nam! v. water (flowers & plants) รถน้ำ

h)rot! nawn n. railway sleeping-car รถนอน

h)rot! pha!-ya-ban n. ambulance รถพยาบาล

h)rot! f)phuang n. trailer (vehicle) รถพ่วง

h)rot! l)pra!-jam! thang bus, passenger bus รถประจำทาง

h)rot! rang n. streetcar, trolley, tram รถราง

h)rot! r)sam-h)law n. samlor, tricycle-taxi. 3-wheeled conveyance รถสามล้อ

h)rot! teen l)ta!-l)khap n. caterpillar tractor รถตีนตะขาบ

h)rot! h)thaek!-f)see n. taxi รถแท็กซี่

h)rot!-yon! n. motor vehicle รถยนต์

f)rua v. leak รั่ว

h)rua n. fence (enclosure) รั้ว

ruam including, add up, total รวม

f)ruam, f)ruam f)duay [f)khao! f)ruam] v. participate, take part in ร่วม, ร่วมด้วย (เข้าร่วม)

f)ruam kan! together (of people) ร่วมกัน

f)ruam meu, f)ruam meu kan! v. cooperate, work together ร่วมมือ, ร่วมมือกัน

f)ruam pai! f)duay v. accompany (go with) ร่วมไปด้วย

ruam h)thang!-l)mot! altogether, total ร่วมทั้งหมด

f)ruap-ruam v. compile (as a book) รวบรวม

ruay adj. rich (financially) รวย

ruh v. belch เรอ

f)ruhm, f)rahm f)ton! v. begin เริ่ม, เริ่มต้น

l)sa!, l)sa! h)nam! n. pond, small lake สระ, สระน้ำ

l)sa! l)ap-h)nam!, l)sa! f)wai-h)nam! n. swimming pool สระลอยน้ำ, สระว่ายน้ำ

l)sa!-l)at adj. clean สะอาด

sa!-bai, sa!-bai dee well, be well, well and happy สบาย, สบายดี

sa!-bai dee r)reu? How are you? Are you well? สบายดีหรือ

l)sa!-l)boo n. soap สบู่, สะบู่

sa!-daeng v. show, demonstrate, express, display แสดง

sa!-daeng khwam yin!-dee congratulate someone แสดงความยินดี

sa!-daeng tua identify oneself, establish one's identity แสดงตัว

l)sa!-l)duak adj. convenient, easy to do สะดวก

f)sae n. whip, mosquito or fly duster แส้

f)sae n. clan, family (Chinese names) แซ่

f)saek-seum v. infiltrate, stealthily penetrate แทรกซึม

r)saen [l)neung! r)saen, r)saen l)neung!] one hundred thousand (100,000) แสน (หนึ่งแสน, แสนหนึ่ง)

saeng v. pass, overtake in driving, cut in front of someone (in driving) แซง

r)saeng n. light, ray, beam of light แสง

r)saeng l)daet n. sunshine, sunlight แสงแดด

r)saeng fai! n. rays of light (from light bulb, fire, etc.) แสงไฟ

r)saeng jan! n. moonlight แสงจันทร์

r)saeng l)sa!-l)wang n light (in general) แสงสว่าง

l)saep v. smart, sting (as a sore place when touched) แสบ

l)sa!-l)euk! v. hiccup, hiccough สะอึก

l)sa!-l)ha! l)pra!-cha-f)chat the U.N. (United Nations) สหประชาชาติ

l)sa!-l)ha!-h)rat! (ah-me-ri-ka) the United States (of America) สหรัฐ (อเมริกา)

sai n. sand ทราย

h)sai, h)sai meu left, lefthand side ซ้าย, ซ้ายมือ

l)sai! v. put in, put on (as clothing) ใส่

r)sai! adj. clear (not muddied or disturbed) ใส

r)sai tardy, late (not on time), late in the morning; transport line; something long and thin, rope, string, wire; a road or other thoroughfare; telephone line สาย

r)sai ah-l)kat, r)sao ah-l)kat n. aerial, antenna (for T.V., radio) สายอากาศ, เสาอากาศ

f)sai!-deuan n. earthworm ไส้เดือน

r)sai fai!-h)fa n. electric wire, power line สาย ไฟฟ้า

r)sai kan bin! n. airline, airline company สาย การบิน

l)sai! l)klap! put on clothing backwards ใส่กลับ

l)sai! klawn v. bolt, bolt a door ใส่กลอน

l)sai! koon-jae v. lock, lock a door ใส่กุญแจ

f)sai!-l)krawk n. sausage (meat) ไส้กรอก

r)sai f)mai! f)wang   the line is busy (telephone)
สายไม่ว่าง

l)sai! h)nam!-man!   v. oil, apply oil, lubricate
ใส่น้ำมัน

r)sai phan   n. belt (for machinery)   สายพาน

r)sai f)sawy, r)sai f)sawy khaw   n. necklace   สาย
สร้อย, สายสร้อยคอ

r)sai tho-ra!-l)sap!   n. telephone line   สายโทรศัพท์

f)sai! l)ting!   (med.) appendicitis   ไส้ติ่ง

r)sai h)wa!!   n. measuring tape   สายวัด

h)sak!, h)sak! f)pha   wash clothes   ซัก, ซักผ้า

l)sak!   about (approximately)   สัก

l)sak!   n. teak, teakwood   สัก

r)sa-r)kha   n. branch (of a company, of an
academic field, etc.)   สาขา

h)sak! f)haeng   v. dry-clean (clothing)   ซักแห้ง

l)sak! f)khroo   just a moment, for only a short
time   สักครู่

l)sa!-l)kot!, l)sa!-l)kot! tua   v. spell, spell a word
สะกด, สะกดตัว

h)sak! f)pha   wash clothes   ซักผ้า

l)sak! l)pra!-r)deeo   just a minute   สักประเดี๋ยว

h)sak! ')reet   v. launder, wash and iron clothes
ซักรีด

l)sak!-l)sit! adj. sacred ศักดิ์สิทธิ์

l)sa!-l)la! v. sacrifice สละ

i)sa!-l)lak [kin] l)baeng! n. lottery สลาก (กินแบ่ง)

l)sa!-lat! n. salad (food); sea pirates สลัด

l)sa!-r)leung! 25 satangs, 1/4 of one Thai baht,
a 25-satang coin สลึง

l)sa!-l)lop! v. faint สลบ

h)sam! repeat, same as before ซ้ำ

r)sam three (3) สาม (๓)

l)sa!-ma-h)chik! n. member, subscriber (to a
periodical) สมาชิก

l)sa!-r)mai! n. period, era สมัย

l)sa!-r)mai! l)kawn in former times สมัยก่อน

l)sa!-r)mai! h)nee nowadays, in present times
สมัยนี้

l)sa!-l)mak! apply (to do, be or get something)
สมัคร

l)sa!-ma-khom! n. association (group, society,
club) สมาคม

l)sa!-l)mak! f)len be or do something as an
amateur สมัครเล่น

r)ra-f)mat able, can, can do, capable สามารถ

l)sa!-r)maw n. anchor (of a ship) สมอ

l)sa!-r)mawng n. brain(s) สมอง

r)sa-mee n. husband [polite term; everyday words are "r)phua" and "faen"] สามี

l)sa!-r)mian n. clerk, office-worker เสมียน

r)sam!-khan! adj. important สำคัญ

r)sam!-h)lak! (h)not! v. choke (on) สำลัก (น้ำ)

r)sam-h)law n. "samlor", tricycle-taxi สามล้อ

r)sam-h)law f)khreuang motorized tricycle-taxi, "samlor" สามล้อเครื่อง

r)sam-lee n. cotton wool สำลี

r)sam-l)liam n. triangle สามเหลี่ยม

r)sam!-h)nak! (ngan) n. office, bureau สำนัก (งาน)

r)sam!-nao! n. copy, duplicate (of papers, documents) สำเนา

r)sam! niang n. accent (in speaking) สำเนียง

r)saw!-nuan n. idiom (in speaking) สำนวน

l)sa!-l)moot! h)not n. small notebook สมุดโน้ต

l)sa!-l)moot! tho-ra!-l)sap! n. telephone directory สมุดโทรศัพท์

l)sa!-mo-r)sawn n. club (usually private) สโมสร

r)sam!-pha-h)ra! n. supplies, materiel สัมภาระ

r)sam!-f)phat n. v. interview สัมภาษณ์

r)sam!-ran adj. luxurious, happy, content สำราญ

r)sam!-l)rap! for, in order to สำหรับ

r)sam!-l)ret! be succesaful, succeed สำเร็จ

r)sam!-l)ret! l)jak.... graduate from.... สำเร็จจาก

r)sam!-l)ruat v. survey, inspect, take a census สำรวจ

h)sam! h)sam! over and over, repeatedly ซ้ำๆ

r)sam-l)sip! thirty (30) สามสิบ (๓๐)

l)sa!-r)muh always เสมอ

l)sa!-r)muh kan! even, equal, a tie score เสมอกัน

f)san! short (in length, duration, not usually for height) สั้น

l)san! v. tremble, shake, vibrate สั่น

r)san n. court (of law) ศาล

l)sa-r)nam n. field, yard, lawn สนาม

l)sa-r)nam bin! n. airfield สนามบิน

l)sa!-r)nam h)kawf n. golf course สนามกอล์ฟ

l)sa!-r)nam kee-la n. sports stadium, (colloq.) the National Stadium สนามกีฬา

l)sa!-r)nam h)ma n. racetrack, horse-racing track สนามม้า

l)sa!-r)nam h)rop! n. battlefield สนามรบ

l)sa!-r)nam f)ya n. lawn, yard, grassy lawn สนามหญ้า

l)sa!-l)nap! l)sa!-r)noon v. support, be in favor of สนับสนุน

r)san!-f)chat n. citizenship สัญชาติ

f)sang v. build สร้าง

l)sang! v. order, command สั่ง

l)sang! ah-r)han order fcod (in a restaurant)
สั่งอาหาร

r)sang!-l)kal-)see n. zinc, galvanized iron สังกะสี

r)sang!-l)ket v. observe สังเกต

r)sang!-khom! society, social สังคม

l)sal-l)ngop! adj. peaceful สงบ

l)sang! h)wail leave a message (as on the phone)
สั่งไว้

l)sal-r)nim!, l)sal-r)nim! f)kheun! rust, rusty สนิม,
สนิมขึ้น

l)sal-!)nook! fun, a food time, enjoyable สนุก

r)san!-l)til-f)phap n. peace สันติภาพ

l)sal-r)nuh v. offer, propose เสนอ

r)san!-ya n. contract, agreement; v. promise
สัญญา

f)saol, f)saol l)sok adj. sad เศร้า, เศร้าโศก

r)saol n. post, pole เสา

r)saol [wan! r)saol] Saturday เสาร์ (วันเสาร์)

r)sao young woman, youthful (for women);
[also shows female gender, as in "r)lan r)sao"
= niece] สาว

r)saol ah-l)kat n. aerial, antenna เสาอากาศ

r)sao h)chai! n. maid สาวใช้

f)sap v. know (know something -- not a person or a place) ทราบ

h)sap! n. wealth, riches ทรัพย์

l)sap! v. chop (as meat) สับ

l)sap!-da, l)sap!-l)pa!-da n. week, a week สัปดาห์

l)sa!-pha n. assembly, council สภา

l)sa!-pha ka f)chat the Thai Red Cross สภากาชาด

l)sa!-phan n. bridge พาน

l)sa!-r)phom! shampoo (wash) the hair สระผม

l)sap!-l)pa!-r)ot! n. pineapple สับปะรด

r)sa-ra-f)phap v. confess สารภาพ

r)sa-ra!-h)wat! police inspector สารวัตร

r)sa-ra!-h)wat! h)thal-r)han military police สารวัตร ทหาร

r)sa-ra!.h)wat l)yai! chief inspector (police) สารวัตรใหญ่

l)sa!-r)som! v. collect (as stamps etc.) สะสม

l)sat! n. animal สัตว์

l)sat v. splash (in, on) สาด

l)sa!-taem, l)sa!-taem prai!-l)sa!-nee n. postage stamps แสตมป์, แสตมป์ไปรษณีย์

l)sa!-tang n. satang, 1/100 of one Thai baht, (colloq.) money in general สตางค์

l)sal!-h)tek! n. steak สเต๊ก

l)sal!-r)than, l)sal!-r)than-f)thee n. place, locality สถาน, สถานที่

l)sal!-r)than bo-f)ling! bowling alley สถานโบว์ลิ่ง

l)sal!-r)tha nee n. station (railway, police etc.) สถานี

l)sal!-r)tha nee wit!-tha!-yoo! n. radio station สถานี วิทยุ

l)sal!-r)than-f)thee n. place, localit, สถานที่

l)sal!-r)than-f)thee l)yoo n. address, place of residence สถานที่อยู่

l)sal!-r)than f)thoot n. embassy, diplomatic office in general สถานทูต

l)sal!-r)tha-l)pal!-h)nik! n. architect สถาปนิก

r)sa-tha-ra!-na! adj. public สาธารณะ

r)sa-tha-ra!-na! l)pra!-l)yot n. public welfare, public interest สาธารณประโยชน์

r)sa-tha ra!-na!-l)sook! n. public health สาธารณสุข

r)sal!-l)ti! n. mind, consciousness, sense สติ

l)sat! h)liang n. pet, domesticated animal สัตว์เลี้ยง

l)sat! f)phaet n. veterinarian สัตว์แพทย์

l)sal-tree n. woman, lady [a polite term; ordinary term for "woman" is "f)phoo-r)ying!"] ศรี

l)sat-l)sal-r)na n. religion ศาสนา

l)sat-l)sal-r)na l)it!-l)sal-r)lam n. Islamic religion ศาสนาอิสลาม

l)sat-l)sal-r)na h)khrit! Christian religion ศาสนา คริสต์

l)sat-l)sal-r)na h)phoot! Buddhist religion ศาสนา พุทธ

l)sat-l)sal-tra-ɹan n. professor ศาสตราจารย์

l)sal-r)wan! n. heaven, paradise สวรรค์

l)sa-l)wang adj. bright, light (not dark) สว่าง

sal-wat!-dee Hello. Goodbye. Good morning. Etc. (general greeting and parting wish) สวัสดี

sal-watl-di!-f)phap n. safety สวัสดิภาพ

f)sawm n. fork (for eating) ส้อม

f)sawm, f)sawm-saem v. repair ซ่อม, ซ่อมแซม

h)sawm v. rehearse, practice ซ้อม

f)sawn v. hide something ซ่อน

r)sawn v. teach สอน

sawng, sawng l)jot!-r)mai n. envelope ซอง, ซอง จดหมาย

l)sawng v. shine light on ส่อง

r)sawng two (2) สอง (๒)

r)sawng h)khrang!, r)sawng r)hon! twice, two times สองครั้ง, สองหน

r)sawng r)sam a few, two or three สองสาม

r)sawng f)thao! twice as, double สองเท่า

r)sawng yam midnight (colloq.) สองยาม

f)sawn tua hide oneself ซ่อนตัว

l)sawp, l)sawp f)lai! take an exam สอบ, สอบไล่

l)sawp f)dai! pass an exam สอบได้

l)sawp-r)suan v. investigate, question สอบสวน

l)sawp-r)tham v. enquire สอบถาม

l)sawp l)tok! fail an exam สอบตก

l)sawt, l)sawt f)khao! v. insert สอด, สอดเข้า

sawy n. soi, lane ซอย

f)sawy, f)sawy khaw n. necklace สร้อย, สร้อยคอ

l)sa! r)yaw Siam (old name of Thailand) สยาม

h)see!, h)si! (emphatic word, usually not translated) ซี

l)see four (4) สี่ (๔)

r)see n. color, paint สี

r)see choml-phoo pink (color) สีชมพู

f)seed, f)seet, f)seed-seeo, f)seet-seeo adj. pale (complexion) ซีด, ซีดเชียว

r)see daeng red (color) สีแดง

r)see dam! black (color) สีดำ

r)see h)fa light-blue (color) สีฟ้า

r)see r)khao white (color) สีขาว

r)see r)kheeo green (color) สีเขียว

f)see khrong n. ribs ซี่โครง

l)see-l)liam n., adj. quadrilateral สีเหลี่ยม

r)see f)muang purple (color) สีม่วง

r)see h)nam!-nguhn dark blue (color) สีน้ำเงิน

r)see h)nam!-tan brown (color) สีน้ำตาล

r)see-l)sa! n. head (of a person) ศีรษะ

l)see-l)sip! forty (40) สี่สิบ (๔๐)

f)seet, f)seet-seeo adj. pale (of complexion) ซีด, ซีดเซียว

r)see thawng gold (color), blond (of the hair) สีทอง

l)see f)yaek n. junction, crossroads (!-way) สี่แยก

sen!, sen! f)cheu v. sign, sign one's name เซ็น, เซ็นชื่อ

f)sen n. line [classifier noun for lines, rope, hair, thread, string etc., as in "f)cheuak r)sawng f)sen = 2 strings] เส้น

r)se-na-thi-kan (mil.) chief of staff เสนาธิการ

f)sen lo-l)hit! n. blood vessel เส้นโลหิต

f)sen f)luat n. piece of wire เส้นลวด

f)sen-l)mee n. Chinese egg-noodles เส้นหมี่

f)sen l)pral-l)sat n. nerves (of body) เส้นประสาท

sen l)til-f)met n. centimetre เซนติเมตร

f)sen trong! straight line เส้นตรง

l)sep-l)tit! addicted (especially narcotics & drugs) เสพติด

l)set!, l)set! h)laeo ready, finished, completed เสร็จ, เสร็จแล้ว

l)set n. remainders, wastes, parts (of something) เศษ

l)set ah-r)han n. scraps of food, leftovers เศษ อาหาร

l)set r)khawng n. waste material, rubbish, scraps, remains เศษของ

l)set l)kral-l)dat n. waste paper, paper scraps เศษกระดาษ

l)set l)suan fraction, part of something [Note. Any fraction may by expressed by the formula "l)set + top number; l)suan + bottom number", as in 3/4 = l)set r)sam l)suan l)see.] เศษส่วน

l)set-l)thal-l)kit! n. economy, the economy
เศรษฐกิจ

f)seu, f)seu-trong adj. honest, faithful ซื่อ, ซื่อตรง

h)seu v. buy ซื้อ

f)seua n. shirt, blouse, coat เสื้อ

f)seua, f)seua f)nawk coat (of man's suit) เสื้อ,
เสื้อนอก

f)seua, f)seua f)pha n. clothes, clothing (in
general) เสื้อ, เสื้อผ้า

f)seua n. mat (or other floor covering) เสื่อ

r)seua n. tiger เสือ

f)seua h)cham!-nai! n. undershirt เสื้อชั้นใน

f)seua h)chuht n. shirt เสื้อเชิ้ต

f)seua r)fon, f)seua kan! r)fon! n. raincoat เสื้อฝน,
เสื้อกันฝน

f)seua kan! r)nao!, f)seua r)nao n. sweater, jacket
(for cold or cool weather) เสื้อกันหนาว, เสื้อหนาว

f)seua khloom! n. overcoat เสื้อคลุม

l)seuam, l)seuam r)sia v. decay, lose vigor,
deteriorate เสื่อม, เสื่อมเสีย

l)seua h)nam!-man! n. linoleum carpet เสื่อน้ำมัน

f)seua-f)pha h)cham!-nai! n. underwear เสื้อผ้าชั้นใน

f)seua l)sal-tree n. blouse (lady's) เสื้อสตรี

l)seuk!, l)seuk! l)awk ma, leave the Buddhist priesthood (after serving as a Buddhist priest) สึก, สึกลาสิกขา

h)seu r)kkawng buy things, do shopping ซื้อของ

l)seuk!-r)sa v. study, learn (on higher levels) ศึกษา

seum! f)khao! v. absorb, seep into ซึมเข้า

f)seung! (relative pron.) who, which, that ซึ่ง

f)seung! kan! h)lae! kan! mutually, to each other, to one another ซึ่งกันและกัน

l)seup v. investigate, pass on (as a tradition) continue (as a family line) สืบ

l)seup r)suan v. investigate, question about something สืบสวน

l)seup l)taw v. continue (as a family line, tradition, etc.) สืบต่อ

f)seu-l)sat! adj. honest, faithful, loyal ซื่อสัตย์

f)sea-trong! adj. faithful, honest ซื่อตรง

r)sew [r)siu] n. pimple สิว

h)si! [h)see!] (emphatic word used at end of phrases or sentences, usually not translated) ซี

l)sia, l)sia l)yai! n. wealthy and successful businessman (usually Chinese or part-Chinese) เสีย, เสียใหญ่

r)sia (v., adj.) waste, spend, worn, worn out, broken, out of order, pay out, spoiled, in a bad way, lose, become less potent เสีย

r)sia-dai v: regret, begrudge เสียดาย

c)sia r)hai damaged, lost เสียหาย

c)sia jai! regret, be sorry, I'm sorry เสียใจ

r)siam n. spade (small, narrow) เสียม

l)siang v. risk, take a risk เสี่ยง

c)siang n. voice, sound, noise, tone เสียง

r)sia nguhn pay out money, waste money เสียเงิน

r)sia l)priap be at a disadvantage, be on losing end of a bargain เสียเปรียบ

r)sia we-la waste time, lose time เสียเวลา

c)sin!-bon! n. bribe สินบน

r)sin!-f)cheua (n., comr.) credit สินเชื่อ

f)sin!-deuan end of month, last day of month สิ้นเดือน

l)sing!, l)sing!·r)khawng n. thing (in general) สิ่ง, สิ่งของ

r)sing!, r)sing!-to n. lion สิงห์, สิงโต

r)sing!·r)ha-khom! August สิงหาคม

r)sin!-h)kha n goods, merceandise สินค้า

h)sin! l)soot! v. expire, terminate, end สินสุด

l)sip! ten (10) สิบ (๑๐)

l)sip! l)ek (mil.) sgt. (3 stripes) สิบเอก

l)sip!-l)et! eleven (11) สิบเอ็ด (๑๑)

l)sip!-r)sawng twelve (12) สิบสอง (๑๒)

l)sip!-tho (mil.) corporal (2 stripes) สิบโท

l)sip!-tree (mil.) lance corporal, pvt. 1st-class
  (1 stripe) สิบตรี

l)sit!, l)sit!-h)thi! n. right, privilege สิทธิ, สิทธิ

f)so n. chain โซ่

so-da n. soda, soda water โซดา

soi (sawy) soi, lane (small road) ซอย

l)sok adj. tragic โศก

l)sok!-l)ka!-l)prok! adj. dirty สกปรก

f)som! n. orange, citrus fruit ส้ม

r)som! adj. suitable, appropriate สม

r)som!-l)bat! n. wealth, treasure สมบัติ

f)som! r)kheeo-r)wan n. tangerine (fruit) ส้ม
  เขียวหวาน

r)som!-khuan adj. suitable, proper สมควร

r)som-h)moot! [t)wa] v. suppose (that) สมมุติ (ว่า)

f)som!-oh pomelo (fruit), grapefruit ส้มโอ

r)som!-h)rot! v. marry, wed สมรส

son! adj. mischievous, naughty (usually said about children) ซน

f)son!, f)son! h)tao! n. heel (of foot) ส้น, ส้นเท้า

song! v. hold up, maintain, stay the same (also used before normal or special verbs to show actions by royalty) ทรง

l)song! v. send, deliver, see someone off (on trip), ship something ส่ง

l)song! l)jot-r)mai mail (send) a letter ส่งจดหมาย

l)song! kheun v. return something, give back ส่งคืน

r)song!-khram n. war สงคราม

r)song!-khram l)jit-l)ta!-wit-tha-ya psychological warfare สงครามจิตวิทยา

r)song!-r)sai! v. doubt, suspect, wonder สงสัย

r)song!-r)san v. pity, feel sorry for สงสาร

l)song!-r)suhm v. promote, foster, support ส่งเสริม

r)son!-jai! interested (in something) ..ใจ

f)soo v. fight, oppose สู้

l)sook! [wan! l)sook!] Friday ศุกร์ (วันศุกร์)

l)sook! ripe, mature (usually of fruit), well-done (as cooked meat) สุก

l)sook-l)kha!-f)phap n. health สุขภาพ

l)sook! l)sook! l)dip! l)dip! rare (as in cooking meat) สุกๆ ดิบๆ

l)soon zero (0) ศูนย์, สูญ (๐)

l)soon, r)soon r)hai v disappear, be lost สูนย์, สูญหาย

l)soon, r)soon klang n center, centre (usually of activities of some sort) ศูนย์, ศูนย์กลาง

l)soong adj. tall, high, great, noble สูง

l)soop [boo-l)ree] v. smoke (cigarettes) สูบ (บุหรี่)

l)soop [(h)nam!] v. pump (water) สูบ (น้ำ)

l)soo!-f)phap adj. polite สุภาพ

l)soo!-f)phap-boo-root! n. gentleman สุภาพบุรุษ

l)soo-f)phap-sa-tree n. lady สุภาพสตรี

l)soo!-ra n. alcoholic beverages สุรา

f)soo-h)rop! kan! v. battle, engage in warfare สู้รบกัน

l)soo!-r)san n. cemetery, graveyard สุสาน

soo-ti!-l)bat! n. birth certificate สูติบัตร

l)soot! l)sap!-pa!-da n. weekend สุดสัปดาห์

l)soot!-h)thai last, final, last or final one สุดท้าย

l)sop! n. corpse, body of deceased ศพ

r)so-phe-nee n. prostitute โสเภณี

l)sot! adj. fresh (not stale) สด

l)sot adj. single, unmarried โสด

f)suam n. toilet ส้วม

r)suam v. wear (clothing), have on, put on (clothing) สวม

l)suan n. part, branch, bureau, portion, share ส่วน

r)suan n. garden, orchard, park สวน

l)suan l)book!·khon! adj. private (not public) ส่วนบุคคล

l)suan f)kwang l)pak l)kra!·l)bawk n. caliber (of barrel of weapon) ส่วนกว้างปากกระบอก

l)suan h)lot! n. discount ส่วนลด

l)suan f)mak most, most of, a majority ส่วนมาก

l)suan h)nawy least, the smallest part, a minority ส่วนน้อย

l)suan ruam collectively, as a whole ส่วนรวม

r)suan l)sa!·r)nam v. parade สวนสนาม

r)suan l)sa!! n. zoo สวนสัตว์

l)suan tua private, personal (of an individual) ส่วนตัว

suay (sway) (colloq., from Chinese) bad luck, nothing goes right ซวย

r)suay, r)suay ngam pretty, beautiful สวย, สวยงาม

r)suhm r)suay get beauty treatments (hair, facials etc.) เสริมสวย

ta n. eye, grandfather (maternal) ตา

ta!-bai! n. file (tool) ตะไบ

ta!-bai! h)lep! n. nail-file ตะไบเล็บ

ta l)bawt blind (without sight) ตาบอด

l)tae, l)tae f)wa conj. but แต่, แต่ว่า

l)tae l)kawn formerly, in the past แต่ก่อน

f)tae-r)jew! Swatow (sua-thao), Taechiu, Tae-
chew (Chinese dialect spoken by majority of
Chinese speakers in Thailand) แต้จิ๋ว

l)taek v. break (something small, fragile), be
wrecked, be smashed แตก

f)taem n. score, mark (in game or contest) แต้ม

l)taeng v. compose, write, decorate, dress (with
clothing) แต่ง

l)taeng kai v. dress oneself, wear clothes แต่งกาย

taeng-kwa n. cucumber แตงกวา

taeng-mo n. watermelon แตงโม

l)taeng-ngan v. marry, wed แต่งงาน

l)taeng-ngan h)laeo married, have a family
แต่งงานแล้ว

l)taeng f)tang! v. appoint (to a position) แต่งตั้ง

taeng thai n. muskmelon, cantaloupe แตงไทย

l)taeng tua dress oneself (with clothing) แต่งตัว

l)tae f)raek originally, at the first แต่แรก

tai! n. kidneys (of body) ไต

tai v. die, pass away ตาย

f)tai! underneath, south (direction), below ใต้

l)tai! v. crawl, creep (as insects), climb (as trees, mountains) ไต่

f)tai!-l)foon! n. typhoon ไต้ฝุ่น

tai jing! Oh no! What a mess! etc. (exclamation, used mostly by females) ตายจริง

tai h)laeo Oh no! What a mess! etc. (exclamation, used by anybody) ตายแล้ว

tai tua adj. rigid, inflexible ตายตัว

l)tak, l)tak l)daet dry in the sun, lie in the sun ตาก, ตากแดด

l)ta!-f)kee h)nee just a moment ago ตะกี้นี้

ta-l)khai n. ball net (as tennis net, etc.) ตาข่าย

l)ta!-kiang n. lamp, lantern ตะเกียง

l)ta!-l)kiap n. chopsticks ตะเกียบ

l)ta!-kon v. shout, yell ตะโกน

l)ta!-f)kra n. basket ตะกร้า

l)ta!-kraeng n. sieve, strainer ตะแกรง

l)ta!-krai n. scissors ตะไกร

l)ta!-f)kraw n. takro (Thai game), rattan ball (used in playing "takro") ตะกร้อ

l)ta!-l)kua n. lead (metal) ตะกั่ว

l)ta!-l)kua l)bat!-kree n. solder, soldering lead
คะตัวบัคครี

l)ta!-l)lat n. market ตลาด

l)ta!-l)lat h)nam! the Floating Market (famous
tourist attraction of Bangkok Metropolis)
ตลาดน้ำ

l)ta!-l)lat h)nat! n. weekend market, market
open only one certain day(s) ตลาดนัด

l)ta!-l)lawt through, throughout, all during ตลอด

l)ta!-l)lawt kan, l)ta!-l)lawt pai! forever, from
now on ตลอดกาล, ตลอดไป

l)ta!-l)lawt we-la all the time, continuously
ตลอดเวลา

l)ta!-l)lok! joking, funny, comical, amusing ตลก

tam! v. pound (as food, in container), puncture,
pierce (as by a thorn) ตำ

tam (v., prep.) follow, in accordance with,
according to, along (a road etc.), around
(somewhere), in (certain places) ตาม

l)tam! low, low-class, low-level ต่ำ

tam!-bon! tambon (subdiv. of amphoe or district), commune, precinct ตำบล

tam!-bon! f)thee l)yoo address, place of residence
ตำบลพอยู่

tam jai! as you wish, as you like คามใจ

tam l)kot!-r)mai according to the law ตามกฎหมาย

tam lam!-l)dap! in order, orderly arrangement by precedence ตามลำดับ

tam lam!-phang alone, by oneself ตามลำพัง

tam!-l)naeng n. position, post (in govt. service, in business etc.) ตำแหน่ง

tam!-l)ni! v. blame, criticize ตำหนิ

tam-ra n. textbook ตำรา

tam-ra ah-r)han n. recipe (for cooking) ตำราอาหาร

tam h)ral-l)biap in accordance with regulations, in the prescribed way ตามระเบียบ

tam rai-kan ah-r)han à la carte (according to menu, item by item) ตามรายการอาหาร

tam!-l)ruat police, policeman ตำรวจ

tam!-l)ruat [l)tral-wen] chai daen border police ตำรวจ (ตวงเวน) ชายแดน

tam!-l)ruat ja-ra-jawn traffic police ตำรวจจราจร

tam!-l)ruat na-khawn ban Metropolitan Police (of Bangkok Metropolis) ตำรวจนครบาล

tam!-l)ruat phoo-thawn Provincial Police (outside Bangkok Metropolis) ตำรวจภูธร

tam!-l)ruat r)san!-ti!-ban Special Branch Police ตำรวจสันติบาล

tam!-l)ruat thang r)luang highway police ตำรวจ
ทางหลวง

tam l)sa!-l)duak at your convenience ตามสะดวก

tam tham!-ma!-da usual, as usual, usually, normally ตามธรรมดา

f)tang!, f)tang! f)kheun! v. set up, begin something, establish, place something somewhere
ตั้ง, ตั้งขึ้น

l)tang, l)tang l)kap! different, be different ต่าง,
ต่างกัน

l)tang jang!-l)wat! upcountry, in the provinces
ต่างจังหวัด

f)tang! f)kheun! v. establish, organize, found
ตั้งขึ้น

f)tang! na-li-ka set a clock or watch ตั้งนาฬิกา

f)tang! na-li-ka f)riak l)plook! set an alarm clock
ตั้งนาฬิกาเรียกปลุก

l)tang l)pral-f)thet foreign, abroad, foreign
countries in general ต่างประเทศ

f)tang! l)tae since, from a certain time until
another time (past or future), beginning (at,
on, in) ตั้งแต่

l)tang l)tang different, various ต่างๆ

f)tang! f)ton! v. begin, commence something ตั้งต้น

tao! n. stove, oven เตา

l)tao! n. turtle, tortoise เต่า

tao! fai!-h)fa n. electric stove เตาไฟฟ้า

tao! kaes (gas) n. gas stove เตาแก๊ส

f)tao! nom! n. breast (female breast) เต้านม

tao! f)op! n. oven (for cooking) เตาอบ

tao! f)reet (f)pha n. iron (for ironing clothes) เตารีดผ้า

l)tap! n. liver (body organ or of animals) ตับ

l)ta!-f)phok n. hips (of the body) ตะโพก

l)tap! r)moo n. pork liver ตับหมู

l)ta!-poo n. nail (for driving with hammer) ตะปู

l)ta!-poo khuang n. screw, threaded screw ตะปูควง

l)tap! wua n. beef liver ตับวัว

ta-rang n. schedule, square measure [as in "ta-rang f)met" = square metres] ตาราง

l)ta!-rang n. jail, prison ตะราง

l)tat! v. cut ตัด

l)tat! l)awk n. cut out, take out, omit ตัดออก

l)tat! r)phom! cut hair, get a haircut ตัดผม

l)tat!-r)sin!, l)tat!-r)sin! jai! v. decide, judge, make up one's mind ตัดสิน, ตัดสินใจ

l)taw (v., prep.) connect, continue, extend, join; per [as in "l)taw f)chua-mong" = per hour] ต่อ

l)taw, l)taw pai! go on, continue ต่อ, ต่อไป

l)taw, l)taw ra-kha v. bargain (over a price) ต่อ, ต่อราคา

ta!-wan! l)awk sunrise, east (direction) ตะวันออก

ta!-wan! l)tek! sunset, west (direction), the West (Europe & Americas) ตะวันตก

l)tawk n. drive a nail, hammer something, pound something ตอก

tawn n. section, period of time, part ตอน

f)tawn v. herd along, round up, trap, corner (by questions) ต้อน

tawn l)bai afternoon, in the afternoon ตอนบ่าย

tawn h)chao! morning, in the morning ตอนเช้า

f)tawng v. must, have to ต้อง

f)tawng-kan v. need, want, require ต้องการ

tawn klang kheun at night, during the night-time ตอนกลางคืน

tawn klang wan! daytime, in the daytime ตอน กลางวัน

f)tawn-h)rap! v. greet, welcome a visitor, entertain someone, receive guests ต้อนรับ

tawn f)ton! the beginning, the first part ตอนต้น

tawn yen! late afternoon, in the late afternoon ตอนเย็น

l)**tawp** v. answer, reply ตอบ

l)**taw** l)**phit!** wrong number, call wrong number (on phone) ต่อผิด

l)**taw ra-kha** v. bargain (for better price) ต่อราคา

l)**taw** f)**soo** v. fight, oppose, struggle ต่อสู้

l)**taw** f)**tan** v. resist, hold back ต่อต้าน

l)**taw wan!** per day ต่อวัน

l)**tawy** v. punch (hit with fist), sting (as a bee) ต่อย

l)**te!**, l)**teh!** v. kick เตะ

tee v. beat, whip, hit, strike; [also used colloquially for hours from 1 a.m. to 5 a.m., to mean "o'clock", as in "tee l)neung!" — 1.00 a.m.] ตี

tem! adj. full, full up เต็ม

f)**ten**, f)**ten-ram!** v. dance เต้น, เต้นรำ

teuan (l)**tak! teuan, teuan jai!**) v. warn, caution, remind เตือน (ตักเตือน, เตือนใจ)

l)**teuk!** n. building (of stone or brick) ตึก

l)**teun**, l)**teun nawn**, l)**teun** f)**kheun!** v. awake, awaken, wake up ตื่น (ตื่นนอน, ตื่นขึ้น)

teung! adj. tight, taut, tense, strained ตึง

l)teun-f)ten adj. excited, exciting ตื่นเต้น

tha v. rub on, apply, put on (as a liquid etc.) ทา

f)tha, f)tha reua n. port; docks, wharf, landing ท่า, ท่าเรือ

f)tha, f)tha l)hak [f)wa] if, provided that, in the event that ถ้า, ถ้าหาก (ว่า)

f)tha ah-l)kat l)sa!-yan n. airport ท่าอากาศยาน

tha!-bian n. register, registry ทะเบียน

tha!-bian h)rot! n. license plate (for an automobile), vehicle registration ทะเบียนรถ

tha!-bian l)tang-f)dao n. alien registration card, alien papers ทะเบียนต่างด้าว

h)thae real, genuine, authentic, really, true, very, very much แท้

h)thaek!-f)see n. taxi, taxicab แท็กซี่

thaen v. substitute, take the place of แทน

h)thaeng, h)thaeng f)look (n., v.) miscarriage, abortion, have a miscarriage แท้ง, แท้งลูก

thaen f)thee instead of, to replace something else แทนที่

r)thaeo n. row, line, section แถว

f)thaep almost, nearly แทบ

h)tha!-r)han n. soldier, military personnel in general ทหาร

h)tha!-r)han, thang h)tha!-r)han adj. military, pertaining to military ทหาร, ทางทหาร

h)tha!-r)han ah-l)kat (mil.) airman, air-force personnel, pertaining to air force ทหารอากาศ

h)tha!-r)han l)bok! (mil.) soldier, ground forces, pertaining to army ทหารบก

h)tha!-r)han f)chang (mil.) engineers ทหารช่าง

h)tha!-r)han l)fai na-wi-ka-yo-thin (mil.) marines ทหารฝ่ายนาวิกโยธิน

h)tha-r)han h)ma (mil.) horse cavalry ทหารม้า

h)tha!-r)han h)ma yan-l)kraw! (mil.) armored cavalry ทหารม้ายานเกราะ

h)tha!-r)han peun-l)yai (mil.) artillery forces ทหารปืนใหญ่

h)tha!-r)han f)rap (mil.) infantry ทหารราบ

h)tha!-r)han reua (mil.) sailors, navy personnel, pertaining to navy ทหารเรือ

h)tha!-r)han yam (mil.) sentry, guard ทหารยาม

h)tha!-r)han yan-i)kraw! (mil.) armored, armored cavalry ทหารยานเกราะ

thai! Thai, Thailand ไทย

thai, thai doo v. guess ทาย, ทายดู

h)thai at the end, the end, rear, last part ท้าย

r)thai! n., v. plow, plough ไถ

l)thai f)roop, l)thai f)phap v. photograph ถ่ายรูป, ถ่ายภาพ

f)thak n. land leech ทาก

h)thak!-thai v. greet, exchange greetings ทักทาย

h)tha!-h)law!, h)tha!-h)law! kan! v. argue. quarrel ทะเลาะ, ทะเลาะกัน

h)tha!-leh n. sea ทะเล

h)tha!-leh l)sap n. lake, inland sea ทะเลสาบ

tham! v. make, do ทำ

f)tham! n. cave ถ้ำ

r)tham v. ask (questions) ถาม

tham! ah-r)han, tham! l)kap!-f)khao cook, make food, prepare food ทำอาหาร, ทำกับข้าว

tham! f)duay made of, made from ทำด้วย

tham! f)hai! v. cause, make happen ทำให้

tham! f)hai! l)beua v. bore, make bored ทำให้เบื่อ

tham! f)hai! f)cheua v. convince ทำให้เชื่อ

tham! jon! khuhy v. become accustomed to, get used to ทำจนเคย

tham! kan thaen v., adj. acting (in place of someone else), act in place of someone else (as in a position) ทำการแทน

ham! l)kap!-f)khao cook, prepare food ทำกับข้าว

am! khwam l)sa!-l)at v. clean up, do cleaning work ทำความสะอาด

ham!-lai v. destroy, ruin, demolish ทำลาย

ham!-ma!-da adj. normal, ordinary, natural, usual, regular ธรรมดา

ham!-mai! why? ทำไม

ham! f)mai! f)dai! can't do something, cannot be done ทำไม่ได้

ham! na v. rice-farm ทำนา

tham!-nai v. predict ทำนาย

ham! ngan v. work, do work ทำงาน

tham!-niam v. custom (of people) ธรรมเนียม

tham! l)phit! v. make a mistake, commit an offense or crime ทำผิด

tham! h)rai v. hurt someone (physically), injure (cause harm) ทำร้าย

tham! f)thot v. punish ทำโทษ

than!, than! we-la in time, on time, timely ทัน, ทันเวลา

f)than (pron., respectful) you, he, she, him, her, they, them (also used respectfully before the names or titles of important people or people worthy of respect) ท่าน

l)than n. battery (small), charcoal ถ่าน

tha!·na!·l)bat! n. banknote ธนบัตร

tha!·nai khwam n. attorney-at-law, lawyer ทนายความ

tha!·na-khan n. bank ธนาคาร

tha!·na-h)nat! postal money-order ธนาณัติ

thang n. way, path, road, route, direction, via, by way of, in the way of, in the field of, method, means ทาง

h)thang! adj. all ทั้ง

r)thang! n. bucket, large can, tank, pail ถัง

r)thang! n. (mil.) tank ถัง

thang ah·l)kat air-mail, via air-mail ทางอากาศ

thang l)awk n. exit, way out ทางออก

thang f)awm n. detour ทางอ้อม

thang l)bok! by land, pertaining to land ทางบก

thang deeo one-way street ทางเดียว

thang duhn n. aisle, pathway, footpath, trail ทางเดิน

thang duhn h)thao! n. sidewalk, pavement (for pedestrians) ทางเดินเท้า

thang f)khao! n. entrance, way in ทางเข้า

h)thang! kheun all night ทั้งคืน

thang r)khwa   right, on the right-hand side
ทางขวา

thang klai! long-distance (telephone) ทางไกล

h)thang!-r)lai all (shows plural, as in "r)khao
h)thang!-r)lai" = they or them) ทั้งหลาย

thang r)luang [l)phaen-din!] n. (national) highway
ทางหลวง (แผ่นดิน)

h)thang! l)mot! adj., pron. all, altogether, all of
something ทั้งหมด

r)thang! r)phong!, r)thang! l)khal-l)yu: ... wastebasket, trash can, garbage can ถังผง, ถังขยะ

thang reua by boat, sea mail (regular mail)
ทางเรือ

thang h)rot!-fai! by train, railroad, railway ทาง
รถไฟ

thang h)sai, thang h)sai meu left-hand side, to
the left ทางซ้าย, ทางซ้ายมือ

h)thang! r)sawng both, both of.... ทั้งสอง

thang h)thao! n. sidewalk, footpath ทางเท้า

than f)khao v. eat, dine ทานข้าว

f)than h)khrap!, f)than h)kha! (polite terms,
respectful) Sir, Madam [when addressing
someone: f)than h)khrap! is spoken by males

f)than h)kha! is spoken by females] ท่านครับ,
ท่านคะ

l)tha!-r)non! n. road, street, avenue ถนน

than!·ta!-f)phaet n. dental surgeon ทันตแพทย์

r)than h)thap! n. military base ฐานทัพ

r)than h)thap! ah-l)kat (mil.) AF base ฐานทัพอากาศ

r)than h)thap! reua (mil.) naval base ฐานทัพเรือ

than!·thee at once, immediately ทันที

than!·wa·khom! December ธันวาคม

than ya take medicine ทานยา

thao! [r)see thao!] gray (color) เทา (สีเทา)

h)thao! n. foot (of body) เท้า

f)thao!-l)kae n. wealthy and successful Chinese
businessman เถ้าแก่

f)thao!-kan! equal, equally เท่ากัน

f)thao!-l)kap! equal to เท่ากับ

f)thao! l)kap! f)wa.... equivalent to saying that....
เท่ากับว่า....

f)thao!-h)nan! only, just, no more than that
เท่านั้น

h)thao! l)plao! barefoot(ed) เท้าเปล่า

f)thao!-rai! how much? how....? เท่าไร

f)thap v. put over, place, lay on top ทาบ

h)thap! on top of, overlay, run over, crush, diagonal mark (/) ทับ

h)thap! (mil.) army, armed forces, troops ทัพ

h)thap! ah-l)kat (mil.) air force ทัพอากาศ

h)thap! l)bok! (mil.) army ทัพบก .

h)thap! reua (mil.) navy ทัพเรือ

h)thap!-thim! n. ruby ทับทิม

tha r)see v. paint, apply paint ทาสี

f)that n. slave ทาส

l)that n. tray ถาด

f)tha thang n. appearance, how one looks ท่าทาง

l)that! pai! next (in a series) ถัดไป

that!-sa!-na! n. attitude, outlook ทัศน

f)thaw n. pipe, tube, hose ท่อ

f)thaw ai!-r)sia n. muffler, exhaust pipe ท่อไอเสีย

r)tha-wawn adj. permanent, lasting, regular ถาวร

tha!-wee, tha!-wee f)kheun v. increase, become larger ทวี, ทวีขึ้น

tha!-f)weep n. continent ทวีป

h)thaw jai! v. despair, be discouraged ท้อใจ

f)thawn n. part, section, piece ท่อน

r)thawn v. withdraw, take out, take back ถอน

thawng, thawng-kham n. gold ทอง, ทองคำ

thawng [r)see thawng] adj. gold, golden, blond(e) ทอง (สีทอง)

f)thawng, f)thawng jam! v. memorize, learn by heart ท่อง, ท่องจำ

h)thawng n. stomach, abdomen ท้อง

thawng brawn n. bronze ทองบรอนซ์

thawng daeng n. copper ทองแดง

h)thawng duhn, h)thawng f)ruang n. diarrhea, upset stomach ท้องเดิน, ท้องร่วง

h)thawng·h)fa n. sky ท้องฟ้า

thawng r)khao n. white gold, platinum, nickel ทองขาว

thawng r)leuang n. brass ทองเหลือง

h)thawng h)nawy n. abdomen ท้องน้อย

h)thawng l)phook constipated, constipation ท้องผูก

f)thawng f)theeo v. tour, sightsee ท่องเที่ยว

r)thawn jai! v. sigh ถอนใจ

f)thawn h)mai! n. block of wood, log ท่อนไม้

r)thawn nguhn v. withdraw money ถอนเงิน

thaw f)pha v. weave ทอผ้า

thaw!·ra!·man v. suffer, torture, torment ทรมาน

thaw!·ra!·yot! v. betray ทรยศ

f)thawt fry, fried (for food) ทอด

l)thawt l)awk take off, take out, remove ถอดออก

l)thawt rawng-h)thao! take off one's shoes ถอด
รองเท้า

f)thawt l)sal-r)maw v. anchor, throw out the
anchor ทอดสมอ

l)thawt f)seua [f)pha] take off clothing, undress
ถอดเสื้อ (ผ้า)

r)thawy, r)thawy r)lang! v. retreat, back up,
back up a vehicle ถอย, ถอยหลัง

the, theh v. pour (a liquid) เท

thee n. instance, occasion, time [as in 2 times
= "r)sawng thee"] ที

f)thee that, that which, where, at, at a place;
which, who, whom (as relative pronouns);
place or thing for doing something; room,
place, space ที่

thee-deeo quite, very, most, exactly ทีเดียว

f)thee-din! n. land, plot of land ที่ดิน

f)thee l)jawt h)rot! bus-stop, parking space,
parking place ที่จอดรถ

f)thee kan! chon! n. bumper (of vehicle) ที่กันชน

f)thee kan! lom! n. windshield (of vehicle)
ที่กันลม

f)thee r)khai! khuang n. screwdriver ที่ไขควง

f)thee l)khia l)boo!-l)ree n. ashtray ที่เขี่ยบุหรี่

thee h)la!........;........at a time [as in "thee h)la!
   r)sawng" = 2 at a time] ทีละ...

f)thee h)laeo adj. last.... [as in "ah-h)thit! f)thee-
   h)laeo" = last week] ที่แล้ว

f)thee h)laeo ma in the past, formerly, up to now
   ที่แล้วมา

thee r)lang after, later, afterwards, some other
   time (any time after the present) ที่หลัง

thee h)la! l)yang item by item, one by one
   ที่ละอย่าง

f)thee r)leua the remainder, what is left ที่เหลือ

f)thee r)nai! where? what place? ที่ไหน

f)thee r)nai! f)kaw! f)dai! anywhere, any place
   will do ที่ไหนก็ได้

f)thee f)nan! there, that place, at that place ที่นั่น

f)thee f)nang! n. seat, place to sit ที่นั่ง

f)thee-nawn n. mattress ที่นอน

f)thee f)nee here, this place, at this place ที่นี่

f)thee l)neep h)nek!-thai! n. tie-clasp ที่หนีบเน็คไท

f)theeo v. go out for a good time, tour, go
   around aimlessly เที่ยว

f)theeo kan-bin! n. airplane flight, airline flight
   เที่ยวการบิน

f)thee l)preuk!-r)sa n. advisor, consultant ที่ปรึกษา

f)thee l)puht l)khuat n. bottle-opener ที่เปิดขวด

f)thee l)puht l)kra!-r)pawng n. can-opener, tin-opener ที่เปิดกระป๋อง

thee f)rack at first, the first time, in the first place ที่แรก

f)thee h)rak! n. dear, sweetheart ที่รัก

f)thee rawng f)thuay n. saucer ที่รองถ้วย

f)thee f)reng [h)nam!-man!] n. accelerator, gas-pedal ที่เร่ง (น้ำมัน)

f)thee l)soot! to the greatest extent [shows superlative, as in "dee f)thee l)soot!" = the best] ที่สุด

f)thee tham!-kan, f)thee tham!-ngan n. office ที่ทำการ, ที่ทำงาน

f)thee tham! kan prai!-sa!-nee n. post office ที่ทำการไปรษณีย์

f)thee l)yoo n. address, place of residence ที่อยู่

h)thet! adj. false, untrue เท็จ

f)theu adj. blunt (not sharp) ทื่อ

r)theu v. carry (something light), hold (in one's hands), believe in (as a religion or superstition) ถือ

r)theung! v. reach, arrive, get to ถึง

r)theung! h)mae f)wa even, even if, even so ถึงแม้ว่า

r)theu oh-l)kst take advantage of (an opportunity) ถือโอกาส

the.wa!-da (theh-wa-da) n. angel เทวดา

thiam adj. artificial, synthetic เทียม

thian n. candle เทียน

f)thiang, f)thiang wan! noon, 12 o'clock noon เที่ยง, เที่ยงวัน

r)thiang v. contradict, argue, talk back, dispute เถียง

f)thiang kheun midnight, 12 o'clock midnight เที่ยงคืน

f)thiap v. compare เทียบ

h)thing! v. discard, throw away ทิ้ง

h)thing! ra!-l)buht v. bomb, drop bombs ทิ้งระเบิด

h)thit!, h)thit!-thang n. direction, way ทิศ, ทิศทาง

h)thit! r)neua north (direction) ทิศเหนือ

h)thit! f)tai! south (direction) ทิศใต้

h)thit! ta!-wan! l)awk east (direction) ทิศตะวันออก

h)thit! ta!-wan! l)awk r)chiang r)neua northeast (direction) ทิศตะวันออกเฉียงเหนือ

h)thit! ta!-wan! l)awk r)chiang f)tai! southeast (direction) ทิศตะวันออกเฉียงใต้

h)thit! ta!-wan! l)tok! west (direction) ทิศตะวันตก

h)thit! ta!-wan! l)tok! r)chiang f)tai! southwest (direction) ทิศตะวันตกเฉียงใต้

h)thit! thang n. direction, way to go ทิศทาง

tho two (2) [in a telephone number, instead of "r)sawng", for clarity]; 2nd-grade [as in "h)chan! tho", 2nd-grade official] โท

f)tho [short for colloq. expression "h)phoot!-f)tho", of vague meaning] Oh my God! โธ่

l)thom! h)nam!-lai v. spit, expectorate ถ่มน้ำลาย

thon! v. endure, tolerate; adj. durable, lasting ทน

thong! n. flag ธง

thong! f)chat n. national flag ธงชาติ

thon! than lasting, enduring, have long life (for things) ทนทาน

r)thoo v. rub, scour, scrub, polish ถู

h)thook!, h)thook! h)thook! adj. every [as in "h)thook! wan!" = every day] ทุก, ทุกๆ

h)thook! n. sorrow, sadness, unhappiness ทุกข์

l)thook adj. cheap, inexpensive, correct, have right number or answer (as on lottery); [also shows passive voice, as in "l)thook tee = be beaten] ถูก

l)thook, l)thook f)tawng adj. correct, right, accurate ถูก, ถูกต้อง

h)thook! l)sing! [h)thook! l)yang!] everything ทุกสิ่ง
(ทุกอย่าง)

f)thoom! (colloq.)....o'clock [7-11 p.m., as in
"r)sawng f)rhoom!" = 2 o'clock in the evening,
or 8 p.m.] ทุ่ม

thoon! n. funds, capital, scholarship, fellowship
ทุน

f)thoon! n. buoy (at sea) ทุ่น

f)thoong! (na) n. rice-field, paddy-field ทุ่ง (นา)

r)thoong! n. bag, sack, pouch ถุง

r)thoong! meu n. gloves ถุงมือ

r)thoong! h)thao! n. socks (for feet) ถุงเท้า

r)thoong! h)thao! yao n. stockings, hose ถุงเท้ายาว

f)thoop n. incense, joss sticks ธูป

h)thoop!, h)thoop! tee v. hit something hard with
a solid object, beat, smash ทุบ, ทุบตี

h)thoo!-h)ra! n. business, affairs, personal business ธุระ

h)thoo!-h)ra!-kan administration, administrative
ธุรการ

h)thoo!-h)ra!-l)kit! n. business (in general) ธุรกิจ

h)thoo!-rian n. durian (fruit) ทุเรียน

f)thoot diplomat, diplomatic, **ambassador**, envoy, attaché ทูต

f)thoot h)tha!-r)han ah-l)kat n. air attaché ทูตทหาร อากาศ

f)thoot h)tha!-r)han l)bok! n. military attaché (army) ทูตทหารบก

f)thoot h)tha!-r)han reua n. naval attaché ทูตทหาร เรือ

tho pai!, tho.ra!-l)sap! pai! v. call (on phone), make a phone call โทร. ไป, โทรศัพท์ไป

tho l)phit! call wrong number (on phone) โทร.ผิด

h)thop!-thuan v. review (as lessons) ทบทวน

tho-ra!-f)lek n. telegram, cablegram โทรเลข

tho-ra!-l)sap n. v. telephone โทรศัพท์

tho-ra!-h)that! T.V., television set โทรทัศน์

f)thot punish, punishment, blame someone โทษ

h)thot!-lawng v. experiment, try out, test ทดลอง

f)thua, f)thua pai! everywhere, in general ทั่ว, ทั่วไป

l)thua n. bean, nut ถั่ว

l)thua li!-r)song! n. peanuts ถั่วลิสง

f)thuam flooded (with water) ท่วม

f)thuay, f)thuay-f)kaeo n. glass (for drinking) ถ้วย, ถ้วยแก้ว

f)thuay-cham n. dishes (for eating) ถ้วยชาม

thuh you (spoken mostly by elders or teachers to children or students and by girls or women to each other); she, her (colloq. for a famous young woman) เธอ

l)thuh!, l)thuht please (polite word used for mild emphasis at end of requests, orders, or suggestions) เถอะ, เถิด

l)ti!, l)tih! v. blame, criticize ติ

f)tia adj. short (for persons), not tall เตี้ย

tiang, tiang nawn n. bed เตียง, เตียงนอน

l)tit! stick to, attach to, be stuck ติด

l)tit!, l)tit!-h)tang! v. install ติด, ติดตั้ง

l)tit!-fai! ignite (start) a fire ติดไฟ

l)tit!-tian v. blame, criticize ติเตียน

tit! l)kap! against, next to, attached to ติดกับ

tit! f)khreuang start a car or motor ติดเครื่อง

l)tit! l)kra!-doom! v. button ติดกระดุม

l)tit! r)sin!-bon! v. bribe ติดสินบน

l)tit! h)tang! v. install ติดตั้ง

l)tit! l)tal-rang be in jail or prison ติดตะราง

l)tit!-l)taw v. contact, communicate with someone ติดต่อ

l)tit! h)wai! v. attach, connect, stick to ติดไว้

to, toh adj. big, large ใต

t)o, to h)laeo big (in age & size), no longer a
baby or child ใต, โตแล้ว

h)to!, h)toh! n. table โต๊ะ

h)to! ah-r)han n. dining table โต๊ะอาหาร

l)tok! v. fall, fall from, fall out of, drop, fail
(an exam etc.) ตก

to f)kheun! increase in size, become larger โตขึ้น

l)tok!-jai! frightened, suddenly surprised ตกใจ

h)to! klang n. coffee-table โต๊ะกลาง

l)tok!-long! agree, O.K., agreed ตกลง

l)tok!-long! ra-kha bargain & come to an agreement on the price ตกลงราคา

l)tok! pla, l)tok! l)bet! v. fish, go fishing ตกปลา,
ตกเบ็ด

tom! n. mud, mire ตม

f)tom! v. boil something, (slang) trick someone
(as a "con" man etc.) ต้ม

f)ton! n. tree, bush, [classifier noun for trees,
plants, columns, pillars, as in "f)ton! r)son!
r)sawng f)ton! = two pine trees] ต้น

ton! eng (tua eng) oneself ตนเอง

f)ton! r)hawm n. green onions ต้นหอม

f)ton! l)het n. cause, reason ต้นเหตุ

f)ton! h)mai! n. tree ต้นไม้

f)too n. cabinet, cupboard, case (as bookcase), wardrobe (for clothing) ตู้

f)too l)jot!-r)mai n. letter-box, mail-box, post-box ตู้จดหมาย

f)too l)kap!-f)khao n. cabinet (for keeping food) ตู้กับข้าว

f)too khrua n. kitchen cabinet ตู้ครัว

h)took!-kae n. gecko, large house lizard ตุ๊กแก

h)took!-l)ka!-ta n. doll ตุ๊กตา

too-la-khom October ตุลาคม

l)toom! n. bump, blister (on the body) ตุ่ม

l)toom!, l)toom!-h)nam! n. large water-jar (for storing water in homes, as in the bathroom) ตุ่ม, ตุ่มน้ำ

l)toom! phawng n. blister ตุ่มพอง

f)too r)nang! r)seu n. bookcase ตู้หนังสือ

f)too f)seua-f)pha n. wardrobe (for clothing) ตู้เสื้อผ้า

f)too l)yai! n. big cabinet, railway boxcar ตู้ใหญ่

f)too yen! n. refrigerator ตู้เย็น

l)top! v. slap (with the hand) ตบ

l)top! meu v. applaud, clap hands ตบมือ

tra n. seal, stamp (official), brand, trademark ตรา

trae n. bugle, horn (of a vehicle) แตร

trae h)rot! car horn, automobile horn แตรรถ

trae wong! n. brass band (musical group) แตรวง

tra kan h)kha n. trademark, brand, seal ตราการค้า

l)tral koon n. family, clan, stock, tribe, lineage, ancestry ตระกูล

triam v. prepare, make ready เตรียม

triam h)phrawm (mil. & police) alert, be on alert (for invasion, for a coup attempt, etc.) เตรียมพร้อม

trong! Attention! (command, in military life and in schools) ตรง

trong! straight, direct; right or exactly at a place; sharp (exactly, for time) ตรง

trong! f)kham opposite, across, on the opposite side, across from ตรงข้าม

trong! pai! straight ahead ตรงไป

trong! [l)taw] we-la punctual, on time ตรง (ต่อ) เวลา

l)truat, l)truat doo, l)truat tra v. examine, check, inspect ตรวจ, ตรวจดู, ตรวจตรา

tua n. animal, (colloq.) body (of a person) ตัว

r)tua n. ticket (for admission etc.) ตั๋ว

r)tua bin! airplane ticket ตั๋วบิน

tua eng (ton! eng) oneself ตัวเอง

tua mia n. female (for animals) ตัวเมีย

tua r)nang!-r)seu n. letter of alphabet ตัวหนังสือ

tuang v. measure (volume) ตวง

r)tua pai!-l)klap! n. round-trip ticket ตั๋วไปกลับ

tua f)phoo male (animals) ตัวผู้

tua l)san! v. tremble, shake (of a person) ตัวสั่น

tua to big-bodied (person) ตัวโต

tua-l)yang n. sample, example ตัวอย่าง

tuhm v. fill up, add to เติม

l)tuhp to [f)kheun!] v. grow (bigger), become
bigger เติบโต (ขึ้น)

h)uak, l)uak (colloq.) vomit, throw up อ้วก, อวก

f)uan adj. fat, big and husky อ้วน

l)uat, l)uat dee v. boast, brag อวด, อวดดี

uay-phawn (f)hai) v. bless, give blessings to
อวยพร (ให้)

wa "wa" (unit of linear measure in Thailand,
equal to 2 metres) วา

f)wa say, tell, scold, [often used as a connecting word and translated as "that", as in
"l)bawk f)wa...." = say that....] ว่า

f)waen, f)waen ta n. spectacles, eye-glasses แว่น, แว่นตา

r)waen n. ring (finger ring) แหวน

f)waen kan! l)daet n. sunglasses แว่นกันแดด

r)waen f)phet n. diamond ring แหวนเพชร

f)wai! v. "wai" (greet someone or sbow respect with clasped hands under chin & slightly bowed head, in traditional Buddhist way) ไหว้

f)wai, f)wai h)nam! v. swim ว่าย, ว่ายน้ำ

h)wai! v. put in place, put away, keep, store [often used after other verbs to reinforce the meaning, as in "l)kep! h)wai!" = put away] ไว้

r)wai! able to do something (physically able) ไหว

r)wai n. rattan, wicker หวาย

wai! fai! adj. inflammable ไวไฟ

h)wai jai! v. trust, have faith in ไว้ใจ

h)wai jai! f)dai! adj. reliable, trustworthy ไว้ใจได้

r)wai!-h)phrip! dee adj. intelligent, alert ไหวพริบดี

h)wai! h)thook! v. mourn, dress in mourning (usually all black) ไว้ทุกข์

wai!-ya-kawn n. grammar ไวยากรณ์

wan! n. day (often used before the name of a day of the week as in "Monday" = either "jan!" or "wan! jan!") วัน

l)wan v. sow (seeds) หว่าน

r)wan adj. sweet หวาน

wan! ah-h)thit! Sunday วันอาทิตย์

wan! angl-khan Tuesday วันอังคาร

,**wan! f)chat** National Day วันชาติ

wang! n. palace วัง

wang, wang long!, wang h)wai! v. lay, lay something down, place, put in a place วาง, วางลง, วางไว้

f)**wang** adj. vacant, not in use, free, not busy ว่าง

f)**wang, f)wang l)plao** adj. empty ว่าง, ว่างเปล่า

r)**wang!** n., v. hope หวัง

f)**wang ngan** adj. unemployed ว่างงาน

wang phluhng v. commit arson วางเพลิง

wan! jan! Monday วันจันทร์

wan! [h)khlai wan!] l)kuht n. birthday วัน(คล้ายวัน) เกิด

wan!-na!-f)rok n. tuberculosis วัณโรค

wan!-h)nee today วันนี้

wan-h)nee [f)meua wan, f)meua wan h)nee] yesterday วานนี้ (เมื่อวาน, เมื่อวานนี้)

wan! [f)kheun!] pee l)mai! New Year's Day วัน (ขึ้น) ปีใหม่

wan! h)phoot Wednesday วันพุธ

wan! h)phreu!-l)hat! Thursday วันพฤหัส

wan! r)sao! Saturday วันเสาร์

wan-seun [h)nee] [f)meua wan! seun] the day before yesterday วานซืน (นี้) (เมื่อวานซืน)

wan! l)sook! Friday วันศุกร์

wan! tham!-ngan work-day, working day วันทำงาน

wan!-f)thee date (of the month) วันที่

wan! l)yoot! holiday วันหยุด

f)wao n. kite ว่าว

h)wat! n. wat, Buddhist temple วัด

h)wat! v. measure (dimensions) วัด

f)wat [f)roop] draw (pictures) วาด (รูป)

f)wat f)phap (nai! jai!) v. imagine วาดภาพ (ในใจ)

r)waw n. siren หวอ

h)wa-l)weh lonely, lonesome ว้าเหว่

r)wee n. v. comb (for hair), bunch (of bananas) หวี

we-la n. time (in general); prep. at a certain time เวลา

we-la l)bai in the afternoon เวลาบ่าย

we-la h)chao! in the morning เวลาเช้า

we-la deeo kan! at the same time, meanwhile
เวลาเดียวกัน

we-la klang kheun at night, during the night-time
เวลากลางคืน

we-la klang wan! daytime, in the daytime เวลา
กลางวัน

we-la nan a long time, for a long time เวลานาน

we-la h)nan! then, at that time, those days
เวลานั้น

we-la h)nee now, at this time, nowadays เวลานี้

we-la f)thao!-rai!? At what time? What time is
it? เวลาเท่าไร

we-la trong! correct time, accurate time of day
เวลาตรง

we-la yen! (in the late afternoon) เวลาเย็น

we-la f)yiam visiting hours (as in a hospital)
เวลาเยี่ยม

h)wen v. omit, skip over, leave (a space, etc.)
เว้น

h)wen l)tae unless, except เว้นแต่

wian r)hua, wian r)see-l)sai feel dizzy เวียนหัว,
เวียนศีรษะ

wiat-nam Vietnam(ese) เวียดนาม

wi-cha n. subject (academic), academic knowledge วิชา

wi-cha-f)cheep n occupation, profession วิชาชีพ

wi!-jai! v. research วิจัย

wi!-h)khraw! v. analyze วิเคราะห์

wi!-na-thee second (1/60 of a minute) วินาที

f)wing! v. run วิ่ง

f)wing! l)khaeng v. race (by running) วิ่งแข่ง

f)wing! r)nee v. run away, escape วิ่งหนี

win!-yan n. spirit, soul วิญญาณ

wi!-thee, wi!-thee tham! n. way or method of doing something วิธี, วิธีทำ

wi!-(r)thee, wi!-r)thee thang n. path, course, way วิธี, วิธีทาง

wit!-sa!-f)kee n. whiskey วิสกี้

wit!-sal-wa!-kam n. engineering วิศวกรรม

wit!-sa!-wa!-kawn n. engineer (civil etc.) วิศวกร

wit!-tha!-ya-lai! n. college, higher school วิทยาลัย

wit!-tha!-ya-l)sat n. science วิทยาศาสตร์

wit!-tha!-h)yoo! n. radio, wireless วิทยุ

wong! don!-tree n. band (musical group) วงดนตรี

wong!-jawn n. electrical circuit วงจร

wong!-klom! n. circle วงกลม

wong!-wian n. traffic circle, compass (for drawing circles) วงเวียน

l)**woot** n. steam whistle หวูด

wua n. cow. วัว

ya n. medicine, drug ยา

f)**ya** grandmother (paternal) ย่า

f)**ya** n. grass, weeds หญ้า

l)**ya** don't!, do not! (imperative word) อย่า

l)**ya** (**kan!**) v. get divorced หย่า (กัน)

f)**yaek**, f)**yaek** l)**awk** v. separate, break apart
แยก, แยกออก

f)**yaeng** (**kan!**) v. compete for, fight over แย่ง
(กัน)

ya l)**fin!** n. opium ยาฝิ่น

yai n. grandmother (maternal) ยาย

h)**yai**, h)**yai** f)**ban** v. move (one's residence) ย้าย,
ย้ายบ้าน

h)**yai** [f)**yok** h)**yai**] v. transfer, move someone
to a new position or assignment ย้าย (โยกย้าย)

l)**yai!**, l)**yai!** **toh** big, large ใหญ่, ใหญ่โต

l)**yai!** f)**kheun!** become bigger, increase in size
ใหญ่ขึ้น

yai! **maeng-moom!** n. cobwebs, spider webs
ใยแมงมุม

f)yak difficult ยาก

l)yak, l)yak l)ja! would like (to) อยาก, อยากจะ

l)ya kan! v. get divorced หย่ากัน

ya f)kha h)cheua f)rok n. antiseptic, germ-killer
ยาฆ่าเชื้อโรค

ya f)kha ma-laeng n. insecticide ยาฆ่าแมลง

ya l)khat! n. scouring powder ยาขัด

ya l)khat! rawng-h)thao! n. shoe-polish ยาขัดรองเท้า

f)yak-jon! very poor, in poverty ยากจน

yam n. guard, watchman ยาม

ya h)met! n. pill, tablet (medicine) ยาเม็ด

f)yam! f)kham! 6 o'clock p.m. (colloq.) ยามค่ำ

f)yam! f)roong! 6 o'clock a.m. (colloq.) ยามรุ่ง

yam! l)sa!-l)lat! Thai-style salad (food) ยำสลัด

yam! l)yai! mixed green Thai-style salad (food)
ยำใหญ่

yang! (prep.) to (a place), bound for (a place)
ยัง

yang!, yang! f)mai! not yet, still, yet ยัง, ยังไม่

yang n. rubber ยาง

yang, yang h)rot! n. tire, tyre (for vehicles) ยาง,
ยางรถ

f)yang v. barbecue, broil ย่าง

l)yang n. thing (in general) อย่าง

---

yang ah!-l)lai! n. spare tire (for vehicle) ยางอะไหล่

l)yang l)det!-l)khat absolutely อย่างเด็ดขาด

yang h)lop! n. eraser, rubber ยางลบ

yang f)mai!.... not yet.... ยังไม่....

yang nai! n. innertube (of a tire) ยางใน

l)yang r)nai!? which one? in what way? in which way? อย่างไหน

l)yang h)nan! like that, in that way อย่างนั้น

yang f)nawk n. outer tire, casing (for vehicles) ยางนอก

l)yang h)nawy at least, as a minimum อย่างน้อย

l)yang h)nee like this, in this way อย่างนี้

yang h)ra!-l)buht, yang l)taek n. blowout (of auto tire) ยางระเบิด, ยางแตก

l)yang rai!? how? in what way? อย่างไร

l)yang-rai! f)kaw f)dai! however, in any way, any way will do อย่างไรก็ได้

l)yang rai! f)kaw dee, l)yang-rai! f)kaw tam in any case, however, nevertheless, anyhow อย่างไรก็ดี, อย่างไรก็ตาม

yang h)rat! [r)khawng] n. rubber band ยางรัด(ของ)

yang h)rot! tire, tyre (for vehicles) ยางรถ

yang f)rua n. puncture (leak in tire) ยางรั่ว

yao adj. long (in size) ยาว

ya om! n. cough drops, lozenges ยาอม

ya om! f)klua khaw n. antiseptic mouthwash
ยาอมกลัวคอ

l)ŗap adj. rough, coarse, vulgar หยาบ

ya h)phit! n. poison ยาพิษ

ya h)ral-bai n. laxative ยาระบาย

ya r)see fan! n. toothpaste ยาสีฟัน

ya l)soop n. tobacco ยาสูบ

f))at n. relatives, kinsfolk ญาติ

ya l)thai n. laxative ยาถ่าย

f.)yat f)phee h)nawŋ n relatives (in general)
ญาติพี่น้อง

f)yaw v. abbreviate, shorten, condense ย่อ

yawm v. yield, give in, agree, allow, let ยอม

yawm, yawm h)hai! v. agree, allow, let ยอม,
ยอมให้

yawm, yawm h)phae v. surrender, give up, give
in ยอม, ยอมแพ้

f)yawm [l)kha!·l)nat f)yawm] small (in size) ย่อม
(ขนาดย่อม)

f)yawm, f)yawm l)ja! liable to, likely to, of
course ย่อม, ย่อมจะ

h)yawm v. dye (change color) ย้อม

yawm h)rap! v. accept (something), admit
(something is true) ยอมรับ

l)yawn adj. slack (as a rope) หย่อน

l)yawn jai! v. relax หย่อนใจ

l)yawn l)sa!-l)mat!-l)tha!-f)phap be lax, negligent in one's duties, inefficient, incompetent หย่อน สมรรถภาพ

f)yawt n. peak, top, tip, topmost, total (in figures) ยอด

f)yawt ban!-chee n. balance (accounting) ยอดบัญชี

f)yawt r)khao! n. mountain-top, mountain-peak ยอดเขา

l)yawt h)nam!-man! v. oil, lubricate หยอดน้ำมัน

f)yee-f)haw n. brand, trade-name ยี่ห้อ

f)yeeo n. v. (colloq.) urine, urinate เยี่ยว

f)yee-l)poon Japan(ese) ญี่ปุ่น

f)yee-l)sip! twenty (20) ยี่สิบ (๒๐)

yen! cool, fresh, in late afternoon เย็น

yen!-h)nee late this afternoon เย็นนี้

yen! f)phroong!-h)nee tomorrow in late afternoon เย็นพรุ่งนี้

h)yep! [l)kra!-l)dat] staple paper (with stapler) เย็บ (กระดาษ)

h)yep! [f)pha] v. sew, make clothing เย็บ (ผ้า)

ye-soo h)khrit! Jesus Christ เยซูคริสต์

l)yeua n. bail, decoy, victim, prey เหยื่อ

l)yeuak n. pitcher (container) เหยือก

yeum, yeum ao!, yeum ma v. borrow, take by borrowing ยืม, ยืมเอา, ยืมมา

yeun v. stand, be standing ยืน

f)yeun v. extend, submit (a form or application) ยื่น

yeun f)kheun! v. stand up ยืนขึ้น

f)yeun meu extend one's hand, stick out one's hand ยื่นมือ

yeun-yan! v. insist, reaffirm, confirm ยืนยัน

h)yeut! v. (leg.) seize & hold ยึด

f)yeut, f)yeut l)awk pai! v. stretch, extend, lengthen ยืด, ยืดออกไป

f)yiam v. visit เยี่ยม

l)yiap v. step on (something) เหยียบ

l)yik! v. pinch (with fingers) หยิก

h)yim! v. smile, grin ยิ้ม

yin!-dee [f)duay] happy, glad, delighted ยินดี (ด้วย)

ying! (peun) v. fire (a gun) ยิง (ปืน)

f)ying! extreme(ly), very (much) ยิ่ง

l)ying! proud, haughty, vain, arrogant หยิ่ง

r)ying! woman (also shows feminine gender) หญิง

r)ying! l)ka!-l)ree (n., slang) whore หญิงคณรที

f)ying! l)kwa h)nan! besides that, moreover, in addition ยิ่งกว่านั้น

r)ying! f)nuat n. masseuse หญิงนวด

r)ying! h)rap! h)chai! n. maid หญิงรับใช้

r)ying! r)so-phe-nee n. prostitute หญิงโสเภณี

yin!-yawm v. consent ยินยอม

l)yip! v. pick up (with fingers) หยิบ

h)yok! n. round (boxing), set of proofs (print-ing) ยก

h)yok!, h)yok! f)kheun! v. lift, raise ยก, ยกขึ้น

h)yok! ah-r)han [f)hai!] v. serve food ยกอาหาร(ให้)

h)yok! f)khreuang v. overhaul (vehicle engine) ยกเครื่อง

h)yok! f)luhk v. annul, abolish, cancel ยกเลิก

h)yok! meu f)wai! (pay respects or express greetings in polite traditional Thai-Buddhist way, with hands brought together at or slightly under the chin) ยกมือไหว้

h)yok! song! (bra-sia) n. brassiere ยกทรง(บราเซียร์)

h)yok! f)thot v. pardon (for crime, offense etc.) ยกโทษ

h)yok! h)wen v. exempt, except ยกเว้น

f)yok h)yai v. transfer (from one position or assignment to another) โยกย้าย

h)yok!-f)yawng v. praise ยกย่อง

yon v. throw โยน

f)yon! wrinkled, folded (as skin) ย่น

l)yoo v. be (in a location), live (in a place), be present, be alive, be located at, be at อยู่

l)yoo dee-dai be lonely, be alone อยู่เดียวดาย

yeeng! n. mosquito ยุง

f)yeeng! adj. confused, troublesome, in a mess ยุ่ง

h)yoo!-f)rop Europe(an) ยุโรป

l)yoot! Stop!, cease, have a holiday (from work or school) หยุด

l)yoo l)taw (pai!) v. stay (on), remain (in a place) อยู่ต่อ (ไป)

l)yoot! ngan take a vacation, stop work หยุดงาน

yoot-ti-tham! adj. just, fair; n. justice ยุติธรรม

l)yoo wen be on duty during non-working hours (according to a roster, as in govt. offices) อยู่เวร

l)yoo yam be on watch, guard duty อยู่ยาม

h)yot! n. rank (as in mil. service) ยศ

l)yot! n. drop; v. drip หยด

yuan Vietnam(ese) ญวน

h)yuh!, h)yuh!-h)yae! (colloq.) very much, a lot เยอะ, เยอะแยะ

yah-ra!-man! German(y) เยอรมัน

เรียนภาษาต่างประเทศสำหรับคนไทย

เรียนภาษาไทยสำหรับชาวต่างชาติ

หนังสือของชำร่วย

อื่นๆ